D0759810

People and Tourism in Fragile Environments

People and Tourism in Fragile Environments

Edited by
MARTIN F. PRICE
University of Oxford, UK

With a Foreword by
VALENE L. SMITH

Published in association with the Royal Geographical Society
(with The Institute of British Geographers)

JOHN WILEY & SONS
Chichester · New York · Brisbane · Toronto · Singapore

National 01243 779777
International (+44) 1243 779777

Other Wiley Editorial Offices

John Wiley & Sons, Inc., 605 Third Avenue,
New York, NY 10158-0012, USA

Jacaranda Wiley Ltd, 33 Park Road, Milton,
Queensland 4064, Australia

John Wiley & Sons (Canada) Ltd, 22 Worcester Road,
Rexdale, Ontario M9W 1L1, Canada

John Wiley & Sons (SEA) Pte Ltd, 37 Jalan Pemimpin #05-04.
Block B, Union Industrial Building, Singapore 2057

Library of Congress Cataloging-in-Publication Data

People and tourism in fragile environments / edited by Martin F. Price
with a foreword by Valene L. Smith.
p. cm.
"Published in association with the Royal Geographical Society
(with the Institute of British Geographers)."
ISBN 0-471-96584-7 (hbk. : alk. paper)
1. Tourist trade–Environmental aspects. 2. Environmental
degradation. I. Price, Martin F.
G155.A1P374 1996
333.7′ 137–dc20 96-1057
CIP

British Library Cataloguing in Publication Data

A catalogue record for this book is available from the British Library

ISBN 0 471 96584 7

Typeset in 10/12pt Times by Saxon Graphics Ltd, Derby
Printed and bound in Great Britain by Biddles Ltd, Guildford
This book is printed on acid-free paper responsibly manufactured from sustainable forestation, for which at least two trees are planted for each one used for paper production.

To James Kishlar

Contents

About the Contributors

Ana Baez is President of Turismo y Conservacion Consultores, S.A., in Tibás, Costa Rica. She was formerly Deputy Director of the National Museum of Costa Rica and Dean of the Faculty of Tourism at the Universidad Latinoamericana de Ciencia y Tecnología, where she co-founded and directed the regional postgraduate ecological tourism programme. She has taught, organized research programmes and conferences, and consulted on environment and development issues in Latin America, Europe, and North America.

Dhyani Berger PhD grew up in Kenya, and has worked in Africa, Asia, and the USA with governments and international and local NGOs. Her academic training and work have linked education and community empowerment to conservation and tourism, especially in pastoralist socio-ecosystems. Her present consulting work in rural development and natural resource management emphasizes participatory and experiential methodologies for community-based programmes and training.

Emile Boonzaier is a Lecturer in the Department of Social Anthropology, University of Cape Town, South Africa. He is currently working on his doctorate in tourism, focusing on the way in which 'brokers' (tour guides, park officials, personnel in tourist organizations, entrepreneurs) mediate the relationship between tourists and local populations. His other research interests include medical anthropology, racism, and ethnicity.

Design Workshop is a planning, landscape architecture, and urban design firm with offices in: Aspen, Denver, Vail, Colorado; Phoenix, Arizona; Albuquerque and Santa Fe, New Mexico; and Sao Paulo, Brazil. The firm also maintains strategic alliances in Vienna and Grenoble. One area of expertise, large-scale master planning, has developed with the completion of plans in Arizona and Colorado. The Flathead County team was comprised of: **Kurt Culbertson** (Partner-in-Charge); **Deanna Snyder** (Project Manager); **Steve Mullen** (GIS Expert); **Bill Kane** (Implementation); **Marty Zeller** (Conservation partners; Agricultural Lands Protection); and **Suzanne Richman** (Visual Quality).

James Enote is a member of the Zuni Tribe and heads the Zuni Department of Natural Resources and the Zuni Conservation Project, which focuses on sustainable development. He is also vice-president of the board of the A:shiwi A:wan Museum and Heritage Center, a farmer, and a consultant to international organizations on issues of environment and development, especially in regard to indigenous peoples.

Martin Fitton is Chief Executive of the Brecon Beacons National Park. He previously worked as a rural sociologist and for the Countryside Commission. In addition to his National Park role, he is chairman of the local Jigsaw Campaign, which encourages people throughout Wales to take community decision-making powers into their own hands. He is also a member of the Executive Committee of the Wales Rural Forum, which brings together rural community organizations to promote sustainable development.

Harold Goodwin PhD is a Research Fellow at the Durrell Institute of Conservation and Ecology (DICE) at the University of Kent, UK, and is Project Director for the DICE/Overseas Development Administration (ODA) Tourism, Conservation, and Sustainable Development Project. His research interests include the politics of conservation and development, and he has lectured widely on political ideologies and industrialization. He has undertaken consultancy work on tourism in more than twenty countries worldwide.

David Harrison PhD is Lecturer in Sociology at the University of Sussex, UK. He has studied the social and cultural consequences of tourism in the eastern Caribbean, Bulgaria, and Swaziland. Author of *The Sociology of Modernization and Development* (1988), he is also editor of *Tourism and the Less Developed Countries* (1992) and joint author, with R. Butler and W. Filho, of *Sustainable Tourism and the Environment, Volume II: Case Studies* (1996).

Bjørn Kaltenborn PhD is Senior Research Scientist at the Eastern Norway Research Institute in Lillehammer. He has undertaken research in many alpine and arctic regions, on themes including recreation and tourism research, use and perceptions of natural environments, place attachment, nature experiences, social values of natural resources, and recreation management planning. He has also taught human geography and resource geography.

Alisa Mallari has a background in applied anthropology. She lived in Zuni for two years, directing the Zuni Youth Environmental Organization and working closely with the Zuni Conservation Project. She is currently working for a social science research organization in California, and coordinated a symposium on indigenous issues in conservation policy for the World Conservation Union (IUCN).

Kirsti Pedersen is Assistant Professor in physical education and sport studies at Finnmark College, Alta, Norway, where she has been teaching outdoor education, dance, gymnasics and pedagogy for the past fifteen years. Her research has been concerned with gender issues, and she is currently working on a doctoral degree on gender relations in outdoor life, based on fieldwork in Finnmark.

Frank Potts MSc is employed by the Zimbabwe Department of National Parks and Wildlife Management as Warden for Main Camp, Hwange National Park. In 1994, he completed the MSc in Conservation Biology at the Durrell Institute for Conservation and Ecology at the University of Kent. He is currently on a two-year sabbatical, teaching at the Botswana Wildlife Training Institute.

Martin Price PhD is Programme Leader of the Mountain Regions Programme in Oxford University's Environmental Change Unit. The main focus of his research has been the interactions of resident and visiting populations with the environments of mountain areas; his other research has considered the societal aspects of climate change and the implementation of interdisciplinary research. He has worked as a consultant to many international organizations, including UNESCO, UNEP, IUCN, and the International Social Science Council.

Valene Smith PhD is Professor of Anthropology at California State University, Chico. She is well known for pioneering work on diverse aspects of tourism: pilgrimages, war and tourism, and tourism in polar regions (including the first publication on tourism in Antarctica). Her edited volume, *Hosts and Guests: The Anthropology of Tourism* (1977, 1989), is a near-classic work. She travels widely to identify changing global trends.

Veronica Strang DPhil is an anthropologist in Oxford University's Environmental Change Unit, where her research and teaching focuses on the cultural construction of environmental values. Before conducting research with Aboriginal groups, cattle farmers, and miners in Far North Queensland, she spent a year there as part of a stock team on a cattle station. Her research in the area led to involvement in local catchment management. Her previous work was on environmental and tourism issues in Canada and the British West Indies.

Arvid Viken is Associate Professor of Tourism at Finnmark College, Alta, Norway, where he has taught for the past seven years. He has done research on tourism as a phenomenon and an industry in the Arctic, where he is currently working on a project on ethnic tourism.

Matt Walpole studied ecology at Cambridge University and is currently a research assistant with the DICE/ODA Tourism, Conservation and Sustainable Development Project. He has studied tourism and protected-area management in southern Africa, India, and Indonesia and is now embarking on a PhD, studying black rhinoceros ecology, conservation, and management.

Christopher Whinney graduated from Trinity College, Dublin, and subsequently worked as a shepherd, farmer, and writer in England and Italy. In 1976, he walked from London to Rome. He founded Alternative Travel Group, of which he is Managing Director, in 1979, and has won national and international recognition for training. He is a Director and Council Member of the Association of Independent Tour Operators.

Foreword

World population has more than doubled in the fifty years since World War II. Post-war technology, including jet aircraft, industrial and office automation and their concomitant social changes, has altered the pre-war work ethic and shortened the work week. Employers in industrial countries now accept the concept of paid vacation and travel away from home as a human right. Multi-national corporations of necessity guaranteed paid vacations and incentive travel to their overseas management, and from there the trend has penetrated almost world-wide. Even in a labour-restrictive society such as the People's Republic of China, one-seventh of the workforce is on holiday one day a week, and the days are staggered in an effort to minimize overcrowding by domestic tourists at prime attractions such as the Great Wall.

The fragile environments of our planet are rapidly disappearing under the impact of greatly increased numbers of leisured people with cash and credit cards, ready to pay for a vacation. Many seek a change from progressive urbanization, crime-ridden cities, and the stress of telephones, social pressure, and pollution. They especially want an experience with Nature and an identity with 'life'—with trees, birds, vistas, and with peoples living 'simpler lives'. The travel industry, recognizing this trend, is marketing wilderness and adventure tourism as its most rapidly developing sector, with cultural-ethnic-tribal tourism as a nascent adjunct.

A satellite view of our world suggests two types of fragile environments. The first type includes areas within highly industrialized countries which, even a century ago, were still wilderness, or at least rural, but are now victims of massive over-use and consequent pollution. National Parks in the USA—such as Yellowstone, Grand Canyon, and Yosemite—are prime examples of little patches of real estate, so much sought after for their 'natural beauty' that four million persons per year try to squeeze into each of them, and park rangers are trained in riot control! In Europe, 45 ski lifts on a single Alpine mountain, impacted by traffic jams 100 km long, with an entire valley floor paved for parking is, indeed, an over-used and now very fragile environment. Fifty million visitors a year descending on Spanish beaches are significant contributors to air, water, and noise pollution. Can these sample categories of abused landscapes survive? Do we as humans have the collective willpower to limit our personal use of these domestic facilities, to let them recover and survive? And what alternative recreation is available to satisfy that craving for the 'unspoilt outdoors'?

The second type of fragile environment includes the world's only remaining wilderness, outside or beyond the industrial or developed boundaries. Unfortunately, these areas, finite in size, are already under attack in the guise of *ecotourism.* Some have termed this *eco*nomic tourism, because it often merely means that tourism is being pushed, for entrepreneurial gain, ever deeper into isolated and heretofore little-visited terrain. The remaining wilderness is in double jeopardy, because the physical landscapes are among the world's most fragile, including polar areas, deserts, and tropical rainforests. These three regions are coincidentally also the homelands of remnant tribal populations whose ethnicity is increasingly a tourist attraction. The geographer Preston James (1966) influenced a generation of scholars with his regional analysis of three areas most 'favourable' to human settlement (oases, Mediterranean littorals, and tropical highlands). The contrasting three areas, whose resources set limits to human land use (or were 'unfavourable') are the three fragile landscapes named previously. Unfortunately, James' statistics are out-dated and his insights therefore largely forgotten, but the significant correlations between aboriginal land use and fragile lands are sharply focused. International visitors to the world-famous Grand Canyon rank 'seeing an Indian' as second only to the geological panorama; Australia's impressive Kakadu National Park also links desert landscapes with aboriginal inhabitants, as is similarly the case for the Arctic and Inuit. Papua New Guinea, Sulawesi, and Sarawak are tropical landscapes whose indigenes are in the forefront of destination attractions.

The impacts of wilderness travel are often irreversible. Arctic tundra, disturbed for construction, averages a regrowth of only one inch in fifty years; indigenous peoples, having tasted the sweet juice of tourist cash, seldom return to subsistence activities. How do we *manage* the fragility of the wilderness, yet provide tourists with their much-sought opportunity to visit these lands? Like the apocryphal lemmings, the tourist march to the perimeter is underway; in this case, it will be the host area—including its people and their cultures—rather than the invading humans, that will die... unless management policies are developed and implemented.

People and Tourism in Fragile Environments is the first book to address these varied issues in depth and is a veritable beacon, alerting public concern. Martin Price is to be highly commended for his vision and effort that contribute to a greater awareness of our precious and perishable global resources.

Valene L. Smith,
Professor of Anthropology,
California State University—Chico

James, P., 1966, *The Geography of Man,* Blaisdell, Waltham, Mass.

Acknowledgements

The evolution of this book began in May 1990, when Dr Thomas Schaaf of UNESCO's Division of Ecological Sciences invited me to prepare a proposal for a research project within the Man and the Biosphere (MAB) programme. The rather ambitious proposal, 'The sustainable future of mountain communities: resources and tourism in the context of climate variability and change', was approved by MAB's International Coordinating Council in November 1990. While the preparation of the proposal led to the establishment of a network of over 100 concerned individuals from around the world, the project was unfortunately never funded.

In early 1993, I met Nigel Winser, Deputy Director of the Royal Geographical Society (RGS), and discussed the project with him. He encouraged me to submit a proposal to the RGS, for a conference focusing on the integration of tourism in mountain communities. Some months later, after discussions with the Director of the RGS, Dr John Hemming, a revised proposal including not only mountains, but also other fragile environments, was approved. The conference took place in September 1994, and was attended by a diverse audience of about two hundred. Alison Glazebrook, Programme Coordinator for the RGS, must be specially acknowledged for her hard work in obtaining financial support and organizing the travel of overseas speakers, in addition to her usual tasks of conference management. The participation of overseas speakers was ensured through the sponsorship of British Airways and Abercrombie and Kent Ltd, whose Managing Director, Martin Thompson, opened the conference. Martin Brackenbury, Director of Thomson Travel, and Charles Secrett, Director of Friends of the Earth, introduced the two sessions and moderated some lively debate.

One of the main aims of the conference was to present a range of case studies from diverse perspectives. Six of the chapters in this book are based on presentations at the conference, and the others were selected to ensure maximum diversity of topics and perspectives, and high quality. I would like to thank all of the authors for contributing excellent papers and their patience with my queries and demands. Finally, the book would not have been published without the continuing support—in spite of missed deadlines—of Iain Stevenson and Katrina Sinclair of John Wiley and Sons.

1 Fragile Environments, Fragile Communities? An Introduction

DAVID HARRISON AND MARTIN F. PRICE

TOURISM IN THE WIDER CONTEXT

In recent years, travel and tourism has become the world's largest industry (World Travel and Tourism Council, 1995). Tourism is a service industry whose primary resource is environments and cultures which differ from those where the tourists usually live (Graburn, 1989) and can therefore be marketed by the industry. As the world's population becomes increasingly urbanized, environments which are less suitable for dense human colonization become increasingly attractive as tourist destinations. This is not only because their biophysical characteristics contrast with those where most tourists live, but also because these environments, which may be found in both industrialized and developing countries, are often the homes of long-established populations of people whose cultures are very different from today's westernized, urban norms. This brings us to one of the central themes of this book; that tourism is an economic activity that is imposed, or at least grafted, on a pre-existing set of economic activities and traditional ways of life.

The case studies in this book focus on a specific set of physical environments: mountains, deserts, savannahs, and the arctic. These environments are not mutually exclusive; there are both desert and arctic mountains, and the dividing line between savannahs and hot deserts is often more a question of biogeographical or climatic definition than a reality for any practical purpose, and they are commonly considered under the more general term of drylands (Beaumont, 1993). Nevertheless, these four environments have a particular set of characteristics in common, notably their marked seasonality, which means that many human activities are limited to quite clearly defined parts of the year. In particular, the season for cultivating crops, collecting naturally growing foods, hunting, or fishing is typically limited to relatively few months—or even weeks—of the year. Not surprisingly, the same period is often the most attractive for tourists. One example is provided by the arctic, where year-round survival has traditionally depended on hunting, fishing, and collecting fruits in the few weeks of summer which have now become the main tourist season. The

People and Tourism in Fragile Environments. Edited by M. F. Price.

introduction and growth of tourism in this crucial annual period can have both positive benefits and negative impacts for local communities, and these are likely to change in importance over time.

Just as tourism should not be viewed in isolation from the environments and cultures on which it is imposed, its effects should not be dissociated from wider trends affecting the communities where it develops. The development of tourism is closely bound up with changes in accessibility to potential destinations, as noted for mountain regions by Price (1992) and for the arctic by Johnston (1995). Increases in accessibility—whether by land, air, or sea—may be driven by a government's desire to develop tourism as a means of increasing national incomes or revitalizing local economies. Yet, just as often, improvements in access derive from military ('security') imperatives or the construction of transport infrastructure to allow the development of other economic resources, such as hydrocarbons, minerals, forests, or grazing land.

Similarly, no community in the world now exists in isolation; few ever did. Willingly or not, all communities are part of nation-states with policies for all aspects of their inhabitants' lives; for education, health care, communications and security (social and otherwise). The impacts of the implementation of these policies inevitably form a framework within which tourism develops. Again, greater integration may be beneficial—for instance, through providing better, more timely information and new skills necessary for dealing with tourists and other imports from the wider world—yet many skills and traditional knowledge may be lost. The loss may be multiple; such skills may belatedly be recognized as a valuable resource for tourism, and can also provide reserves for survival if income from tourism and other external sources declines.

Thus tourism must be regarded as part of a dynamic societal system. It is a competitive industry with many components and products, and tourist areas tend to go through a life cycle that is likely to involve stagnation or decline (Butler, 1980). In mountain areas, which were among the first rural tourist destinations (Price, 1992), there are many examples of decline (eg, Dearden, 1989; Direction du Projet MAB Pays d'Enhaut, 1985) and, in all of the environments considered in this book, the long term should always be considered. This is especially because many of these environments are distant from sources of tourists, so that transportation accounts for a significant component of the total costs of tourism to these remote destinations. While world fuel prices are not rising significantly at present, they can be expected to do so in future decades. This is likely to result not only from increased scarcity of resources, but also from carbon taxes, introduced by governments as a means to decrease the rate of consumption of fossil fuels, in accordance with their responsibilities under the Framework Convention on Climate Change and whatever instruments follow it (Dower and Zimmerman, 1992). Consequently, people who have come to rely on tourism in these fragile environments may be subject not only to the vagaries of fashion that characterize this competitive industry but, paradoxically, also victims of the inaccessibility that has been one of their greatest attractions.

FRAGILE ENVIRONMENTS

The concept of fragile environments is complex. While 'fragile' is defined in all dictionaries, we have not been able to find a published definition of 'fragile environment'. However, in Collins' *Dictionary of Environmental Science,* there is a definition of 'fragile ecosystems', which are considered:

> those plant and animal communities which are particularly vulnerable to damage caused by human activity. All ecosystems can be damaged or destroyed by humans but those in slow-growing alpine regions and those in high-latitudes in particular have suffered very considerable destruction due to the low powers of regeneration and recovery. Wetland communities... are also considered fragile communities in that they require very specific conditions of wetness and pH for their survival. (Jones et al., 1990: 180–181)

This definition effectively identifies two types of fragile ecosystem or environment: those that are inherently fragile (eg, wetland communities), and those that are fragile in relation to human activities. As discussed below, this includes not only the alpine (and other mountain) and high-latitude ecosystems mentioned in the definition, but also most desert and savannah ecosystems. In both cases, there is a clear link to the understanding of fragility in ecology, effectively an antonym to 'resilience' in Holling's (1973) theory of resilience and stability in ecological systems (see also May, 1974; Holling, 1986; Pimm, 1991).

In recent years, a third use of 'fragile environment' has emerged, recognizing that human beings have become agents of environmental change at the global scale (Fyfe, 1981; Clark and Holling, 1985). Two books, both entitled *The Fragile Environment* (Friday and Laskey, 1989; Mohan, 1991) cover the wide range of themes—including human population growth, urbanization, industrialization, pollution, and climate change—that are included in this use of the term. Many of the papers in the latter book, as well as a recent book by Wright (1992), argue for major changes in societal and educational systems. Thus, this rather generic global version of 'fragile environment', like the related term 'global change' (Price, 1989) tends to be used by an author or editor more or less according to his or her whims.

The widespread perception of the whole Earth as a fragile environment was one of the catalysts to the United Nations Conference on Environment and Development (UNCED), held in Rio de Janeiro in 1992 (Strong, 1992). Agenda 21, the plan for action approved at UNCED, identifies six 'fragile ecosystems' for specific actions by governments and the international community: deserts, semi-arid lands, mountains, wetlands, small islands, and certain coastal areas (Johnson, 1993). Chapters 12 and 13 of Agenda 21 are both titled 'Managing Fragile Ecosystems', with the respective subtitles 'Combating Desertification and Drought' and 'Sustainable Mountain Development'. The measures indicated in these chapters clearly indicate that the delegates at this unique global meeting perceived fragility as resulting from the interactions of human beings with the biophysical environments which they inhabit or use in other ways.

This is very close to the concept of 'fragile lands' developed in a book edited by Browder (1989): 'lands that are potentially subject to significant deterioration under agricultural, silvicultural, and pastoral systems... (they are) only fragile in terms of (1) specific types of use systems, and (2) specific intensity and frequency levels of usage' (Denevan, 1989: 11). These lands include mountain areas, savannahs, and other drylands: 45 per cent of the area of Latin America. Both Denevan (1989) and Wilken (1989) stress that these fragile lands should preferably be managed according to traditional land use systems. Yet Denevan (1989: 23) also recognizes that 'social fragility, in terms of organization, markets, prices, incomes, social relationships and politics... can be more critical than environmental fragility'.

This argument has been further developed by Turner and Benjamin (1994) in their review of land use in fragile lands. They propose that the degradation of an environment results from interactions between its biophysical characteristics and the ways in which it is used. In particular, degradation appears most likely with rapidly changing land use, conflicting incentives to land use, extreme land pressures, frontier conditions, poverty, external control of resources or decision making, and aridity. Although their discussion applies principally to communities which depend primarily on agriculture, the focus on stresses on cultural and social systems is equally valid when one considers the development of tourism in the fragile environments considered in the following case studies. Parenthetically, it should be noted that aridity—lack of available water—is a major constraint for much of the year not only in deserts (hot or cold) and savannahs, but also in mountain and arctic environments, especially in winter when water supplies are frozen.

Of the fragile ecosystems identified in Agenda 21, the four discussed in this book are the most significant in terms of the proportion of the Earth's surface they cover, as well as being differentiated from the others by their seasonality and patterns of water availability. In both developing and industrialized countries, they are also characterized by the continued existence of a significant number of the world's remaining indigenous people although, as discussed in many of the chapters of this book, they often live somewhat uneasily with more recent immigrants.

Most of the literature that explicitly refers to drylands as fragile environments (or ecosystems), considers the expansion of agriculture or the introduction of new grazing systems: eg, in Botswana (Handscomb, 1990); China (Zhao, 1988); Egypt (Briggs et al., 1993); Ghana (Nsiah-Gyabaah, 1994); South Africa (Jocum et al., 1992). These papers emphasize the need to use limited resources carefully, and the related need to minimize or reverse desertification. However, as El-Ashry and Ram (1991) note for East Africa in general, these activities must be seen in the context of population growth, recurring droughts, ill-advised government policies and international assistance, and years of over-exploitation; integrated approaches to agriculture, forestry, energy and rural development are needed, combined with economic incentives, education, and an improved knowledge base.

There are similar emphases in the literature on mountains as fragile environments, which mainly focuses on the introduction of new agricultural and forestry land uses and technologies, often associated with immigration. Examples include Cameroon (Tchawa, 1993); the Canary Islands (Rodriguez et al., 1993); Ecuador (Bebbington et al., 1993); Himachal Pradesh and Sikkim, India (Kapoor and Bhagat, 1990; Rai et al., 1994); Nepal (Tamang, 1993); Sabah, Malaysia (Voon and Teh, 1992); and, more generally, Latin America (Browder, 1989) and the Mediterranean (Poly, 1991). These papers stress a variety of common themes, notably the risks of the rapid introduction of new land uses in the place of traditional resource management techniques. They emphasize that much can be learned from traditional soil and water management practices, and that care must be taken to minimize deforestation and to avoid excessive additions of fertilizers and other chemicals to soils. In most cases, increased population pressure and integration into external economic systems, often with changes in patterns of land tenure, are major contributing factors to undesirable changes in the biophysical environment. The need for a close relationship between tourism and conservation is a secondary emphasis of some of this literature, especially from the Himalaya (eg, Gurung, 1992; Karan, 1989; Singh, 1989). Referring particularly to Nepal's Annapurna Conservation Area, Gurung (1992) notes the urgent need for environmental education.

The primary emphasis of the literature which refers to the arctic as a fragile environment relates to the long time taken for its ecosystems to recover from disturbance (eg, Sugden, 1989), particularly resulting from the introduction of tourism. With regard to Canada's Northwest Territories, Hamley (1991), notes that not only the biophysical environment but also social structures are fragile. This is a major theme of the first book on polar tourism (Hall and Johnston, 1995), which describes both environmental and societal impacts and diverse means to avoid them.

In summary, the concept of fragile environments used in this book is a wide one. It recognizes that certain environments have biophysical characteristics that render them particularly susceptible to damage by human activities, with relatively slow rates of recovery. Yet, as noted by Denevan (1989), fragility is a relative concept, and must include not only the biophysical but also the human constituents of these environments—and their interactions. Just as traditional uses of soils, water, plants, and animals—often developed over centuries (or longer) of experimentation to minimize change in a community's biophysical life-support system—may be rapidly degraded by external influences, the community's societal structures are equally susceptible to change by external human forces, whose magnitude and potential impacts are not always predictable.

PEOPLE, TOURISM AND 'FRAGILE' COMMUNITIES

If arriving at a definition of a fragile physical environment is difficult, it is well nigh impossible to define a fragile community. In a physical sense, certainly, communities can be damaged, sometimes to the point of extinction, as numerous tragic photographs of bombed villages and columns of refugees so regularly testify. Yet, physical structures are often rebuilt, and much wartime experience suggests, albeit in retrospect, that feelings of social solidarity may actually increase when a population is under attack. There may be a parallel here with tourism.

Some Western critics of tourism, especially in island communities, have focused almost entirely on its allegedly destructive effects on local culture, prompting MacNaught (1982) to deride such critics' 'fatal impact' thesis and the way they ignore attitudes of the islanders themselves. By contrast, it might be argued that human cultures are highly durable, and able to withstand considerable external pressures for change. As has been indicated elsewhere (Harrison, 1996), much depends on the extent to which modifications to a society's social structure or culture are depicted as changes in degree or changes in kind. Ultimately, such assessments are likely to be highly evaluative, involving judgements on how far 'development' is said to have occurred.

Nevertheless, current concerns about the nature of development, especially in less-developed countries, are reflected in studies of international tourism. Perhaps more than any other industry, tourism is closely associated with globalization, of which it is both a cause and an effect. Improvements in transport infrastructure, commencing with the railways in the mid-nineteenth century, extending to sea travel, and later to the conquest of the air and to electronic communications, have brought the possibility of mass travel to virtually every part of the globe. In today's shrinking world, economic, social and cultural isolation are increasingly difficult to sustain; indeed, as globalization has increased in momentum, 'sustainable development' has become the key focus of development studies, a focus as relevant to social structures and cultures as to the relationship of human society with the wider environment (Redclift, 1984, 1987; Adams, 1990; Lélé, 1991; Yearley, 1991; World Bank, 1994) In this context, where tourism is increasingly promoted as a form of 'development', it is not surprising that attention has also shifted to the problems and potentials of sustainable tourism (Cater and Lowman, 1994; Archer et al., 1996; Briguglio et al., 1996).

Although they tend to focus more precisely on the physical environment, the case studies in this book also deal with societies whose way of life is perceived, at least by some, to be 'under threat'. As a consequence, they raise important issues of social and cultural sustainability, which we discuss below. However, before turning to these, it is vital to make the obvious but necessary point that social change is not new. Indeed, sociology and its related disciplines came into existence to describe and explain social upheavals in both the industrialized West and the 'primitive' societies which were brought, for good or ill, under its influence. From early on in these studies, notions of diffusion and evolution were employed in the attempt to understand processes of social and cultural change (Harrison, 1988).

In particular, sociologists emphasized that communities and societies respond to and act directly upon their wider physical and social environments. In the structural functionalism of Radcliffe-Brown, for instance, social systems are depicted as 'adaptational systems', divided into three aspects:

> There is the way in which the social life is adjusted to the physical environment, and we can, if we wish, speak of this as ecological adaptation. Secondly, there are the institutional arrangements by which an orderly social life is maintained.... This we might call, if we wished, the institutional aspect of social adaptation. Thirdly, there is the social process by which an individual acquires habits and mental characteristics that fit him for a place in the social life and enable him to participate in its activities. This, if we wish, could be called cultural adaptation.
>
> (Radcliffe-Brown, 1952: 9)

A similar but more extensive emphasis on adaptation was provided by Talcott Parsons, whose work, in this respect, leaned heavily on that of Malinowski (Parsons, 1957). This is not the place to indulge in a detailed account of Parsonian functionalism which has, in any case, been subjected to many critiques and has recently been undergoing extensive reassessment (Hamilton, 1985; Holton and Turner, 1986; Robertson and Turner, 1991). However, it is essential to note that, for Parsons, systems of any kind, including social systems, need to meet four basic requirements if they are to survive. Best remembered through the acronym AGIL, a social system must ADAPT to its environment, through the economy; meet its GOALS by mobilizing its resources, carried out in the political sphere; INTEGRATE its component parts to keep deviance and conflict to a minimum, through institutions of social control; and maintain patterns of social action (LATENCY) through socialization processes (Rocher, 1974; Craib, 1984).

There is no need to accept Parsonian functionalism in its entirety to recognize, first, that human societies must adapt to external pressures to survive and, secondly, that we need to examine the role played in social change by economic, political, social and cultural institutions. This does not avoid the difficult question of how far a community or society has to adapt before it changes into another kind of society. However, it is perhaps a useful position to take when asking what lessons, if any, can be learned from the case studies in this book about the response of several different societies to tourism.

The reactions of individual members of 'host' societies to tourism have been well documented in previous research. At Byron Bay, in New South Wales, Australia, for instance, residents pointedly adjusted their daily timetable of activities to avoid contact with tourists (Brown and Giles, 1994), and there are numerous examples of communities changing the timing or nature of their festivals, either to accommodate tourists (Brandes, 1988; Greenwood, 1989; Picard, 1990) or to prevent tourists attending them (Boissevain, 1996). Elsewhere, Dogan (1989) has noted that resident strategies vary from active resistance, retreatism into traditional language and culture, and the deliberate maintenance of boundaries, to the more positive revitalization of arts and crafts and the adoption of tourist lifestyles, especially by the young. In Greek resorts, by contrast, some young Greek men, the *kamakia*, reportedly compensate for feelings of cultural inferiority 'by lying, tricking and sexually conquering foreign tourist women from the supposedly superior societies' (Zinovieff, 1991: 203): an outcome much desired, but perhaps less often achieved, by young Arab men in Jerusalem (Cohen, 1971; Bowman, 1989). There is evidence, too, that when faced with an 'invasion' of tourists, local communities underline their own sense of identity in other ways. Tourists may be given nicknames. In the southwest of England, for example, they are referred to as 'grockles', 'emmets' (ants), or 'boat people', and elsewhere they are the butt of local humour, as among the native Americans studied by Evans-Pritchard (1989) and Sweet (1989).

It is a moot point as to how far individual resident reactions can be represented as community responses to tourism, and care must be taken in too readily interpreting such actions as functional adaptations of the social system. However, when such behaviour is patterned, regular and widespread, it may have social effects far beyond those intended by individual actors. As Boissevain (1996) suggests:

> communities visited by tourists adapt surprisingly quickly. They rapidly adopt businesslike attitudes to maximize profits. They are creative in inventing and staging events that furnish entertainment and provide information on their culture. These attractions, while usually not explicitly developed to protect back regions [i.e., areas of a host society reserved only for local residents, where tourists are not welcome], function to deflect the tourist gaze from private space and activities. Host communities take specific, active measures to protect their values and customs threatened by outsiders. The means they utilize include covert action, hiding from tourists, communal celebrations, fencing them out, organized protest and even overt aggression to protect their interests.

Although community responses to tourism inevitably vary across time and space, the case studies in this book give some clues as to factors which may be especially important. Among these, access to local resources, the amount of consensus and cohesion in the host community, and the degree to which its existing political and other institutions are able to work with outside agencies are the most noteworthy.

ACCESS TO LOCAL RESOURCES

All the societies discussed in this volume are part of wider social units and it is clear that, with the possible exception of the Zuni of New Mexico (Chapter 2), none have complete control over their resources. Indeed, the Zunis' negotiation over the lands to be ceded to the National Park Service, although not yet complete, is a signal that they, too, will surrender some access and control over land in return for the economic advantages tourism is expected to bring. In 1999, a similar reliance on outsiders for economic development will accompany the creation of semi-autonomous Nunavut, when less than 20 000 Inuit will become citizens of an area of the Canadian Arctic three times the size of France (Chapter 3). Control over mineral resources (mined by outsiders) will provide most of their income, but their new status will include responsibility for a pristine but highly fragile arctic environment, along with opportunities for increased interaction with tourists. As Smith notes in Chapter 3, and as others have noted elsewhere (eg, Johnston, 1995), such encounters may not always cement international understanding on the most appropriate exploitation of the local wildlife.

The other communities discussed in the following chapters have less control than either the Inuit or the Zuni. Like the Inuit, the Aboriginal people of Australia (Chapter 4) have long been marginalized by the dominant white society, and Sapmi (formerly known as Lapland) and Svalbard, both administered by Norway (Chapters 5 and 6), are subject to that country's legislation concerning the public's free access to the rural areas. However, people in these societies share a concern about the degree to which their own freedoms are or will be limited by tourism. They want the economic benefits brought by tourism, but also want to minimize the economic and other costs which tourism incurs.

COMMUNITY COHESION AND CONSENSUS

Partly because they vary greatly in population size and geography, the degree of social cohesion manifested in the communities described in this volume is also subject to much variation. As described by Mallari and Enote in Chapter 2, the Zuni of New Mexico are perhaps the most close-knit. With a population of less than 10 000, they are cautious about tourism development, which is in its early stages, and although they encourage big-game hunting, with Zuni guides, other forms of tourism are less favoured. Despite the agreement of the Zuni Tribal Council to the formation of a National Historical Park in the region, parts of which would then be leased to and managed by the National Park Service, the Zuni and their religious leaders worry about the possible effects of tourism on their culture and sacred sites. As a consequence, the plans have not yet been implemented. Indeed, inappropriate behaviour by tourists has periodically prompted the Zuni Tribal Council to ban them from Zuni ceremonial dances.

The Zuni seem to have a high degree of social cohesion and a representative government sensitive to the needs of the community. Sooner rather than later, they will need to take important decisions about further tourism but, so far, they have withstood its onset. In a very different context, another indigenous group, also a minority in its own land, has been more accommodating. As described by Strang in Chapter 4, the thousand or so Aboriginal people living on Cape York, Australia and, to a lesser extent, the white cattle farmers in the area, have gradually welcomed tourism. For both groups, tourism is not only a source of income, but also a positive affirmation of their cultures, which they have steadfastly maintained in the face of persistent persecution by people who, until recently, have been socialized into despising them.

In some respects, the Inuit of Nunavut (Chapter 3) are similar to the Zuni and the Aboriginal people of Cape York. Their culture, too, has been subject to denigration from outside, and yet has remained resilient. However, separated by a vast expanse of territory, the Inuit rely on air transport to maintain contact with family and friends and, so far, tourists visiting the region have tended to prefer the comfort of cruise ships to the more rudimentary (but nevertheless expensive) accommodation available on land. In these circumstances, both the cohesion of this 'new nation' and the threats to it may be a matter of future possibility rather than present reality. However, it is noteworthy that the Inuit of Nunavut are being advised to develop community-based tourism with assistance not only from the Inuit of Alaska, who have had more experience of tourism, but also from the World Tourism Organisation, and thus to protect their cultural integrity with support from a new set of 'insiders' and a major participant in international tourism.

There seems little consensus and community cohesion among the 75 000 Sami, who live mainly in Norway, but whose territory straddles Norway, Finland, Sweden, and Russia. Like the Zuni and the Aboriginal people of Cape York, they are an indigenous minority in their own land but, according to Pedersen and Viken in Chapter 5, this highly modernized population has little sense of its own identity. After generations of persecution and exploitation, Norwegian-educated Sami return to Sapmi having learned of their 'own' culture elsewhere.

It is noticeable that the two smallest groups, the Zuni and the Aboriginal people of Cape York, have proved more resistant to incursions of modernity than the larger indigenous groups. It may be that once a critical point is reached in the decline of a culture, resistance to change takes on a new urgency. But modernity can also be used as a resource, and the Inuit are clearly using modern methods of communication to their own advantage. Social change need not follow the same pattern everywhere. While some societies may remain in special 'niches' in a symbiotic relationship with more developed societies (Parsons, 1964), others may be more adaptable.

Much may depend on the length of time cultural instutions have had to take root in a given environment. In the Norwegian Arctic, permanent communities have only recently been established on the archipelago of Svalbard, and most have been based on coal-mining. According to Kaltenborn in Chapter 6, as this industry has declined, the five thousand permanent residents have warmed to tourists, who are increasingly seen as an alternative source of income. At the same time, increased awareness of the possible dangers of tourism to such an environmentally sensitive area has prompted several research and planning initiatives by the national government. Local reactions are harder to gauge: although some local residents want to work in tourism, there is no evidence in this chapter of any strong community feelings on the matter. Perhaps because settlements are so diverse and so recent, most initiatives appear to be taken by government, with little or none at grass-roots level.

The five thousand people in the numerous small communities in the region of the Monteverde Cloud Forest Reserve (MFCR) of Costa Rica include native Costa Ricans and more recent Quaker settlers from the USA. Described by Baez in Chapter 7 as 'a very special community', the region indeed seems to be characterized by a high degree of consensus and participation, as well as by a prominent presence of non-governmental organizations. The focus on eco-tourism as a form of sustainable tourism fits in with the local ethos of cooperation, and local people and outsiders apparently work together in a highly productive and unusual partnership which, despite some problems, sounds almost too good to be true.

In some circumstances, tourism may itself lead communities to become more cohesive, perhaps with varying degrees of assistance from outsiders. As Boonzaier points out in Chapter 8, the process of the establishment of a national park in the Richtersveld, in the Republic of South Africa, led prominent outsiders to form a Community Committee to oppose an official body that was negotiating away many of the rights of the local coloured population. From his account, it is clear that a partnership of local residents, NGOs, and academics was able to substantially alter the conditions under which the park was established, much to the benefit of local people. Most importantly, his account also shows that the local population, encouraged by success in the negotiations, by national changes and by tourist interest, consequently became more confident in its dealings with outside agencies and is in the process of developing a more positive, measured, approach to its own culture, which until recently had been much derided.

Self-protection of a similar order is evident among the residents of Flathead County, Montana, in the USA, where tourism is already highly developed, and in the Brecon Beacons National Park of Wales. As Culbertson and his colleagues report in Chapter 9, Flathead County is part of a region that has increasingly acted as a magnet for tourists and second-home owners. In response to this situation, a highly diverse group of citizens has come together in a series of action sets (Mayer, 1966). Forming a pressure group designed to bring future development under control, members of the public engaged an outside consultant to assist them in producing a plan for sustainable growth in the area. They then participated in a wide range of public meetings, goal-setting sessions, and work groups, which led to the formulation, though not without opposition, of a Master Plan to guide future decisions on land use and resource protection.

In Chapter 10, by contrast, Fitton points to two separate sets of interests in two national parks in South Wales and shows how the National Parks Authorities (NPAs) were able to work with both, to achieve quite different aims. In Llanthony Valley, in the Brecon Beacons, a community of ninety people strongly objected to tourists, who brought them no economic benefits and considerable annoyance, merely passing through the area in their cars. Following a process of consultation with the NPA, it was agreed that road signs in the area would be removed. For car drivers, at least, the valley was simply removed from the map. By contrast, the South Pembrokeshire Partnership for Action with Rural Communities (SPARC), a community development project involving 37 small communities, is a group of community associations devoted to the development of small-scale, community-based tourism. Prompted by local activists and supported by numerous grants, including funds from the European Union, SPARC worked with the NPA in involving residents in widespread discussion and consultation, formulating Action Plans for tourism development (and other activities) for each participating community.

While the NPAs in South Wales were able, at least to some extent, to work with two groups with quite different attitudes to tourism, the situation is very different among the Kenyan Maasai. As Berger indicates in Chapter 11, their pastoral way of life has long been under attack by a 'modernization' programme that has reportedly demeaned their culture, privatized their lands, removed them from national parks, and encouraged them to become commercial farmers. Although there is now an increasing awareness that their knowledge of arid and semi-arid lands, and their pastoralism, may have some kind of 'fit' with tourism and wildlife conservation, the Maasai themselves are divided. Some are indeed benefiting from tourism—for example, from partnerships with safari operators—and parts of the tourism industry, as well as government agencies, are taking a more active role in encouraging the Maasai to participate in and benefit from wildlife conservation. However, many Maasai continue to regard tourism as a threat, and participation in the industry is said to increase communal divisions, which are already considerable. As Berger comments:

> The monopoly of power by a few has divided communities who have not found it easy to unite, organise, and claim what is rightfully theirs. Ironically, some aspects of tradition—respect for elders, the recognition of life-long office of a leader, and age-group or section solidarity—have made the Maasai majority vulnerable to abuse of power and customary respect, and hence to political manipulation.

The problem is not unusual. It is one thing to encourage 'community participation' and advocate links between tourism and traditional cultures, but quite another to face the possibility that some 'traditional' cultures may themselves be thoroughly inegalitarian. In such circumstances, to argue that tradition (or what it has become) should be respected, and simultaneously to encourage participation, is simply contradictory (Harrison, 1996). However, without consensus at local level, protection of an indigenous culture becomes more difficult (and more difficult to justify), even with the active assistance of outside agencies which, in any case, may have several different axes to grind.

Where only a minority benefits from wildlife conservation, only a minority is likely to support it, as has been shown, for instance, in Zambia's ADMADE programme, which is operated through the chiefs (Gibson and Marks, 1995). In

Chapter 12, as part of their examination of Zimbabwe's Hwange National Park, Potts and his colleagues briefly discuss the CAMPFIRE initiative, which followed the 1975 Parks and Wildlife Act, through which local people and landowners were allowed to benefit directly from wildlife conservation. It should be noted that no local people live in the Park itself, and that much of the surrounding area is sparsely populated. However, since 1991, several wards in Tsholotsho Communal Land, south of the Park, have participated in the CAMPFIRE project, thus gaining fees from hunting, and employment opportunities, and the authors note that 90 per cent of the total income to Zimbabwe's CAMPFIRE districts came from sport hunting. That said, the programme is an aspect of government policy and, as its organizers and critics suggest, the success of every CAMPFIRE project depends, at least to some extent, on the willingness of local authorities to encourage genuine participation at local levels (Zimbabwe Trust et al., 1990; Gibson and Marks, 1995).

It should be clear, even from this brief survey, that the level of consensus in the communities studied in this volume varies considerably. Although the evidence is sketchy, there is perhaps a case for arguing that where absolute population numbers are small, as among the Zuni and the Aboriginal people of Cape York, cultures may be more resilient. However, much also depends on the regularity of contact and the extent to which a local culture is 'rooted' in the community. The Inuit of Nunavut apparently think nothing of travelling long distances by air to retain contact with one another, while among the five thousand residents of Svalbard, for instance, which was permanently settled only in this century, there is little evidence of community cohesion. By contrast, the Costa Rican communities discussed by Baez, with the same population size as Svalbard, seem to have greatly benefited from a relatively recent influx of Quaker immigrants and to have specialized in a form of tourism which was appropriate to their ethos.

Small size is certainly not everything. The case studies suggest that several communities, large and small, developed consensus as a response to tourism, or to plans for tourism-related projects. In their different ways, the residents of Flathead County, the Brecon Beacons, and the Richtersveld illustrate a tendency to unite around a common purpose. Even the Turkish villagers whose initial hospitality was replaced by hostility, greeting tourists with stones, as described by Whinney in Chapter 13, were reinforcing their community's identity in the face of what they perceived to be an attack on their culture.

EXTERNAL INVOLVEMENTS

A striking feature of the communities discussed in the following chapters is extensive outside involvement in their destinies. Few of these communities are autonomous and all are well on the path of modernization, a path they do not appear to want to leave. As the residents of Richtersveld made clear, they were happy to be empowered and to cater for tourist interest in their culture, but they had no intention of faking authenticity by returning to 'traditional' dress and housing for the benefit of the tourists. Only among the relatively homogeneous Zuni, perhaps, is there an apparent lack of outside influence. In seeking to re-establish local control over local resources, other communities have drawn on outside agencies for varying amounts of support. Although the Aboriginal people and cattle ranchers of Queensland have developed their own organizations to ensure their voice was heard, they have also entered partnerships with tour operators, as have the Kenyan Maasai and the Zimbabwean participants in the government-run CAMPFIRE scheme.

An even more organized response to tourism is seen in Monteverde, Costa Rica, where, according to Baez, there are probably 'more NGOs than any other community in the country'. In the Richtersveld Reserve in South Africa, too, local empowerment in response to tourism expansion was not achieved alone, but from within a kind of rainbow coalition, which included trades unionists, NGOs, politicians and academics. Indeed, if the Inuit of Nunavut follow Smith's advice and make common cause with the Inuit of Alaska and enlist the assistance of the World Tourism Organisation, they will follow an established pattern. Only in the heterogeneous communities of Svalbard and among the acculturated and highly modern Sami, both administered by Norway, does it seem that 'development' is being imposed from above. The moral, perhaps, is that we should no longer seek to know how far 'development' is either 'top-down' or 'bottom-up', but rather ask which institutions, local and outside, are involved in tourism, and how they articulate with one another.

CONCLUSION

It is quite clear that local communities can develop institutionalized responses to tourism. What matters, if 'fragility' is to be protected, is to ensure that local voices are heard and that the goals of the community are sensibly framed and—equally importantly—efficiently implemented: 'the most formidable task on the road to sustainable development, and tourism development, is that of building the institutions needed for policy implementation' (de Kadt, 1992: 73). This is a construction project in which insiders and outsiders, the state and the private sector, must be involved.

As Whinney makes clear in Chapter 13, despite the good intentions of some tour operators, tourism development can easily move out of the control of local people. It may be that Doxey's (1975) index of irritation, where initial euphoria is replaced by apathy, annoyance and then antagonism, is not universally applicable; indeed, there is evidence in the following chapters that the unwillingness of some communities to receive tourists has been replaced by a warmer welcome. However, like other uncontrolled forms of migration, rapid tourism development clearly causes problems, and the best counter to this, again, may be found in institutions strongly supported, if not initiated, at local level, and in the sensible implementation of policies that carry a wide range of community approval.

Communal 'fragility' is hard to define and even harder to demonstrate, and Boissevain (1996) may be correct in suggesting that 'communities visited by tourists adapt surprisingly quickly'. There is certainly no justification for wanting to preserve 'traditional' societies in aspic. Nevertheless, even at a common-sense level, it seems reasonable to suggest that, at least in the short term, rapid tourism development can overwhelm small communities, especially those with a widely different culture from the tourists. In such circumstances, it seems wise to advocate—and encourage—the development of local organizations, albeit with appropriate outside support, that can maximize the economic benefits on offer and minimize the economic, social and cultural costs. The tourism industry can play its part in this process. A sensitive approach by tour operators, for example, perhaps supported by an industry-wide code of ethics, sensible training programmes, and close liaison with residents of tourist-receiving areas, may help to guard against get-rich-quick operators and, at the same time, promote slower but more sustainable tourism. However, if 'the sweet juice of tourist cash', as Smith defines it in the foreword to this volume, enables communities to improve their standard of living, maintain a clear idea of the goals they wish to achieve, and socialize their young into a community which—although subject to change—remains under the substantial control of its members, they can hardly be said to be compromising the ability of future generations to meet their own needs.

REFERENCES

Adams, W.M., 1990, *Green Development: Environment and Sustainability in the Third World*, Routledge, London.

Archer, B., Briguglio, L., Jafari, J. and Wall, G. (eds), 1996, *Sustainable Tourism in Islands and Small States, Vol. I: Theoretical Issues*, Cassell, London.

Beaumont, P., 1993, *Drylands: Environmental Management and Development*, Routledge, London.

Bebbington, A.J., et al., 1993, Fragile lands, fragile organizations: Indian organizations and the politics of sustainability in Ecuador, *Transactions of the Institute of British Geographers*, 18(2), 179–196.

Boissevain, J., 1996, Introduction, in J. Boissevain (ed.), *Coping with Tourists: European Reactions to Mass Tourism*, Berghahn, London.

Bowman, G., 1989, Fucking tourists: sexual relations and tourism in Jerusalem's Old City, *Critique of Anthropology*, 9(2), 73–93.

Brandes, S., 1988, *Power and Persuasion: Fiestas and Social Control in Rural Mexico*, University of Pennsylvania Press, Philadelphia.

Briggs, J., et al., 1993, Sustainable development and resource-management in marginal environments—Natural resources and their use in the Wadi-Allaqi region of Egypt, *Applied Geography*, 13(3), 259–284.

Briguglio, L., Butler, R.W., Harrison, D. and Leal Filho, W. (eds), 1996, *Sustainable Tourism in Islands and Small States, Vol. II: Case Studies*, Cassell, London.

Browder, J. (ed.), 1989, *Fragile Lands of Latin America: Strategies for Sustainable Development*, Westview, Boulder.

Brown, G. and Giles, R., 1995, Coping with Tourism: an examination of resident responses to the social impact of tourism, in A.V. Seaton (ed.), *Tourism: The State of the Art*, John Wiley and Sons, Chichester, 755–764.

Butler, R.W., 1980, The concept of a tourism area cycle of evolution: Implications for management of resources, *The Canadian Geographer*, 24, 5–12.

Cater, E. and Lowman, G. (eds), 1994, *Ecotourism: A Sustainable Option?, John* Wiley and Sons, Chichester.

Cohen, E., 1971, Arab boys and tourist girls in a mixed Jewish–Arab community, *International Journal of Comparative Sociology*, 12(4), 217–233.

Clark, W.C. and Holling, W.S., 1985, Sustainable development of the biosphere: Human activities and global change, in T.F. Malone and J.G. Roederer (eds), *Global Change*, Cambridge University Press, Cambridge, 474–490.

Craib, I., 1984, *Modern Social Theory: From Parsons to Habermas*, Wheatsheaf, Brighton.

Dearden, P., 1989, Tourism in developing countries: Some observations on trekking in the Highlands of North Thailand, in L.J. D'Amore and J. Jafari (eds) *Tourism—A Vital Force for Peace*, International Institute for Peace Through Tourism, Montreal, 207–216.

de Kadt, E., 1992, Making the alternative sustainable: lessons from development for tourism, in V. Smith and W. Eadington (eds), *Tourism Alternatives: Potentials and Problems in the Development of Tourism*, University of Pennsylvania Press, Philadelphia, 47–75.

Denevan, W.M., 1989, The geography of fragile lands in Latin America, in Browder, J. (ed.), *Fragile Lands of Latin America: Strategies for Sustainable Development*, Westview, Boulder, 11–25.

Direction du Projet MAB Pays d'Enhaut, 1985, Tourisme Pays d'Enhaut, *Schlussbericht Schweizerisches MAB-Programm 15*, Bundesamt für Umweltschutz, Bern.

Dogan, H.Z., 1989, Forms of adjustment: sociocultural impacts of tourism, *Annals of Tourism Research*, 16(2), 216–236.

Dower, R.C. and Zimmerman, M.B., 1992, *The Right Climate for Carbon Taxes: Creating Economic Incentives to Protect the Atmosphere*, World Resources Institute, Washington DC.

Doxey, G.V., 1975, A causation theory of visitor–resident irritants: methodology and research inferences, *Proceedings of the 6th Annual Conference, Travel and Tourism Research Association*, Salt Lake City, TTRA, 195–198.

El-Ashry, M.T. and Ram, B.J., 1991, Natural resource management and agricultural development in the arid areas of East Africa, in Bishay, A. and H. Dregne (eds), *Desert Development, Part 2: Socio-Economic Aspects and Renewable Energy Applications*, Harwood Academic, 85–96.

Evans-Pritchard, D., 1989, How 'They' see 'Us': native American images of tourists, *Annals of Tourism Research*, 16(1), 89–105.

Friday, L. and Laskey, R. (eds), 1989, *The Fragile Environment*, Cambridge University Press, Cambridge.

Fyfe, W.S., 1981, The environmental crisis: quantifying geosphere interaction, *Science*, 213, 105–110.

Gibson, C.C. and Marks, S.A., 1995, Transforming rural hunters into conservationists: an assessment of community-based wildlife programs in Africa, *World Development*, 23–(6), 941–957.

Graburn, N.H.H., 1989, Tourism: The sacred journey, in V.L. Smith (ed.), *Hosts and Guests: The Anthropology of Tourism*, 2nd edn, University of Pennsylvania Press, Philadelphia, 21–36.

Greenwood, D.J., 1989, Culture by the pound: an anthropological perspective on tourism as cultural commoditization, in V.L. Smith (ed.), *Hosts and Guests: The Anthropology of Tourism*, 2nd edn, University of Pennsylvania Press, Philadelphia, 171–185.

Gurung, H.B., 1992, Environmental education in Nepal: A mechanism for resource conservation, *World Leisure and Recreation*, 34(2), 18–22.

Hall, C.M. and Johnston, M.E. (eds), 1995, *Polar Tourism: Tourism in the Arctic and Antarctic Regions*, Wiley, Chichester.

Hamilton, P. 1985, *Talcott Parsons*, Horwood, Chichester.

Hamley, W., 1991, Tourism in the Northwest Territories, *Geographical Review*, 81(4), 389–399.

Handscomb, S., 1990, Production in a fragile environment, *Food Matters*, 4, 27–30.

Harrison, D., 1988, *The Sociology of Modernization and Development*, Routledge, London.

Harrison, D., 1996, Sustainability and tourism: reflections from a muddy pool, in B. Archer, J. Jafari and G. Wall, (eds), *Sustainable Tourism in Islands and Small States, Vol. I: Theoretical Issues*, Cassell, London, 69–89.

Holling, C.S., 1973, Resilience and stability of ecological systems, *Annual Review of Ecology and Systematics*, 4, 1–23.

Holling, C.S., 1986, The resilience of terrestrial ecosystems: local surprise and global change, in W.C. Clark and R.E. Munn (eds), *Sustainable Development of the Biosphere*, Cambridge University Press, Cambridge, 292–317.

Holton, R.J. and Turner, B.S., 1986, *Talcott Parsons on Economy and Society*, Routledge and Kegan Paul, London.

Jocum, I., Groenewald, J.A. and Maree, C., 1992, Toward integration of ecological and economic principles in beef ranching, *South African Journal of Agricultural Extension*, 21, 42–55.

Johnson, S.P., 1993, The Earth Summit: *The United Nations Conference on Environment and Development (UNCED)*, Graham and Trotman, London.

Johnston, M.E., 1995, Patterns and issues in arctic and sub-arctic tourism, in Hall, C.M. and Johnston, M.E. (eds) *Polar Tourism: Tourism in the Arctic and Antarctic Regions*, Wiley, Chichester, 27–42.

Jones, G., et al., 1990, *Dictionary of Environmental Science*, Collins, Glasgow.

Kapoor, K.S. and Bhagat, S., 1990, Resource potentials of Spiti—The cold mountain desert of Himachal Pradesh, *Annals of Arid Zones*, 29(4), 243–249.

Karan, P.P., 1989, Environment and development in the Sikkim Himalaya: A review, *Human Ecology*, 17(2), 257–271.

Lélé, S.M., 1991, Sustainable development: a critical review, *World Development*, 19 (6), 607–621.

MacNaught, T.J., 1982, Mass tourism and the dilemmas of modernization in Pacific island communities, *Annals of Tourism Research*, 9(3), 359–381.

May, R.M., 1974, *Stability and Complexity in Model Ecosystems*, 2nd edn, Princeton University Press, Princeton.

Mayer, A.C., 1966, The significance of quasi-groups in the study of complex societies, in M. Banton (ed.), *The Social Anthropology of Complex Societies*, Tavistock Publications, London, 97–122.

Mohan, I. (ed.), 1991, *The Fragile Environment*, Ashish, New Delhi.

Nsiah-Gyabaah, K., 1994, *Environmental Degradation and Desertification in Ghana: A Study of the Upper West Region*, Avebury, Aldershot.

Parsons, T., 1957, Malinowski and the Theory of Social Systems, in R. Firth (ed.), *Man and Culture: an evaluation of the work of Bronislaw Malinowski*, Routledge and Kegan Paul, London, 53–70.

Parsons, T., 1964, Evolutionary universals in society, *American Sociological Review*, 29(3), 339–357.

Pearson, P., 1993, *Drylands: Environmental Management and Development*, Routledge, London.

Picard, M. 1990, 'Cultural tourism' in Bali: cultural performances as tourist attraction, *Indonesia*, 49, 37–74.

Pimm, S.L., 1991, *The Balance of Nature? Ecological Issues in the Conservation of Species and Communities*, University of Chicago Press, Chicago.

Poly, J.P., 1991, Agrosylvopastoral practices in Mediterranean Europe, in M.K. Muthoo and M.E. Chipeta (eds), *Trees and Forests in Rural Land Use*, Food and Agriculture Organization, Rome, 137–151.

Price, M.F., 1989, Global change: defining the ill-defined, *Environment*, 31(8), 18–20, 42, 44.

Price, M.F., 1992, Patterns of the development of tourism in mountain environments, *GeoJournal*, 27(1), 87–96.

Radcliffe-Brown, A.R. 1952, *Structure and Function in Primitive Society*, Cohen and West, London.

Rai, S.C., Sharma, E., and Sundriyal, R.C., 1994, Conservation in the Sikkim Himalaya: Traditional knowledge and land use of the Mamlay watershed, *Environmental Conservation*, 21(1), 30–34.

Redclift, M. 1984, *Development and the Environmental Crisis: Red or Green Alternatives?*, Methuen, London.

Redclift, M., 1987, *Sustainable Development: Exploring the Contradictions*, Routledge, London.

Robertson, R. and Turner, B.S. (eds), 1991, *Talcott Parsons: Theorist of Modernity*, Sage, London.

Rocher, G., 1974, *Talcott Parsons and American Sociology*, Barnes and Noble, London.

Rodriguez, A.R., et al., 1993, Assessment of soil degradation in the Canary-Islands (Spain), *Land Degradation and Rehabilitation*, 4(1), 11–20.

Singh, T.V., 1989, *The Kulu Valley: Impact of Tourism Development in the Mountain Areas*, Himalayan Books, New Delhi.

Strong, M.F., 1992, Environment and development—The United Nations road from Stockholm to Rio, *Interdisciplinary Science Reviews*, 17(2), 112–115.

Sugden, D.E., 1989, The polar environment: illusion and reality, *Ambio*, 18(1), 2–5.

Sweet, J.D., 1989, Burlesquing 'the Other' in Pueblo performance, *Annals of Tourism Research*, 16(1), 62–75.

Tamang, D., 1993, *Living in a Fragile Environment*, International Institute for Environment and Development, London.

Tchawa, P., 1993, La degradation des sols dans la Bamileke medidional, conditions naturelles et facteurs anthropiques, *Cahiers d'Outre-Mer*, 46(181), 75–104.

Turner, B.L. and Benjamin, P., 1994, Fragile lands: identification and use for agriculture, in V.W. Ruttan (ed.), *Agriculture, Environment, and Health: Sustainable Development in the 21st Century*, University of Minnesota Press, Minneapolis, 104–145.

Voon, P.K. and Teh, T.S., 1992, Land use and the environment in the South Kinabalu highlands, Malaysia, *Malaysian Journal of Tropical Geography*, 23(2), 103–118.

Wilken, G.C., 1989, Transferring traditional technology: A bottom-up approach for fragile lands, in J. Browder (ed.), *Fragile Lands of Latin America: Strategies for Sustainable Development*, Westview, Boulder, 44–57.

World Bank, 1994, *Making Development Sustainable*, The World Bank, Washington, D.C.

World Travel and Tourism Council, 1995, *Travel and Tourism's Economic Perspective*, World Travel and Tourism Council, Brussels.

Wright, W., 1992, *Wild Knowledge: Science, Language, and Life in a Fragile Environment*, University of Minnesota Press, Minneapolis.

Yearley, S., 1991, *The Green Case*, HarperCollins, London.

Zhao, S.Q., 1988, Desertification and de-desertification in the Hexi Corridor, *Chinese Journal of Arid Land Research*, 1(2), 117–124.

Zimbabwe Trust, Department of National Parks and Wild Life Management and the Campfire Association, 1990, *People, wildlife and natural resources—the CAMPFIRE approach to rural development in Zimbabwe*, Zimbabwe Trust, Harare.

Zinovieff, S., 1991, Hunters and hunted: Kamaki and the ambiguities of sexual predation in a Greek town, in P. Loizos and E. Papataxiarchis (eds), *Contested Identities: Gender and Kinship in Modern Greece*, Princeton University Press, Princeton, N.J., 203–220.

2 Maintaining Control: Culture and Tourism in the Pueblo of Zuni, New Mexico

ALISA A. MALLARI AND JAMES A. ENOTE

INTRODUCTION

Many mistakes have been made in the name of economic development and there are many examples of the ill effects of tourism development. Communities that are just beginning to consider tourism development are at an advantage, in that they can learn from the experience of negative examples in order to prevent unsustainable development practices. Taking advantage of this experience has contributed to some positive examples of communities that are taking control of development. One of these communities is the Zuni Indian Tribe in the Southwest United States:

> Zuni needs to develop tourism in ways compatible with maintaining and enhancing the lifestyle and sense of community that presently exists in Zuni, and in ways that conserve the natural and cultural resources of Zuni. Tourism is a double-edged sword. More often than not tourism destroys what it originally set out to enhance. The Tribe must know exactly what it does and doesn't want from tourism before tourism is developed.
>
> (Anyon, 1994)

Much of the tourist appeal of the Southwest United States is based on the continued existence of Native American communities and the indigenous culture. The main tourist centres—such as the cities of Santa Fe, Taos, Sedona, and Gallup—are defined by their connection to, and expression of, the Indian cultures that surround them. The tourist industry contributes significantly to the economy of the Southwest and also to some Tribal economies. However, much of the tourist industry is not controlled or directly accessed by the Native American communities. Tribes have responded in a variety of ways. Methods of tourist management and decisions with regard to the double-edged sword of the tourist industry are constantly being negotiated. Many Tribes have benefited from the influx of tourist dollars and yet have also found it necessary to restrict

People and Tourism in Fragile Environments. Edited by M. F. Price.

access to their lands and culture in order to prevent encroachment and loss of control. Researchers such as Evans-Pritchard (1989) and Sweet (1991) have elaborated on other examples of Native American responses to tourism.

This chapter takes a brief look at the Zuni community in west central New Mexico in its struggle to define the issues and needs involved in the discussion of tourism. The Zuni case illustrates the cultural and environmental complexities involved in a particular setting and contributes to a more comprehensive understanding of the dynamics involved in planning to safeguard social, cultural, and environmental needs. As one of many indigenous communities with much experience in negotiating development within local social, cultural, and religious protocols, the experience of Zuni is particularly important to the discussion of socio-cultural impacts of tourism.

In order to successfully achieve development that truly meets the needs of the community, it must maintain control—not only in managing the means of development but, more importantly and essentially, in directing the process and course of development. Community control is predicated by a thorough and sensitive understanding of the community's particular goals, needs, and limitations and of its ability to negotiate within these parameters in order to successfully guide the sustainable development of tourism.

GEOGRAPHY AND HISTORY OF ZUNI

Zuni Indian lands include 462 406 acres (187 136 hectares) in the state of New Mexico and 12 500 more acres (5051 hectares) in the state of Arizona (Figure 2.1). The main reservation is 448 567 contiguous acres (181 535 hectares). Situated on the Colorado Plateau, Zuni lands were once part of a large inland sea and riverine system which deposited the thick layers of sediment that now form the characteristic red striped sandstone mesas and parent material for fertile soils. Zuni is situated at an average altitude of 6500 feet (2000 m) with elevations ranging from 6000 to nearly 8000 feet (1850–2400 m). The climate is generally characteristic of a high semi-arid landscape. The average total annual rainfall is approximately 12 inches (30 cm), although variation is significant, with years of above-average moisture and others of relative drought. It snows during the winter, and temperatures frequently drop below zero degrees Fahrenheit (–18°C). The summers are generally warm, reaching 90–95°F (29 to 32°C), and dry, though relieved by monsoons that typically bring rain during the late summer.

Zuni is located in a remote area of one of the most sparsely populated regions of the USA. The nearest small town is 20 miles (32 km) to the east of Zuni Village. The distance to the nearest large town and interstate highway is approximately 40 miles (64 km), and to the nearest large city, Albuquerque, about 200 miles (320 km).

The total population of Zuni is 9562 (Pueblo of Zuni Census Office, 1995). Zuni Indians comprise 95 per cent of the population, with the remainder con-

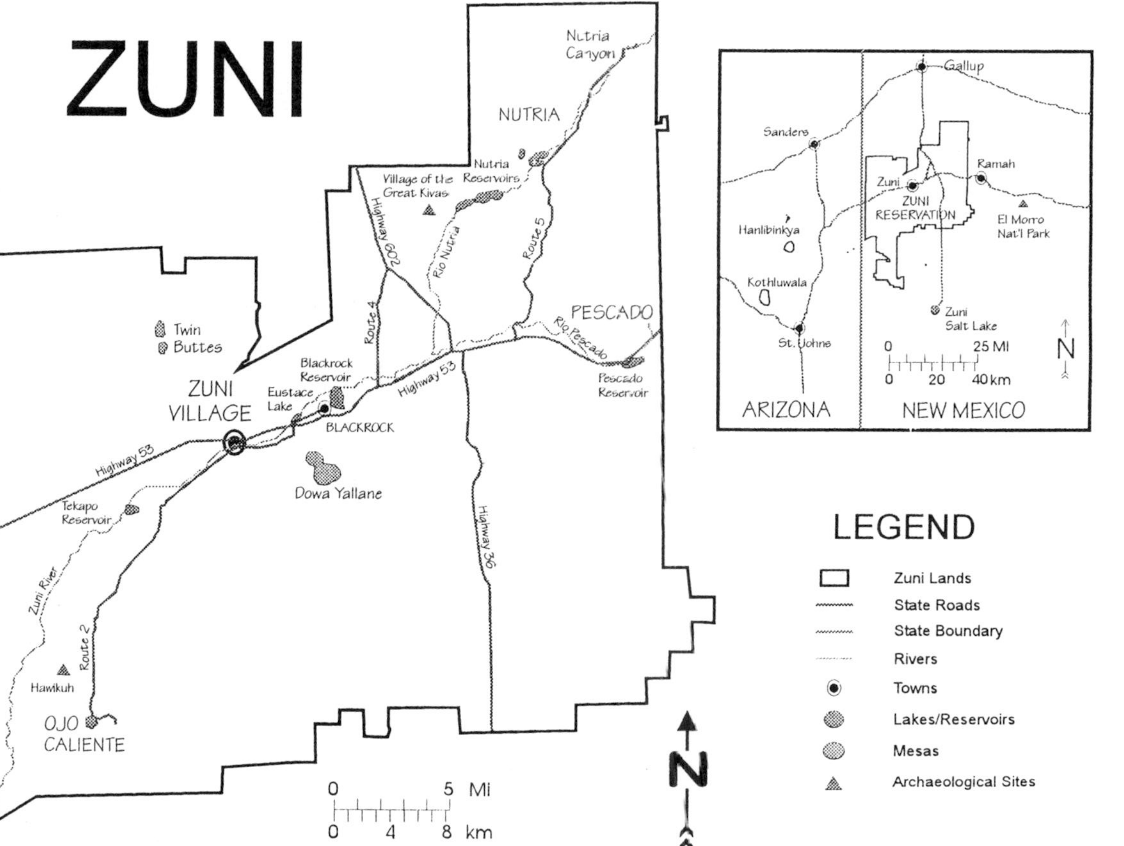

Figure 2.1 Zuni Indian lands

sisting of 4 per cent non-Zuni Indians and 1 per cent non-Indians. The population was severely affected by the immigration of Europeans and Americans to North America. At the turn of the century, the population was at an all-time low of 1000, but is now growing fast towards pre-contact numbers (Ferguson and Hart, 1985). Nearly all of the population live in the main village of Zuni and the nearby satellite community of Blackrock. Traditionally, Zunis lived in large extended family units, and the whole village (or pueblo) consisted of aggregations of these extended family units. Today, many Zunis choose to live in the main village, and extended family units exist, especially in the older parts of the village. Although nuclear family units are becoming more standard, relatives usually are neighbours.

The Zuni people are one of the 15 Pueblo Indian Tribes in the US Southwest. Today, the Puebloan heritage and history are represented in monumental structures such as those at nearby Chaco Canyon and Mesa Verde which were built and occupied around 1200 AD. The Zunis continue to occupy their ancestral lands, although their total land use area was significantly diminished as a result of Spanish, Mexican, and subsequent US encroachment. Aboriginal Zuni land encompassed nearly 15 million acres (6 070 500 hectares) over the present states of New Mexico and Arizona (Ferguson and Hart, 1985). According to Zuni oral history, a long time ago, the Zuni people came to the present site of Zuni Village from their origin near the Grand Canyon. Archaeologists have been able to trace human presence in the Zuni area to the Paleo-Indian period, 5–10,000 years ago (Cordell, 1984). Archaeological evidence identified in Zuni Village has been dated at 650 AD (Ferguson and Hart, 1985). Zuni Village is only one of the settlements occupied by Zuni people at the time of Western contact.

Needless to say, Zunis have been living in Zuni for a very long time. To a visitor Zuni appears, at first glance, like any other small rural town in the West. Yet closer observation shows that the Zuni people still live according to their traditional way of life. Alongside the modern conveniences—televisions, computers, and telecommunications—the Zuni religion, language, agriculture, and other traditions continue to be essential parts of Zuni life and are passed on from one generation to the next.

TOURISM IN ZUNI

The first Europeans who made their way to Zuni in the sixteenth century were the Spanish explorers Fray Marcos de Niza and Francisco Coronado who came to Zuni in search of the fabled cities of gold (Hammond, 1940; Preston, 1992). Subsequently, more foreign colonizers and missionaries found their way to Zuni to exert their influence. In the last century, American anthropologists including Frank Hamilton Cushing (1882–83), A.E. Kroeber (1917), and Ruth Benedict (1934) were attracted by the exotic and the esoteric. They, like many of the present visitors to Zuni, came for many different reasons and each brings to Zuni their ideas, ideology, and influences.

Many visitors today are familiar with Zuni because of the reputation of Zuni jewellery and arts and crafts. Zuni artists are well known for their high-quality hand-made inlay and needlepoint jewellery, as well as their animal carvings or fetishes, traditional pottery, and paintings. Zuni art and jewellery are sold and collected all over the world. Visitors invariably stop at the numerous trading posts to buy a few items for gifts; others come to Zuni as traders who buy from Zuni artists or local trading posts for their retail or wholesale businesses. Others are intrigued by the archaeology, the culture, and the living traditions. Handfuls of people come for the opportunity to visit ancient ruins, and several hundreds travel great distances to witness the ongoing practice of Zuni traditional religion. All visitors to Zuni are no doubt attracted to the beautiful and unadulterated landscape of the Zuni River valley, the dramatic sandstone mesas, riparian areas, woodlands, and accompanying wildlife.

Zuni is part of the Southwest tourist agenda as one of the stops in Indian Country. However, it is definitely off the beaten path, so that travellers must consciously make Zuni a destination and take a significant detour to visit it. According to Butler's (1980) resort cycle model, Zuni tourist development is in the 'exploration stage' of the cycle. According to the model, tourism in this stage is not well developed, and there are few or no resources specifically directed at servicing tourists. There are no hotels or other accommodation for tourists in Zuni; visitors who need lodging find it in the neighbouring towns. There is no tourist centre, and only within the past year has a one-person Tribal office been dedicated to tourism in Zuni. As a result, practically no statistical information on the number of tourists and the economic benefits of tourism in Zuni exists. The typical tourist who comes to Zuni is for the most part operating on his or her own initiative. Few are resourceful enough to find their way to the few government agencies or individuals which direct visitors to places of interest.

Economic viability is obviously an important concern of the Tribe. With high unemployment and an increasing population, the Tribe is faced with the task of encouraging development that will provide more local jobs and a better standard of living for the community. At present, the art industry provides most of the population with an income; the Tribe is the second largest employer; and there are efforts to further develop local land-based industries such as agriculture and livestock grazing. Another development option is tourism, which has been under consideration by the community and the Tribal government for many years. Yet it remains a hotly debated topic, invariably countered with strong sentiments of caution and opposition. Zuni has learned by experience, as well as by example, of the ill-effects of tourism development, and is aware of the potential of long-lasting negative consequences of unregulated and hasty tourism development. However, tourism remains an attractive option, as it has for many other Tribes in the Southwest, because of the relatively low capital investment and potentially high economic returns.

Development proposals have ranged from very large-scale projects with heavy external investment to small local community efforts. Zuni's tourism goals originate from a desire to increase revenue from the present, albeit limited, tourist activity, but these goals are tempered by mixed sentiments about the desirability of increasing activity. Besides generating economic benefit for the Tribe, the most crucial need with regard to tourism is to provide tourists with information regarding respectful and proper behaviour within the community. It is also important to control and limit tourist activity which may adversely interrupt daily life.

Thus, on one hand, the interest of economic development weighs heavily as many Zunis seek alternate incomes because of diminishing markets for Zuni art and increasing costs of living. On the other hand, the interest in cultural preservation and environmental protection have also become important community concerns. As a result, general reactions to efforts promoting tourism development have been negative, citing insensitivity or even blasphemy for Zuni religion and concern over sovereignty of Zuni land use.

RECENT HISTORY OF TOURISM IN ZUNI

In 1965, a Zuni government door-to-door survey was conducted to ascertain individuals' goals for the Zuni community. Among the ideas suggested were establishing a tourist information centre, creating recreation areas and rest areas, training tourist guides, building motels, and developing archaeological sites (Pueblo of Zuni, 1965).

In 1976, the Zuni Comprehensive Development Plan outlined an extensive tourism development plan:

> The increase in tourism in the Zuni area and the spending pattern of the non-local tourist indicate that there is significant potential, from the tourist dollar, to the economy of Zuni. The Zuni Reservation, endowed with many historic sites, scenic vistas, sufficient surface water, and a relatively high elevation, can readily be developed into an attraction for such [tourist] activities.
>
> (Pueblo of Zuni, 1976: 3–A–7)

The Plan made provisions for a motel complex, public campgrounds, and archaeological site development as well as a large-scale proposal sponsored by the National Park Service (NPS). First drafted by the NPS and the Zuni Tribe in 1971, this proposal described the establishment of a Zuni-Cibola National Historical Park (ZCNHP). This was to be planned and managed by the National Park Service, in consultation with an Advisory Commission consisting of the Governor of the Zuni Tribe, the Director of the National Park Service, the Secretary of the Smithsonian Institution, the State Historic Preservation Officer of New Mexico, and three members appointed by the Secretary from recommendations made by the Governor of the Zuni Tribe (United States, 1988: Sec. 6(a)(1)).

The Zuni Tribal Administration supported the concept of establishing the Park as a means to foster the development of a self-sustaining and viable tourism industry (Pueblo of Zuni, 1976: 3-A-7). It would provide for the development and management of selected historical areas on the reservation for tourism, as well as for archaeological site conservation. The proposal was approved at the national level and became an Act of Congress in 1988 (United States, 1988). It stated that Zuni would lease designated sites of 'national and historical' interest to the National Park Service who would then provide for the development and management of these selected historical areas:

> In order to preserve and protect for the benefit of present and future generations certain nationally significant historical, archeological, cultural, and natural sites and resources associated with the Zuni Tribe, and in order to assist members of the Zuni Tribe in preserving and interpreting their tribal culture, there is hereby established the Zuni-Cibola National Historical Park. The park shall consist of lands with respect to which the Secretary of the Interior has accept a leasehold pursuant to ... this Act.
>
> (United States, 1988: Sec. 2(a)).

However, no action has yet been taken by the Zuni community in fulfilment of this Act because Zuni community response terminated its implementation in 1988, as described by the director of the National Park Service, James Ridenour (1990):

> Since the enactment of the authorization act for the establishment of Zuni-Cibola National Historical Park in 1988, the National Park Service has worked very closely with the elected authorities of the Zuni Tribe to prepare a draft statement .... During the process of preparing preliminary documents for the operation of the park, various individuals in the Zuni Tribe became concerned about the details of the proposed leasehold agreement with the Federal Government .... As a result of concerns by some tribal members, Zuni Pueblo Governor and the Tribal Council decided to have an election on the issue of establishing the park on the basis of the 1988 legislation. On January 30, 1988, the Zuni Tribe held an election on the park issue. The result of this election was that 863 Zuni voters cast votes against the park concept and 125 voted in favor of the leasehold and proceeding with the park.

Zuni community action suspended the implementation of the Act because it was felt that the NPS would not give sufficient consideration to Zuni religious activities near or in the Park, and because the Tribal Council did not adequately consult the Zuni public about the establishment of the Park and the ramifications to Zuni tribal sovereignty. As a result, the terms of the Act have been extended in order to provide time to amend it to suit the needs of the community (United States, 1990). The A:shiwi A:wan Museum and Heritage Center, a not-for-profit non-governmental organization located in Zuni and composed of Zuni Tribal members, is seeking opportunities to re-negotiate the terms of the Act to utilize potential funds in a manner acceptable to Zuni's mainstream and culturally sensitive interests.

There have also been a series of small-scale, locally initiated efforts to facilitate tourist activity in Zuni. In the 1970s, the Tribe published a widely distributed tourist information brochure that was intended to attract travellers to Zuni. In 1988, a group of local businesspeople established the Zuni Area Chamber of Commerce. One of its goals was to develop tourism on a small local scale. They published a tourist information newspaper 'Experience Zuni, New Mexico' and a tourist brochure that was distributed throughout the Southwest region. At present, *Zuni History* (Ferguson and Hart, 1991), a locally distributed publication, and a small independent regional monthly newspaper, *Highway 53*, serve as visitor-orientation materials. There are also a few local individuals who occasionally serve as tour guides to interested visitors.

In 1994, the Tribal Government's Business Development, Sustainment and Finance Committee was established for the Zuni Comprehensive Development Plan Update, 1994. Tourism development once again was among the major topics of discussion. Presently, the A:shiwi A:wan Museum and Heritage Center is conducting a community survey of feelings and attitudes concerning tourism, development, and cultural preservation. This organization has an important place in the discussion of tourist development because the community survey gives voice and attention to individual testimony from Tribal members. Preliminary results show that the overwhelming majority of those surveyed are concerned about the preservation of Zuni cultural traditions and sites. Issues such as the need for law enforcement and protection of Zuni sacred sites are perceived as very critical.

SOCIO-CULTURAL CONCERNS

The need for control over the development of tourism is, primarily, to safeguard against negative consequences that will permanently affect the social and cultural life of Zuni. Zuni is an example of a community that is proceeding cautiously to develop a sustainable and appropriate course for involvement in the tourist industry, and has been relatively fortunate that its remote location has kept large-scale tourist activity and outside intrusion to a minimum. As a result, there has been very limited external involvement and influence in the demand for escalated efforts to develop tourism. Although grand proposals for motel complexes, casinos, and even golf courses have repeatedly moved through preliminary and even secondary stages of planning, none of these proposals has been implemented. In fact, Zuni can be thought of as a counter-example to rampant tourism growth in the name of development. Much of this caution is a result of Zuni's cultural and social environment and highly theocratic governing system.

The issues that face Zuni in determining its position toward development are common to many other indigenous communities in the 1990s. These communities must not only work to remain viable and sustainable within a global industrialized economy, but also struggle to retain their individuality, customs, and traditions. These often opposing goals lie at the crux of decision-making in indigenous communities. Tourism brings these issues to the forefront in perhaps the most dramatic way.

Zuni culture continues to retain its integrity and social traditions in spite of its existence within the greater United States culture. There are very distinct aspects of Zuni life that may not be understood or even recognized by a visitor. For example, the oral tradition is a very different method of communication than a written tradition. Religion is passed and communicated orally and by example. Knowledge, practices, and all that is sacred are taught by apprenticeship and practised by memory. The esoteric knowledge is sacred and is not public property. For example, photographic, audio or video recordings, drawing, or any other documentation of Zuni religious events is strictly prohibited by Zuni law. Although signs are posted in the village, tourists often do not see them, do not understand the reasons for the prohibition, or do not take the warnings seriously, and consequently violate the law. Visitors are not allowed to capture Zuni religion on video, for example, because what they have witnessed is not theirs to take home. This would be sacrilegious. It is for these reasons that it is essential to have informed visitors who are respectful of Zuni culture.

Another example of culture and control in Zuni tourism is illustrated by the government edict to close all Zuni religious events to non-Indians in June 1990. Tour buses are still not allowed to enter Zuni during the summer rain dances and the large winter ceremony Sha'lako. One reason for the restriction is that there are no facilities to accommodate such a large influx of tourists. The main reason, however, was that the tour companies were selling Sha'lako and other Zuni religious events as an attraction. Zuni religion was being used to make money. The exchange of money for religious knowledge, ceremonies, or iconography is strictly prohibited and denounced in Zuni culture. This is an example of the cultural differences and misunderstandings that tourism (and tourists) often neglect. This cultural conflict is evident in an article on the ban in the *Gallup Independent*, a local newspaper:

> Zuni tribal officials have 'closed to non-Indians' all religious ceremonies, including summer rain dances and the popular winter dances, they said Thursday. Zuni's biggest tourist attraction is Sha'lako.... The traditional ceremonies bring thousands of tourists—and dollars—to the pueblo each year, and many of those who profit from the influx of tourists are not happy with the tribal council's decision to close the ceremonies to the public.
>
> (Dubin, 1990)

In 1995, there were several tourist incidents involving photography and inappropriate behaviour at Zuni religious events. In response, the Zuni Tribal government and religious leaders have installed an interim ban of all non-Indians from all religious dances.

NATURAL-RESOURCE AND ENVIRONMENTAL CONCERNS

The effects of development on natural resources and the environment cannot be separated from planning for tourism. In the Zuni community, the rhetorical distinctions between land, people, society, culture, religion, and environment become meaningless. The word Zuni means the land, the people, the village, the religion, and the language; they are inseparable. As such, natural-resource concerns are directly linked to issues of cultural preservation and social needs. Protection of Zuni natural resources is necessary for the Tribe's continuance. Water, air, soil, and biodiversity are resources that can be easily affected by tourism. Environmental concerns are supposedly implicit in terms such as sustainable development, ecotourism, and sustainable tourism development.

The degradation of natural resources and the environment is a primary concern in any sort of development. This is especially true for tourism which, due to its often rapid growth, may have unforeseen results and environmental impacts which must be carefully assessed. One recent example is the recent proposal to develop a casino and hotel complex on Zuni land. Real estate was identified and contributing investors were contacted. However, the impact assessment was incomplete, especially with regard to water. This is always a basic issue to be explored carefully, whatever the scale of development, as Zuni's domestic water supply is limited and the system needs repair and upgrading.

In more remote settings, tourism would have relatively little impact because access to backcountry areas is greatly restricted (Figure 2.2). However, many visitors have expressed an interest in viewing the culture of land use and the settings of activities such as farming and livestock grazing. The pastoral nature of these activities is a strong attraction to visitors from large cities and those with an interest in the conservation of natural resources. Some visitors would also like to see major archaeological sites described in historical literature. Currently, restrictions for non-Zunis visiting many areas of the reservation need

Figure 2.2 Visitor access to backcountry Zuni land is greatly restricted

clarification. The restrictions are loosely defined and are always changing in the process of determining what measures are required to adequately safeguard Zuni cultural resources. Thus, in general, organized discussion and policy-making on the subject of backcountry visitors are needed. However, the policy for big-game hunting by non-Indians is an example of approved organized harvesting of Zuni resources by non-Indians. Non-Indian hunters are permitted to hunt with a Zuni guide. This form of tourism has been very successful and has been supported by the community. In this case, religious, economic, and societal needs were discussed together in several meetings by representatives from the various interests involved, leading to a commonly understood policy.

As such, tourists are secondary in issues of environmental protection. This is because cultural preservation and concern for the protection of Zuni religious areas prohibit tourists from visiting backcountry areas of Zuni lands as would normally be the case on state or federal lands. Because Zuni is a sovereign state, Tribal laws can dictate where visitors may and may not go. Consequently, minimal tourist impact to the Zuni environment is assured as long as tourist travel is controlled by cultural concerns.

For the tourist, Zuni is a magnificent place to see how culture, environment, and survival have evolved together in a form of sustainable development that has been practised for many thousands of years. If planned wisely, tourism in Zuni will not destroy what it seeks to share: 'I think that what the Zunis want, above all, is to have outsiders understand the depth of feeling which they have for their landscape and understand that they have treated their environment with the same kind of respect which they have for their friends and for their families' (Hart, 1991).

SUMMARY

Tourism generally has a negative connotation to many Zunis because of bad examples seen elsewhere and experienced locally. With no clear and consistent direction with respect to Zuni tourism, it has been difficult to see any benefits, protective or otherwise, to the Zuni people as a whole. But in fact, a process is occurring. Hidden in Zuni attitudes and social customs, there are voices of people who are leading Zuni to a definition of what kind of tourism will be allowed and how Zuni will benefit.

When the Zuni Tribal Council recently took emergency measures to make Zuni ceremonial dances off-limits to non-Indians, they were reacting to the request of Zuni religious leaders. The Tribal Council admits that it does not have an answer and a plan for tourism development, but has taken a responsible approach in the process. Eventually, tourism will almost certainly become a part of Zuni society and, in these early stages, Zuni is being careful to weigh all foreseeable social and economic costs. The strict measures by the Tribal Council and religious leaders are part of a conservative approach that allows

Zuni to look for a sustainable solution, and should not necessarily be seen as anti-growth.

Tourism development need not necessarily be 'folly if it is carefully planned and integrated into the local economy and society' (Wilkinson, 1989). Experience from elsewhere has shown that:

> Only the firsthand experience of the industry's negative impacts may finally convince authorities of the prudence involved in proceeding more cautiously through the introduction of environmental controls and destinations. This post facto approach to planning arrives too late to rectify the sector's serious externalities.
>
> (Ionnides, 1995)

Zuni needs a systematic approach and management plan to develop, guide, and maintain a tourism industry that incorporates and responds to community values and opinion. The world is shrinking quickly and Zuni will be exposed to other cultures in one form or another. Likewise, other cultures have met and touched Zuni and will continue to do so. The process of defining Zuni needs with respect to tourism is occurring in a characteristic Zuni style. These needs typically concern the individual and family first, and many Zuni people want the opportunity to earn a living immediately. Tourism is seen as a quick way to generate jobs and strengthen the local economy. It is essential for any tourism development to support these immediate economic needs while maintaining the perspective of the long-term sustainability of a Zuni tourism industry. The scale of development must also be maintained in perspective, as hasty planning may not take into account the market, management, and human resource factors that will determine the extent to which the industry can develop.

The issues are also being defined in a manner which is typically Zuni and is familiar to other developing communities with strong cultural roots. While a host of issues pose challenges to an organized plan, they are surmountable. The foremost issues pertain to religious and traditional views, inadequate infrastructure, and minimal capital to stimulate economic rewards. Another key challenge is the definition of the direction and integration of tourism into Zuni society. A sustainable tourism industry is feasible, provided that development serves the community's needs, and works within the parameters set by the community. This form of tourism has the potential to enhance the Zuni way of life, rather than eroding it. However the process proceeds, Zuni will come to terms with the development of tourism through a thorough mixing of ideas and expressions—just as Zunis have done for thousands of years.

REFERENCES

Anyon, R., 1994, Tourism Development, *Report for Zuni Comprehensive Development Plan Update*, June 8, 1994, Pueblo of Zuni.

Bender, N.J. (ed.), 1984, *Missionaries, Outlaws and Indians: Taylor F. Ealy at Lincoln and Zuni, 1878–1881*, University of New Mexico Press, Albuquerque.

Benedict, R., 1934, *Patterns of Culture*, Mentor Books, New York.
Bowekaty, M., 1994, *Report for Zuni Comprehensive Development Plan Update*, July 28, 1994, Pueblo of Zuni.
Butler, R.W., 1980, The concept of a tourist area cycle of evolution: Implications for management of resources, *Canadian Geographer*, 14: 5–12.
Cordell, L., 1984, *Prehistory of the Southwest*, Academic Press, New York.
Cushing, F.H. [1882–83], 1967, *My Adventures in Zuni*, Filter Press, Palmer Lake, Colorado.
Dubin, M., 1990, Zuni religious events all shut, *Gallup Independent*, June 15, 1990: 1.
Evans-Pritchard, D., 1989, How 'They' see 'Us': Native American images of tourists, *Annals of Tourism Research*, 16, 89–105.
Ferguson, T.J. and Hart, E.R., 1985, *A Zuni Atlas*, University of Oklahoma Press, Norman.
Ferguson, T.J. and Hart, E.R. (eds), 1991, *Zuni History*, 3rd edn, Pueblo of Zuni.
Hammond, G.P., 1940, *Coronado's Seven Cities*, US Coronado Exposition Commission, Albuquerque.
Hart, R.E., 1991, Historic Zuni Land Use, in *Zuni History: Victories in the 1990's*, 2nd edn, Pueblo of Zuni, Institute of the North American West and Zuni Archaeology Project: 1–5.
Ionnides, D., 1995, Planning for International Tourism in Less Developed Countries: Toward Sustainability, *Journal of Planning Literature*, 9: 235–254.
Kroeber, A.E., 1917, Zuni Kin & Clan, *Anthropological Papers of the American Museum of Natural History*, 18, pt.2.
Preston, D.J., 1992, *Cities of Gold*, Simon and Schuster, New York.
Pueblo of Zuni, 1965, Tribal Goals, *Zuni Comprehensive Development Plan, 1965*, Pueblo of Zuni.
Pueblo of Zuni, 1976, *Zuni Comprehensive Development Plan, Toward Zuni, 1985*, Pueblo of Zuni.
Pueblo of Zuni Census Office, 1995, *Population of the Pueblo of Zuni, September 1995*, Pueblo of Zuni.
Ridenour, J., 1990, Statement of James Ridenour, Director, National Park Service, Department of the Interior, in United States, 1990, Congress. Senate. Amending the Zuni-Cibola National Historical Park Establishment Act of 1988 to enlarge the time in which the Secretary of the Interior may accept a leasehold interest for inclusion in the park. Senate Report 101–323. June 8, 1990: 4.
Sweet, J.D., 1991, 'Let 'em Loose': Pueblo Indian Management of Tourism, *American Indian Culture and Research Journal*, 15(4), 59–74.
United States, 1988, Public Law 100–567, Oct. 31, 1988. [Zuni-Cibola National Historical Park Establishment Act of 1988].
United States, 1990, Congress. Senate. Amending the Zuni-Cibola National Historical Park Establishment Act of 1988 to enlarge the time in which the Secretary of the Interior may accept a leasehold interest for inclusion in the park. Senate Report 101–323, June 8, 1990.
Wilkinson, P., 1989, Strategies for tourism in island microstates, *Annals of Tourism Research*, 16(1), 153–177.
Zuni Area Chamber of Commerce, 1989, *Experience Zuni New Mexico*, 1989. Pueblo of Zuni.

3 The Inuit as Hosts: Heritage and Wilderness Tourism in Nunavut

VALENE L. SMITH

Nunavut is a new semi-autonomous Inuit (Eskimo) territory (or 'nation' as the term is now used by Native American tribes in the USA) in the northeastern Canadian Arctic. It was officially approved on May 25, 1993 and, following nearly six years of implementation, will be formally launched on April 1, 1999. The largest aboriginal land claim settlement in history, it is rooted in archaeological evidence of Inuit land use spanning at least four millennia (Schledermann, 1990).

The development and management of Nunavut is certain to be carefully monitored by indigenous peoples and political entities around the world, for the implications of its creation are manifestly political, social, and economic. They are also touristic, offering to the resident Inuit an opportunity to control and manage their visitor industry to a degree seldom attained elsewhere. The Nunavut people as a whole can choose to encourage, limit, or even disallow tourism; and within that framework, individual communities can creatively develop local tourism to reflect their resource base and their social preferences. The effectiveness of their tourism planning may also figure importantly in the economic success of the entity, providing employment and a renewed awareness of heritage, as has been noted elsewhere in the Arctic (Smith, 1989).

This chapter addresses some of the important factors to be considered in planning for tourism: namely, the four H's of tourism—habitat, heritage, history, and handicrafts (Smith, 1996)—as they apply to Nunavut.

NUNAVUT: THE NEW STATE

Nunavut, Inuktitut for 'Our Land', grants to some 17 500 resident Inuit outright ownership of approximately one-fifth the total land area of Canada (or an area three times the size of France) (Figure 3.1). The 1993 Agreement between the Inuit and Canada identifies the areas only by coordinates, not by areal extent, which is estimated at 353 610 km^2 (136 493 square miles) of land, which con-

People and Tourism in Fragile Environments. Edited by M. F. Price.

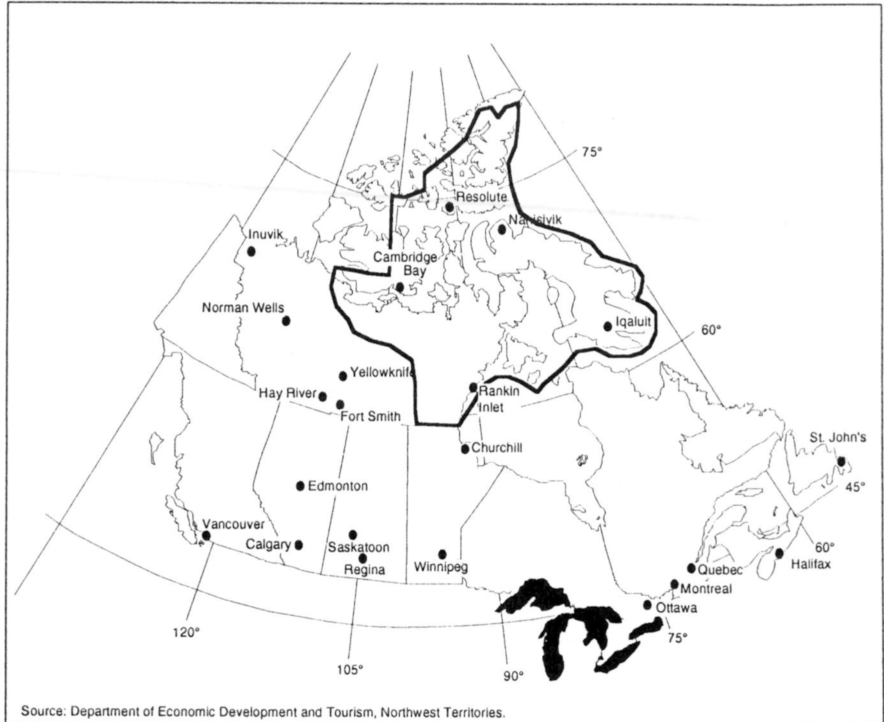

Source: Department of Economic Development and Tourism, Northwest Territories.

Figure 3.1 Nunavut: general location

Source: Department of Economic Development and Tourism, Northwest Territories

stitutes about 18 per cent of the total entity. The remaining 82 per cent—an additional 1.6 million km² of land—is to be held in joint Inuit-Canada control (for subsistence pursuits). The settlement also awards C$1.15 billion for an Inuit-controlled trust fund, the proceeds from which are to provide small loans for Inuit businesses, for educational scholarships, and as an income support subsidy for full-time hunters.

The 282-page Agreement, printed in English, was mailed to every Inuit resident prior to their vote in 1993. The award further granted to the new government their choice of 36 257 km² of subsurface mineral rights. Their selection included some 80 per cent of the known mineral reserves within the area, including copper, lead, zinc, gold, and silver. The first new resource to be developed is a copper and zinc mine 300 km south of Coppermine, near Nunavut's western border. Initial development includes building a haul road to deliver ore to a deep-water port to be created on Coronation Gulf. Two operating lead and zinc mines, one on Little Cornwallis Island and the other at Nanisivik on northern Baffin Island, already benefit the Inuit. Overall, the eventual mineral royalties are projected to have a value of millions of dollars.

Multiple challenges confront the Nunavut Implementation Commission

(NIC), headed by John Amagoalik, termed by some 'father of his country'. The NIC must decide upon a site for the new capital, plan a legislative body, and draft a legal system. The working language for Nunavut will be Inuktitut. A traditional problem in the North still persists: communication and transportation costs among the remote small villages are expensive. However, thanks to far-sighted Canadian educators, many Inuit schools are computer-equipped, and the NIC leadership expects to rely heavily on the so-called electronic highway already in place. *Footprints in the Snow,* the 1995 NIC interim report, states 'Pathways of the past were forged by dogsled and snowmobile... pathways of the future will be travelled electronically' (Pelly, 1995: 9). As part of the effort to distribute economic benefits more widely, Nunavut stresses government decentralization, with no more than 12 per cent of employees expected to be resident in the capital; in contrast to the 40 per cent of Northwest Territories (NWT) employees who live in Yellowknife.

The Nunavut Agreement of 1993 followed twenty years of land claims agitation and was fraught with controversy and delay (Duffy, 1988; Purich, 1992). A private report commissioned by Canada's Federal government illustrates some of the economic concerns, and suggests that establishing the new government will cost C$850 million between 1999 and 2008 (Facts on File, 1993). Thereafter, the Canadian government's annual commitment to Nunavut is scheduled to be C$84.6 million, an amount which will cost Canadian taxpayers about 12 per cent more per year than the total Federal 1993 budget for supporting the same population on the same lands. In addition, Canada will have foregone substantial mineral rights and their generated income.

The Agreement is very complex with reference to non-Inuit who may vote and hold office. It also details joint Federal–Nunavut management for wildlife, fisheries, and parks. The potentially extensive mineral development of the Canadian Shield—including diamonds, oil, gas, gold, and other minerals—will be subject to regulations which are detailed and deemed by some outsiders to be restrictive and one-sided. Three implementation levels are outlined (Mablick, 1995). First, an Inuit-Owned Lands (IOLs) Prospecting License is issued to 'facilitate easy access to Inuit Mineral Lands and to encourage grass-roots exploration of those lands'. Success at this level is prerequisite to a second phase, negotiation of an IOLs Mineral Concession, 'designed to encourage more extensive exploration and development of specific property through provision of secure tenure'. This may then lead to the third level, and issuance of a Production Lease. Quarrying rights are dealt with differently; all soapstone is reserved to Inuit only; uranium and related rights are reserved from any grant; and the oil and gas regime is still undecided.

Despite the effort to encourage 'grass-roots' exploration, the geological nature, minerals, and isolation of the region combine to make all production very costly. In August 1995, the author observed the *Federal Baffin,* a 40 000-ton vessel loaded with lead and zinc concentrates, being escorted through Lancaster Sound by the Canadian ice-breaker, *Terry Fox.* As of mid-1995, the

Canadian government continues to provide free escort service for ore ships in support of the export industry. However, a Federal government faced with budgetary shrinkage could well decide to privatize such industry support; operational costs for a privately operated ice-breaker like the *Terry Fox* average C$35 000 per day. Mineral revenues are important both to the national and the Nunavut economy. Yet, with mining operations almost completely automated, local employment is very limited, especially for the Inuit, because they generally lack the necessary skills and education to function in a highly technical environment.

NUNAVUT SOCIETY

The creation of Nunavut is a psychological triumph of self-determination for the Inuit, but mere existence of an enabling entity does not automatically resolve prevailing social problems. Unemployment ranges between 30 and 50 per cent, and is likely to increase because 40 per cent of the Inuit population is under 15 years of age (Pelly, 1994). For men, subsistence hunting/fishing is not a 'sport'; it is hard work, dependent on acquired skills and good (and expensive) equipment. The food quest is not dependable, and subsistence food does not generate income to buy petrol, snowmobiles, fishing boats, or ammunition. Many younger Inuit are disinterested in this life-style, but wage employment (or welfare) are the only alternatives except for re-location outside the Arctic which, to date, has not been widely successful. Despite decades of Canadian investment in well-equipped schools and well-trained teachers, only 15 per cent of students complete high school (Pelly, 1994). Others are too poorly prepared to move into positions of responsibility in government jobs, independently to innovate viable businesses, or to manage their new-found wealth effectively.

The Inuit have long suffered from a negative self-image, dating from early contacts with outsiders, whether Hudson Bay storekeepers, Royal Canadian Mounted Police (RCMP), teachers, or missionaries. Eskimos became ashamed of their culture, especially when forced off the land into villages for administrative convenience in health and education. Attending school was not compatible with migratory subsistence; children 'got behind' in their studies, lost interest, and eventually gave up, since school did not seem to lead to anything. Among a generation still living, some youths were sent to high schools at cities 'in the South', or to sanatoria for tuberculosis treatment. These experiences altered their family status and values; many learned English. When they returned home after several years absence, their traditional parents and other elders attributed the changes to a type of shamanistic *kipio* or 'soul loss' whereby *Kabloona* (the Inuit term for white man) had captured their spirit. Welfare cheques—the principal source of income in most Canadian Inuit communities—further undermined self-reliance.

Nunavut has materialized as a pivot of change: throughout the North in the 1990s it is evident that Canadian Inuit have come almost full circle. The youths who once were said to have 'lost their soul' had in reality learned English and become rather politically astute. They formed the nucleus of the land-claim movement and the consequent formation of Nunavut. Today, their children and grandchildren are articulate young people, some of whom are staffing computers, publishing newspapers, operating radio stations, and travelling. They are role models, as participants in the new 'state', and exist in sufficient numbers to validate both the value of education and the consequent Inuit ability to compete with the rest of the world on its own terms. Tiny Grise Fiord, the farthest north continuously occupied Inuit village in Canada, boasts a well-known teenage choir. A visiting maritime officer recalls a girl wearing a jacket emblazoned with a 'Moscow' logo. Upon inquiry, she explained in English, 'Oh, I've been everywhere—Moscow, Paris, New York...'.

Canadian Inuit routinely travel by air throughout their North to visit family and friends, as well as to circumpolar sports competitions, exhibitions, church functions, and political meetings. Inuit are frequent customers for charter air services, and their travels provide domestic tourism revenues to support air carriers, hotels, and stores. Similarly, individuals and communities host visitors, sometimes from as distant as Siberia, Greenland, and Scandinavia. Almost every community now has at least one inn owned by the Arctic Cooperatives Ltd Hotel Division (Figure 3.2). With basic infrastructure in place, increased tourism from other parts of Canada, the USA and abroad may serve here, as elsewhere, as a developmental tool, providing some much-needed employment, and as an industry that reinforces Inuit identity.

CANADIAN ARCTIC TOURISM: AN OVERVIEW

Canada's Far North is a landscape little known outside Canada, except for scholars with Arctic interests and the few visitors who have already ventured there. Even jet-setters flying the Great Circle route from Europe to North America seldom have an aerial view. Attendants usually close window shades to show a film or encourage passengers to sleep because 'there's nothing to see out there'. Yet most jet routes between London and Pacific Coast cities overfly significant portions of Nunavut, as they enter Canadian airspace soon after leaving Greenland's western shores. They pass over Iqaluit (formerly Frobisher Bay) on Baffin Island, then westward to their destination. Even from 35 000 feet, many Nunavut landmarks such as Baker Lake (described below) are discernible on a clear day, and the flight becomes a visual experience revealing the vastness of this sparsely populated land.

The Canadian North sprawls over nearly 2.8 million km^2 of land lying north of approximately 60°N. The Arctic is better defined climatically by the mean July isotherm of 50°F (10°C), which serves as the growth boundary between coniferous forests to the south, and the northern Arctic tundra vegetation of low-growing mosses, sedges, and lichens (Sugden, 1982: 17). This remote area,

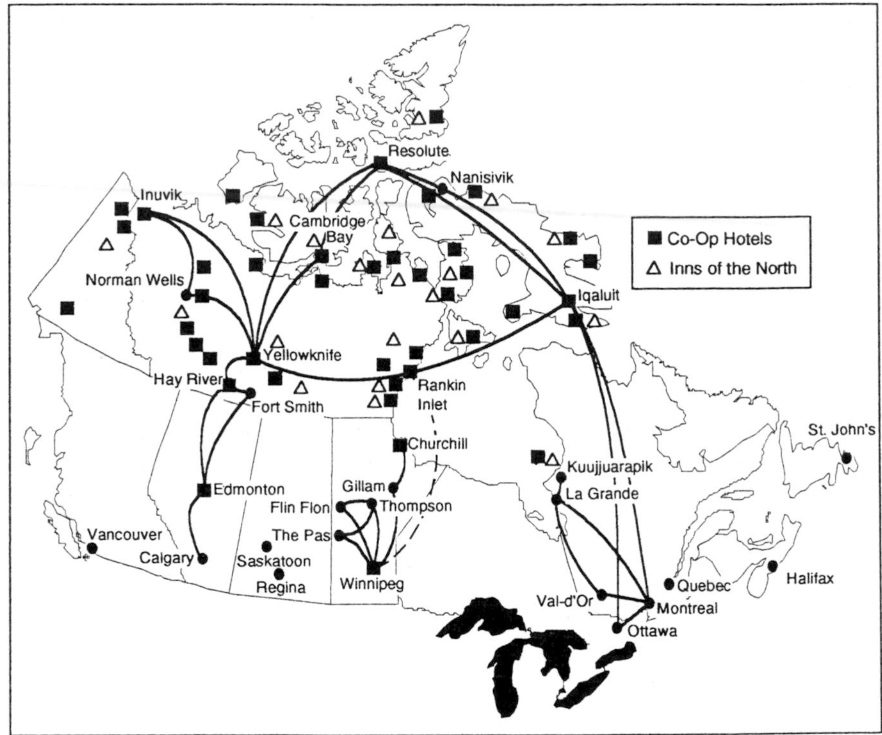

Figure 3.2 Canadian Pacific system route map and local accommodations, 1995

10 per cent larger than the State of Alaska or 12 times the size of the United Kingdom, is divided into two topographic provinces. The larger eastern area, mostly within Nunavut, includes the rugged islands of Baffin and Ellesmere with their dramatic headlands and bird rookeries as well as the treeless, gently undulating heavily glaciated barrens of the Laurentian Shield. West of Nunavut lie the Yukon and excluded portions of Northwest Territories, including the historically important administrative city of Yellowknife.

For perspective, tourism analysis must include this western area because Yellowknife remains the regional capital until a Nunavut site is readied. In addition, Canadian federal and territorial offices in Yellowknife have been actively involved for several decades in the use of tourism for economic development. Their data and orientation are of importance to future policy and management in Nunavut.

Tourism developed quite differently in the western areas of the Yukon and Northwest Territories, primarily because of geographic factors. A brief review is instructive. The construction of the 2400 km Alaska Highway (Alcan) from Dawson Creek, Canada to Fairbanks, Alaska during World War II was the initial link that opened tourism to the western Canadian North. In 1979, the Dempster

Highway, a 730-km gravel road connecting Dawson City to Inuvik on the MacKenzie delta, split off from the Alcan. Thus, in western Canada as in northern Europe, vacationers can drive to the Arctic (Sandell, 1995). The government of the Northwest Territories has actively solicited this wilderness recreation market through an innovative publication, *The NWT Explorer's Guide*, published annually for the past 25 years and distributed free of charge. The 1995 edition (Office of Economic Development and Tourism, 1995b), with 128 slick pages and many excellent full-page photographs, is financially supported by private suppliers: outfitters, charter aircraft companies, guides, hotels, and tour operators. Of the 130 000 copies of this edition, 46 000 were mailed in response to direct inquiries by mail or phone. The NWT maintains a toll-free number in both Canada and the USA, to supply more detailed information for interested individuals. Other copies of the Guide are distributed through offices of the American Automobile Association, Canadian provincial offices and tour operators. The Territory has also actively supported tourism training, policy design and management, and research for the past fifteen years (Haywood, et al., 1993).

The NWT Office of Economic Development and Tourism (1994) extensively surveyed the 1994 visitors through an exit survey. Between May and September, 48 262 people visited the NWT, a figure that had changed only a modest six per cent since the previous exit survey, in 1989. The largest number of visitors came from Canada, and the second largest number from the USA. The primary reason for travel was to visit family and friends (28 per cent), followed by an almost equal division between such varied motives as 'see the Arctic', 'on the map', 'word of mouth', and 'magazine articles'. The exit study differentiated the visitor count in three areas: Dempster/Inuvik; South MacKenzie (South Slave, North Slave); and Nunavut. In all areas, leisure travel predominated, but of particular significance to this chapter is the observation:

> A wide range of activities were enjoyed by non-resident visitors, but those activities which encompassed the unique culture and the natural assets of the Northwest Territories [sic. including Nunavut] were the most popular. Overall, community tours (19%), canoeing/boating (15%), fishing (13%) and hiking (11%) were the four most popular activities indicated by respondents. These activities correlated well with the high ratings attributed to natural assets as attractions.
>
> (Office of Economic Development and Tourism, 1995a: 5)

In contrast to Western Canada, Nunavut and the eastern Arctic have no road links with metropolitan Canada. The air network operates from central hubs which provide service to outlying communities (Figure 3.2). Distances are great, and travel is notoriously expensive (Johnston, 1995). A few 1995 comparisons are instructive: because of traffic volume and airfare wars, a round-trip coach ticket between San Francisco and Denver (1019 miles) cost as little as US$228, and between San Francisco and Washington DC (2419 miles), only US$388. A similar air ticket from Ottawa to Iqaluit, approximately the same distance, cost US$1986; and between Iqaluit (the largest community in Nunavut with 3500 inhabitants) and Yellowknife (population 10 000), US$1224.

Many other factors contribute to expensive travel to any Arctic destination, and especially Nunavut with its dependence on air transport. Building construction on a permafrost foundation requires special standards, as the weight of buildings can cause subsurface melting, especially over an ice lens, and the foundation sinks unevenly; building materials have to be freighted 'from the South'. Food for tourist consumption is necessarily imported (except for caribou or fish). The Arctic is truly a 'polar desert'; culinary water is scarce and often trucked to the site from a distant source; many smaller communities have no sewage system, and must rely on chemical toilets; and heating is an almost year-round requirement. Consequently, accommodation reflects these costs. In August 1995, a tiny two-bedded room with public toilet and shower was US$200 per night at Resolute, and full board added another US$75 per person.

Summer cruises to the Arctic, popular in European waters for more than a century, are increasing in North America, and include Hudson Bay, the High Arctic, and the Northwest Passage (Marsh and Staple, 1995). Their appeal is multiple: tour operators negotiate low group or charter fares from air gateways in the USA or southern Canada; using zodiacs (rubber rafts) the vessels can bring passengers to historic sites (such as Beechey Island, identified with the ill-fated 1845–46 Franklin Expedition) and locate polar bears on the ice, herds of musk ox, and bird rookeries. The vessels normally operate from November to late February in Antarctica, then go into dry-dock for repairs and crew vacation, and operate in the Arctic from June through September.

Most ships retain a staff of natural history lecturers to interpret topics as diverse as geology, archaeology, and ice navigation. In many instances, the passengers develop friendships with lecturers and fellow passengers, and may form an 'associative group' who plan to travel together on another polar cruise. At an average cost of US$500 per day, many passengers are 'repeaters', for several itineraries already exist, and more are being added, including a circumnavigation of Baffin Island scheduled for August 1997. To duplicate such a trip by other means would necessitate chartering helicopters and private yachts. An inducement for adventure cruising is the informality; no dressing for dinner, no floor shows, no casinos; instead, a meal may become cold while the diner frantically photographs a passing whale or a polar bear.

Summer cruise tourism does not substantially benefit Nunavut and/or its residents. On an August 1995 High Arctic cruise, the ship visited three Inuit villages (and paid US$500 as goodwill to each community). It is indicative of the need for tourism development in Nunavut that none of the three had a local guide available; only one of the three had an arts and crafts store. Passengers ashore wandered about taking photos, and were 'thrilled' when they had some direct interaction with a local resident. Yet, following these three exposures, passengers were vocal, informing the Cruise Director, 'no more villages', and 'when you've seen one Inuit village, you've seen them all'. This experience differs from a similar visit several years previously at Rankin Inlet, where a well-organized tour programme, including Inuit music and dancing, delighted the cruise passengers. A young bilingual Inuit woman had initiated the programme, and provided an interesting summary of traditional customs.

NUNAVUT TOURISM: POTENTIALS AND PROBLEMS

Nunavut has two important tourism attractions: Inuit heritage and pristine wilderness. In 1995, nature tourism is the fastest-growing sector of the US and European travel market. This trend is certain to expand, especially with increasing numbers of visitors from densely populated Pacific Rim countries whose art forms have long stressed the beauty of nature. Taiwanese groups first booked Arctic cruises in 1994, and their popularity is growing rapidly among compatriots.

Wilderness is a vanishing asset. The global village of high-rise apartment complexes linked to CNN and virtual reality places a premium on any community that retains some ties with tradition, other than via cultural reconstruction and a heritage 'village'. Nunavut is one of the few remaining areas in the world where inhabitants still live 'close to the land'; where visitors can ride dog teams and see drying racks covered with filleted fish and strips of seal. Sufficient space still exists for individuals to survive with only aboriginal skills, if they choose to do so. Nunavut sued and won its legal case on this premise.

Tourism creates both positive and negative impacts and the people of each community must first decide if they want tourism. Planeloads of visitors are not always compatible with a subsistence lifestyle, as the 1950s Inuit experience at Kotzebue demonstrates (Smith, 1989). There, Inuits were embarrassed by tourist photographs of butchering scenes, and incensed when visitors removed fish from drying racks, smelled it, and threw it on the ground. Also, tourism introduced from outside the community (by government, or the airlines as in the Alaskan Arctic) may generate resistance and/or community divisiveness about who benefits and who loses in the touristic transactions. Downie (1993) provides an example of a professional appraisal that could assist Inuits to determine the economic value of tourism, but such analysis should not substitute for a self-assessment.

'Community-based tourism' became a favoured title for the activities of the Yellowknife-based Office of Economic Development and Tourism, especially with the publication of *A Strategy for Northwest Territories Tourism Industry* (Office of Economic Development and Tourism, 1983). This 12-part study addressed many traditional aspects 'for achieving destinational uniqueness (economic/financial capability, strategic/marketing capability, technological capacity)' (Haywood, et al., 1993: 36), but the authors correctly note that the manual suffers from four deficiencies:

1 disregard for cultural, historical, and management-style factors in decision making
2 a static view of competitive advantage that underplays the need to develop the capacity to manage changing strategy
3 a focus on strategy formulation rather than strategy execution—tourism strategy formulation ignores the need to generate commitment from people to implement or to accomplish a strategy, and
4 inadequate attempts to integrate the three traditionally acknowledged sources of uniqueness.

The field-work of geographer Alison Woodley in Baker Lake is particularly instructive here. She addresses five barriers to a community-based approach to tourism development as initiated by NWT government: lack of vision, low interest awareness, training, economic factors and, most importantly, cultural barriers. Tourism is a cross-cultural industry, involving hosts' and guests' perceptions of each other, and when there are both significant cultural and linguistic differences, misunderstandings are not uncommon. In addition, most visiting planners stay only a few days, which permits neither an adequate understanding of local culture, nor sufficient time 'to develop enough credibility among residents to encourage effective participation in the planning process'... most of the so-called 'community-based' tourism efforts have to date been lip service (Woodley, 1993: 144).

To remedy these shortcomings, the author suggests that the Inuit Circum-Polar Conference innovates some tourism training sessions, patterned after or perhaps assisted by the courses developed by World Tourism Organization (WTO). Ideally, they should draw upon the experiences of Inuit communities, such as the North Alaska Native Association (NANA) based in Kotzebue, Alaska. Further, to preserve the integrity of each Nunavut community, the new state-wide Economic Development and Tourism Board should address now the pattern of tourism in the entire area. Tourists, as contrasted to hunters or fishermen, like to make circuits, visiting a variety of destinations. If every Inuit village is a 'look-alike', the mystique is wasted. Thus the author suggests that each community should undertake a self-assessment based on the four Hs of tourism—habitat, heritage, history and handicrafts—to determine the specific areas in which their individual strengths lie. A suggested list of questions for a series of self-assessments might include:

Habitat

What are the access routes to our community? By air? By sea?

What does air fare cost and how does this compare with other Inuit communities?

What landscape features do we have that are different from other Nunavut communities? Are these unique or interesting to tourists?

What other Nunavut communities are on the same air route, so tourists could make a circle trip, and see different things?

What time(s) of year has special interest to outsiders—such as polar bears, migrating birds, caribou hunting, fishing, dog sledding, canoeing?
Are there seasons when we do not want tourists, or when they would be uncomfortable—insects, barge season?
How do we set trails to protect the tundra, monitor overuse, and control camping by tourists?
How can we control the problem of litter, which offends tourists?

Heritage

What can we show tourists of our traditional way of life? Museum? Traditional camp? Inukshuks? Archaeologic sites: Dorset? Thule? Interpretive Centres? Spokespersons? Story-tellers?
Are there cultural aspects we choose not to share?
How can we give visitors an understanding or experience of our culture and life? Home stays? Hunting trips? Dog sledge journeys? Guided fishing/hunting trips?
Will tourism reinforce our Inuit heritage, especially for traditional values?
Do we want to permit liquor in our community? Even for tourists?
How do we monitor heritage sites, and who will take responsibility?

History

What historical events occurred in our area, of interest to outsiders? Early explorers? Historic buildings such as Hudson Bay Company stores? Missions?
What kind of interpretive centres or leaders can be provided?
Will tourism create divisiveness in our community because of associations with outsiders?
Are there individuals who are willing, or unwilling, to interact with tourists?
Who will make the community decisions—and will everyone agree with these decisions? How will tourism income be used in our community? To benefit all, or the few who 'work' at it?
Do we have good recorded history of our community? Should we be doing oral histories? With whom? Who will do it?

Handicrafts

What are the distinctive crafts of our community, and how do they differ from other Nunavut communities?
Do we have a craft cooperative, so all artisans benefit? Is it actively working to promote tourism and sell products?
Can we sponsor a local craft artisan event to attract tourists? Who will develop this, and how will it be funded? What will we feature, to be distinctive?
How can we market our handicrafts to attract tourists to meet the artisan? Or do some craftsmen not want tourism? If so, why?

Through regional coordination, tourism could be greatly strengthened by virtue of diversity based on geographic and cultural uniqueness.

Tourism will not be the panacea to total employment, however, because of seasonality. The average traveller is afraid of the characteristic for which the Arctic is most noted: the cold. To go North in winter for a vacation borders on lunacy, unless to visit family or friends. However, dog-sledding trips during March and April, after the equinox lengthens the days, are a source of income (and high adventure). Autumn brings the hunters, for caribou, musk ox, and polar bear. In the 1994–95 winter season, the Resolute area, for example, was allotted 38 bears, of which 12 tags were reserved for non-Inuit sports hunters. The Hunters and Trappers Association in Resolute rotated guiding service among their members, and divided the revenues among all member families. Each hunter paid US$12–15 000 for his week-long bear hunt and took the hide home as a trophy, and the meat was distributed among the community members who consider it a delicacy.

Inuit handicrafts have become world renowned, especially the stone carvings which differ from one community to another, dependent upon available stone. Similarly, the prints from Cape Dorset are collector's items; art dealers visit each spring to purchase and stock their shelves 'in the South'. Most visitors do not realize that neither of these crafts were 'aboriginal' but were developed thanks to the leadership of government arts and crafts officers, stationed in each village.

The 'real' Inuit handicrafts used the raw materials from the hunt, especially sealskin and walrus ivory. However, the import ban in the USA on products made from these natural sources has seriously harmed the local economy. Inuit still hunt but leave the hide to rot at water's edge, since it has no value; if anything, the ban has denied Inuit substantial income and fewer seal are now taken. As a direct consequence of the increased seal numbers, fishermen report many fewer fish, and thus their income declines still another notch. The 1995–97 president of Inuit Circumpolar Conference (a Nunavut, Rose Marie Kuptana), elected in Nome, Alaska, in July 1995, has adopted a strong platform to reverse this policy and prevent a similar ban from being imposed by European countries. It is a travesty of scientific investigation that the emotionalism of Hollywood film stars and others can prevail on a nation, to the detriment of both humans and animals. A few items are carved from caribou antler but they are seldom in high demand.

Baker Lake, the only inland Inuit community, is determined to develop tourism. The townspeople take pride in their renovated, historic Hudson Bay Company store which has been converted to a fine interactive museum (Figures 3.3, 3.4). Thanks to a matriarchal Jessie Oonark, who pioneered wallhangings, her work is now copied and augmented by other artists in an array of T-shirts, aprons, handbags, and stationery. The Co-op employs a dozen artisans and staff. Indicative of community efforts (aided by white residents), Baker Lake hosted the opening of a major Canadian Inuit art exhibit in 1994, a 'first ever' because

Figure 3.3 The Akumalik Visitor Centre occupies the original 1940s Hudson Bay Trading Post, now an interactive museum

Figure 3.4 The interior of the restored trading post showing white fox skins that were trapped in the region and traded for tinned food and other western goods

some thirty curators from major North American galleries came to Baker Lake for the gala opening on a four-day tour costing US$2500. The hangings were mounted in the high school gymnasium and, for two days, Inuit artists

(a)

(b)

Figure 3.5 A fashion show of traditional Inuit clothing (a) and modern hand-embroidered vests (b) at the Baker Lake Art Festival

Figure 3.6 The Baker Lake Inuit camp demonstrates the traditional inland Inuit summer camp of caribou-skin tent and family life

explained their innovative designs while video cameras whirred (Figure 3.5a, b). In addition, guests visited the 'model camp' (Figure 3.6), took a walk on the tundra, some flew out to fish Thelon River (see below); and they shopped, leaving in the community untold tens of thousands of US dollars in craft purchases alone. Other communities are taking a cue from this event, as a model for an annual or at least an occasional festivity for tourism.

Nunavut has launched a modest give-away replica of the NWT Explorer's Guide but, as yet, there are insufficient entrepreneurs to sponsor a sizeable publication. Time will resolve that lack, for Nunavut is blessed with some outstanding natural resources. Canada has designated 12 Heritage Rivers, and the Thelon is among them (Figure 3.7). The entire 'nation' was extensively mapped during the land claims actions (Riewe, 1992), and many other valuable maps are available from NWT offices as tourist information handouts. The Thelon region has a creditable history, as it was visited by the Greenland explorer, Knud Rasmussen on his epic Fifth Thule Expedition (1929). Unfortunately, the caribou on which Inuit survival depended 'disappeared' during World War II years. Journalist-author Farley Mowat played out the tragedy of Inuit starvation in his novels, *The Desperate People* and *People of the Deer* (Mowat, 1975, 1989).

The Thelon River is a fisherman's paradise and a canoeist's dream. However, residents in Baker Lake are discovering what others have experienced; that 'backpackers' and campers leave very little money in a community, and may create serious problems. The open spaces are hard to police, and visitors have been found removing heritage items as souvenirs. The RCMP officer stationed

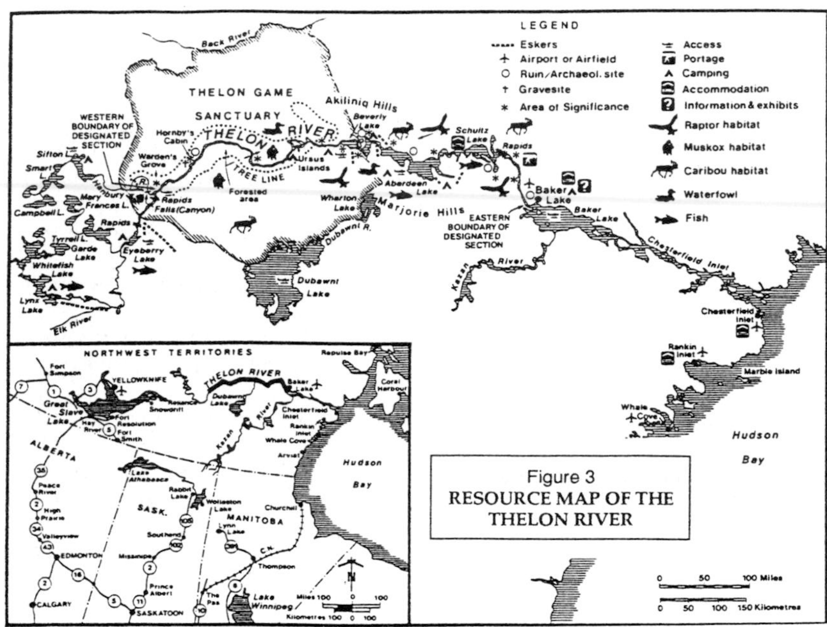

Source: The Canadian Heritage Rivers System, Government of Canada.

Figure 3.7 Resource map of the Theolon River
Reproduced with permission from the Canadian Heritage Rivers System, Government of Canada

in Resolute in 1995 meets every arriving aircraft, to forestall problems. On August 20, 1995 a French couple arrived with a tent among their baggage; seeing him they inquired 'where do we pitch it?'. He indicated 'anywhere' but they found no grassy plot on the rock-hard Shield, and could not drive a single stake. 'What is the alternative?' they asked, to which he replied 'the hotel—$200 per night'. The couple departed on the outbound plane next day. More worrisome to the RCMP are the 'backpackers' who arrive wearing only shorts and a T-shirt; the average temperature in July is 4°C. Having trekked in Nepal or New Zealand, they know nothing of Arctic survival, cold fogs, white-outs, magnetic declination on their compass—and they have no rifles for protection against polar bears. Since Resolute is often a base for expeditions to the North Pole, the RCMPs collect a bond for those participants but, to date, no fees are levied in advance for search and rescue of over-due and lost hikers.

THE NUNAVUT INUIT AND TOURISM

The Inuit have opportunities to develop their own businesses as hotel-keepers, chefs, pilots (there are Inuit pilots in Alaska), outfitters—and more. Unfortunately, such youth role models are still few in number. Time will solve that here, as it has in Alaska. Under the land claims agreement, loans are available, and some have taken advantage of them. Churchill (outside Nunavut) is the 'polar bear capital' of the world in autumn, around the garbage dump. But the bears go north in summer, and one Inuit family now operates a successful summer polar bear lodge at Wager Bay where visitors see the animals in their natural habitat. An enterprise of this type—a modest lodge, six guests for four days—provides substantial income to augment subsistence hunting. This is an effective model that can be replicated, comparable to the Baker Lake Handicraft Show.

A very important facet of tourism that is often overlooked is the electronic highway. As the high school principal of Baker Lake explained, 'Internet is revolutionizing the Arctic'. Economic and tourism development advocates still seem to focus primarily on providing 'service employment' for the 'minimally educated'. US Treasury Secretary Lloyd Bentsen is quoted thus: 'although travel and tourism provided a lot of jobs, they were mostly low-skilled "hamburger flipper" positions'. Instead, in accord with the World Travel and Tourism Council (WTTC), an industry research-oriented organization, Inuits should be thinking 'High Tech and High Touch' (Langton, 1995: 29).

The electronic highway makes it possible to carry on almost any service industry, anywhere. United Airlines processes its daily passenger sales by transporting collected tickets as cargo on their daily flight to Beijing, for Chinese computer personnel to tabulate; and the documents are flown back to the USA 24 hours later. Hotel reservations systems can be operated as easily in Iqaluit as Omaha, thanks to the satellites. Through the DEW (Distant Early Warning) Line system dating from the Soviet nuclear-threat era, some Inuits have strong technical skills that need to be turned from war to recreation. It will take innovative thinking and substantive planning, but the intuitive desire to survive and to continue to live on their homeland is a powerful incentive.

Inuit pride in their new homeland is justified, but with ownership comes responsibility. The Arctic may seem vast because of the low population density, estimated to average at no more than one person per 100 square miles. Although glaciers are powerful and the mountains seem so permanent, underfoot is the permafrost lying atop the granitic mass. In many places, the overlying tundra is barely an inch thick, and once disturbed by a foot, a shovel, or a snowmobile, the scar will remain fresh for decades. Regrowth is at least fifty years to the inch. Ecotourism could profitably push back the frontiers of present habitation, as in the Wager Bay polar bear lodge discussed above, but leaves the polar desert forever marred. Inuits survived here for 4000 years but will the people of Nunavut be as careful as their forebears?

REFERENCES

Downie, B., 1993, Katannilik Territorial Park, in M.E. Johnston and W. Heider (eds), *Communities, Resources and Tourism in the North*, Centre for Northern Studies, Lakehead University, Thunder Bay, 51–60.

Duffy, R.Q., 1988, *The Road to Nunavut: The Progress of the Eastern Arctic Inuit since the Second World War*, McGill-Queen's University Press, Montreal.

Facts on File, 1993, *World News Digest*, 53(2722), 55A3 (January 28, 1993).

Haywood, K.M., Reid, D.G. and Wolff, J., 1993, Establishing Hospitality and Tourism Education and Training in Canada's Northwest Territories, in M.E. Johnston and W. Heider (eds), *Communities, Resources and Tourism in the North*, Centre for Northern Studies, Lakehead University, Thunder Bay, 35–50.

Johnston, M.E., 1995, Patterns and Issues in Arctic and Sub-Arctic Tourism, in C.M.E. Hall and M.E. Johnston, (eds), *Polar Tourism*, John Wiley & Sons, Chichester, 27–42.

Langton, B.D., 1995, High-tech high-pay: Travel and tourism creates quality jobs, *Viewpoint*, 1(2), 26–31.

Mablick, D., 1995, Prospecting and Exploration Activities on Inuit Owned Lands, *Above and Beyond*, 7(3), 60.

Marsh, J. and Staple, S., 1995, Cruise Tourism in the Canadian Arctic and its Implications, in C.M.E. Hall and M.E. Johnston (eds), *Polar Tourism*, John Wiley & Sons, Chichester, 63–72.

Mowat, F., 1975, *The Desperate People*, McClelland and Stewart-Bantam, Toronto.

Mowat, F., 1989, *People of the Deer*, revised edition, Souvenir, London.

Office of Economic Development and Tourism, 1983, *A Strategy for North West Territories Tourism Development*, Government of the Northwest Territories, Yellowknife.

Office of Economic Development and Tourism, 1994, *Visitor Exit Survey*, Government of the Northwest Territories, Yellowknife.

Office of Economic Development and Tourism, 1995a, *Executive Summary, 1994 Visitor Exit Survey*, Government of the Northwest Territories, Yellowknife.

Office of Economic Development and Tourism, 1995b, *1995 Explorer's Guide*, Government of the Northwest Territories, Yellowknife.

Pelly, D., 1994, Birth of an Inuit Nation, *Geographical*, 66(4), 23–25.

Pelly D., 1995, Footprints in the Snow. The March toward Nunavut, *Above and Beyond*, 7(3), 7–10.

Purich, D., 1992, *The Invit and Their Land: The Story of Nunavut*, James Lorimer and Co., Toronto.

Rasmussen, K., 1929, Intellectual culture of the Iglulik Eskimos, in *Report of the Fifth Thule Expedition*, 1921–24, VII:1, Gyldendalske Boghandel, Copenhagen.

Riewe, R. (ed.), 1992, *Nunavut Atlas*, Canadian Circumpolar Institute and Tungavik Federation of Nunavut, Calgary.

Sandell, K., 1995, Access to the 'North'—But to What and for Whom? Public Access in the Swedish Countryside and the Case of a Proposed National Park in the Kiruna Mountains, in *Polar Tourism*, C.M.E. Hall and M.E. Johnston (eds), John Wiley & Sons, Chichester, 131–146.

Schledermann, P., 1990, *4000 Years of Inuit History*, Arctic Institute of North America, Calgary.

Smith, V.L., 1989. Eskimo Tourism: Micro-Models and Marginal Men, in *Hosts and Guests: The Anthropology of Tourism*, 2nd edn, Smith, V.L. (ed.), University of Pennsylvania Press, Philadelphia, 55–82.

Smith, V.L., 1996, Indigenous Tourism and the 4 H's, in R.W. Butler and T. Hinch (eds), *Tourism and Indigenous Peoples*, Routledge, London, in press.

Sugden, D., 1982, *Arctic and Antarctic: A Modern Geographical Synthesis*, Barnes and Noble, Totowa.

Woodley, A., 1993, Tourism and Sustainable Development: The Community Perspective, in J.G. Nelson, R. Butler and G. Wall (eds), *Tourism and Sustainable Development: Monitoring, Planning, Managing*, Department of Geography, University of Waterloo, Waterloo, 135–148.

4 Sustaining Tourism in Far North Queensland

VERONICA STRANG

In recent years, tourism has commonly been presented as the self-indulgent activity of wealthy, dominant societies; an industry which, once imposed on the fragile environments and cultures of small indigenous populations, disrupts and destroys both with the poison of technology and consumerism. This view has been useful in raising ethical questions about the imposition of Western culture on others, and in creating awareness of the effects of tourism on vulnerable ecologies. However, it also tends to cast non-Western or minority cultural groups as naive and dependent on outside decision-makers, and to underline a vision of them as frozen in some kind of static 'traditional way of life' which can be instantaneously overwhelmed by a superior economic force.

In this chapter, I hope to challenge some of these assumptions and to consider tourist activities as a two-way street—as cultural interactions in which economics are only a part of a much more complex exchange. I will focus, in particular, on the least tangible parts of this interaction—the exchange of ideas and values that invariably accompanies the meeting of diverse cultural groups.

Two minority groups whose response to tourism has been anything but passive are the Aboriginal communities and the white cattle farmers who inhabit the western plains of Australia's Cape York Peninsula, a large triangle of land in Queensland's tropical north (Figure 4.1). Rainforested mountains run up its east coast, but most of the area across to the Gulf of Carpentaria consists of flat savannah grassland, woodland and scrub. There are distinct wet and dry seasons: the peninsula receives about 1200 mm of rain between December and March and little for the rest of the year, so it is either flooded—providing rich wetlands for many species of birds and fauna—or rapidly parching, providing little of anything except dust. It is thus a genuinely fragile environment, with delicate friable soils and, for much of the year, only scattered and minimal sources of fresh water.

THE ABORIGINAL POPULATION

The Aboriginal population has inhabited the peninsula for many thousands of

People and Tourism in Fragile Environments. Edited by M. F. Price.

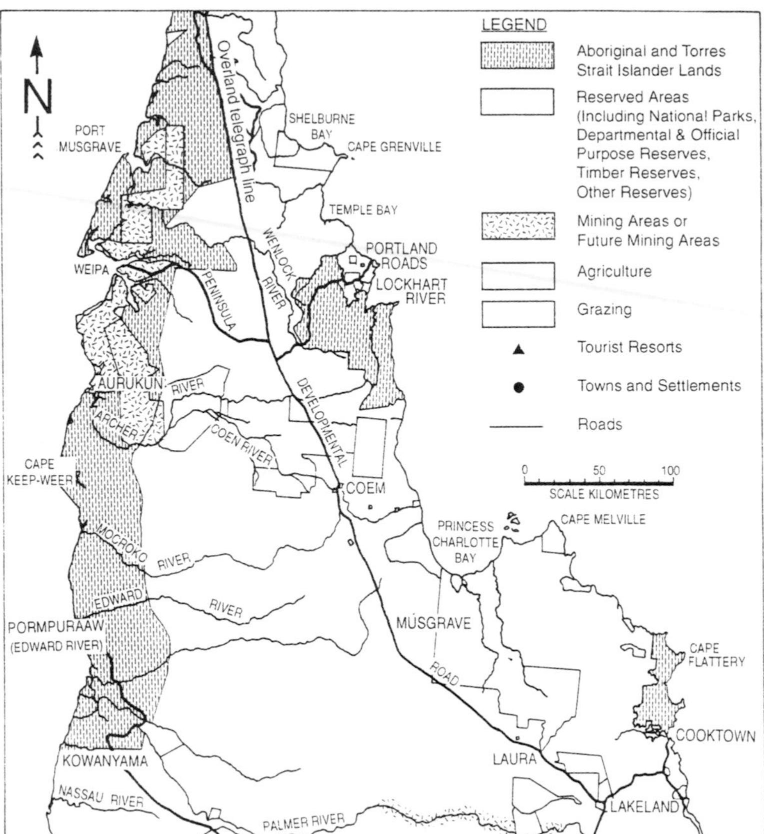

Figure 4.1 Land use on Cape York, North Queensland
(Adapted from Connell Wagner, 1989)

years—some archaeologists would say from 40 to 50 thousand—living in small language groups, further subdivided into land-owning clans (Berndt and Berndt, 1977; Flood, 1983; Mulvaney and White 1987; McConnel, 1957). Until the beginning of this century, they lived as hunter gatherers, maintaining a sustainable lifestyle through careful use and management of their environment.

This way of life depended on highly detailed knowledge of the local ecology and its resources, and on close and continuous interaction with the land. The continuity of this association was maintained by traditional law firmly linking kinship with communal landownership (Sharp, 1933; 1937; 1939; Peterson, 1972). According to Aboriginal Law the members of each clan inherit rights to land and resources, and responsibility to care for these in both spiritual and practical terms. Through a belief system centred on human spiritual conception from within the land, each person acquires an identity linking them with a particular place as well as a kin group and clan. This is a permanent relationship: in

Aboriginal terms, people and their 'country' are not seen as divisible. It is also holistic: the land mediates every aspect of traditional life, binding people and country together socially, spiritually and economically. It is thus a very intimate environmental relationship which engenders highly protective and emotionally laden values about the land, and creates links with clan country that are as strong as family ties (Sharp, 1933; Kolig, 1987; Strang, 1994).

The first intrusions into this relationship were made by explorers who first came to the peninsula in the 1600s, but the real colonization of the peninsula was carried out by the miners and cattle ranchers who came into the area in the late 1800s (Merlan, 1978; Rose, 1984; Done, 1987). Each stage of this contact history was characterized by extreme violence against the indigenous people, beginning with killings and kidnappings carried out by the first explorers and ending with the virtual genocide perpetrated by some of the early settlers (Reynolds, 1987; Willshire, 1896). The Aboriginal people who survived this aggressive process of colonization found themselves shunted onto mission reserves or pushed into providing a cheap labour force on the vast cattle properties that were established on their traditional land. Their normal patterns of movement around clan country were disrupted, and they were forced to adopt the economic mode and way of life of the colonists. Like most subject peoples, they found themselves leading double lives—conforming on the one hand to the demands of European domination, and on the other attempting, quietly, to maintain their traditional use and care of the land (McGrath, 1987; Stevens, 1974; Berndt and Berndt, 1987).

Despite the gloomy predictions that they and their culture would die out (Sharp, 1952), Aboriginal people and their beliefs and values have proven very resilient. Within a few decades they had successfully incorporated cattle work into their lives and found ways to balance this with traditional priorities, finding that stock work made good use of their bush skills and allowed them to remain on their own country. They achieved a workable *modus vivendi* with the pastoralists, exchanging stock work and domestic labour for food and tobacco, and setting up extended family communities at each station homestead. Under the protective wing of the station owners they were no longer considered 'wild blacks' and could thus continue many of their traditional activities.

This balance suffered in the 1960s when new legislation setting minimum wages meant that resident Aboriginal groups were increasingly excluded from the cattle stations and moved onto the Mission Reserves to be under the wing of first the Church, and later the State (Stevens, 1974; Strang, 1994). These were much more repressive regimes which separated people from their land, enforced a European 'education' and actively discouraged many traditional practices (Chapman, undated; Strang, 1994).

In recent years, many groups have begun to shrug off the heavy paternalism of the State: old Missions have become self-governing Aboriginal communities on Reserve land, with their own elected Councils empowered to make major social and economic decisions. Communities such as Kowanyama, on the western coast of the Peninsula, now have a 'mixed economy'. Kowanyama is a typical ex-Mission community: it is comprised of three language groups totalling about a thousand people, and holds about 1000 square miles of land. The community runs its own herd of cattle and a few men still work on neighbouring white-owned stations, although in the present political climate, this is becoming increasingly rare. Most people supplement their cash income by hunting and gathering. There are some ideas about starting up a fish or prawn farm, although such projects require a lot of capital and technical expertise.

> Under its broader philosophy of the management of marine and land resources for the benefit of the community, the Council has also considered the establishment of aquaculture operations as a source of economic revenue for the community. In particular, it has recently considered the establishment of an experimental eeltail catfish and redclaw crayfish farming operation.
>
> (Dale, 1991:7)

In financial terms, it is difficult for the community to break even: the minimal stockwork wages and income from the Reserve's cattle operation are wholly inadequate for supporting a thousand people. The population remains heavily dependent on State support, and one of the community's major aims is to create sufficient employment and income to render this unnecessary. Thus, like many other Aboriginal people, the inhabitants of Kowanyama are searching for a new formula in their environmental relationship: one that re-establishes economic self-sufficiency within a modern context, but also upholds traditional values and maintains spiritual and emotional connection with the land (Sinnamon, 1992; Taylor, 1984; Dale, 1992; Kowanyama Aboriginal Council, 1990; Hill, 1992).

THE WHITE PASTORALISTS

On the surrounding cattle stations, the white pastoralists are also struggling financially. The savannah country does not provide rich grazing land, and the properties are therefore, on average, one to two thousand square miles in area. Each supports only a few people and most of the work is seasonal. More often than not, the peninsular cattle industry hovers on the edge of financial viability. Many of the stations were established in the late eighteenth century to supply beef to the miners during the gold rushes on the eastern peninsula, and when these waves receded, the 'frontier' became a 'remote area'—poor grazing country, a long way from markets and infrastructure.

> After 100 years of pioneering effort, the Cape York Peninsula cattle industry has failed to become permanently established . . . If current trends and land use policies are maintained, the industry will continue to retract from the more isolated areas.
>
> (McKeague, 1992: iv)

The result of the stations' long isolation and limited economic choices is a distinct subculture which, until recently, remained well insulated from the mainstream of Australia, holding onto many old-fashioned beliefs and values, and a way of life that, even today, retains many features of the colonial era. It is a tough kind of life, very physical and aggressive: most of the stock work is still done on horseback; and, running loose in the vast paddocks for months and sometimes years at a time, both cattle and horses tend to be wild and unruly. The young men who work on the stock teams—and it is almost always men—are there to prove themselves in a challenging rite of passage. Codes of conduct are often harsh and uncompromising, and the land is seen, in many respects, as an adversary to be subjugated and tamed—a hostile environment of floods and drought, crocodiles, wild pigs and snakes, sharp thorns and strangling vines.

Despite its marginal profitability, the station subculture is framed, primarily, as an economic endeavour. Like the early settlers, the pastoralists see the land as an alienable commercial resource, valuing it largely according to its ability to support cattle—in terms of its grasses, water sources, paddocks and roads. The adverse ecological effects of the cattle are denied, and the pastoralists rarely question the sustainability of the industry, in either environmental or financial terms. However, their environmental relationship is more complex than this overtly commercial frame suggests. Founded on the battles of the early pioneers, the industry remains as much a way of holding land as an economic enterprise. Beneath the apparently adversarial environmental interaction, some of the families who have been there for generations are fiercely attached to their land, which provides them with a clear sense of identity, freedom from the pressures of urban life, and a small-scale and close-knit station network in which everyone is known and familiar. For the young men on the stock teams, the duel with the environment is a necessary and romantic part of their passage into manhood, with the land providing an imaginative resource and a backdrop to their activities. It could also be argued, though few station folk would admit absorbing Aboriginal values in any way, that long-term association with Aboriginal people has encouraged a closer relationship with the land than might otherwise have been constructed.

Thus we have two groups, each experiencing, using and valuing the same land in its own way, according to its particular cultural precepts. The Aboriginal community remains closely tied into an intense and holistic environmental relationship in which the land provides the central theme for every aspect of their lives. The pastoralists, while framing the land as both frontier adversary and temporary economic resource, have, in isolation from the mainstream, constructed a way of life containing its own beliefs and values, and become—sometimes—quite strongly attached to the land as a retreat from urban life and as an important part of their identity.

Though there is little common ground in their respective environmental relationships, the two groups do share some common features: both are small-scale, cohesive communities with a particular identity and culture; both rely on the land as a primary economic resource; both are struggling to achieve or maintain financial independence and political self-determination; both are accustomed to a way of life separate from that of the wider Australian population.

CAPE YORK JOINS THE MAINSTREAM

Links with the mainstream are seen by Aboriginal people and pastoralists as a distinctly mixed blessing, combining the possibility of economic gain and a better standard of living, with the threat of interference, disruption and unwelcome changes. Closer links are, however, inevitable. In the last decade the mainstream has begun to flood onto the peninsula with unstoppable momentum. It has come partly through increasingly sophisticated communications—telephones, televisions, better roads and infrastructure; and partly through increasing State involvement in the area. More than anything, however, it has come through tourism. The last decade has seen Far North Queensland become one of the most desirable tourist destinations in Australia.

The tourist industry reached the Cape York Peninsula in the early 1980s, with small numbers of fishermen from the heavily populated east coast braving many hours of dirt road to the Gulf for the sake of adventure, uncrowded fishing places, and a freezer full of barramundi to pay for the holiday. As word got out, their numbers began to increase. Cairns, in the south-east corner of the Peninsula, stopped being a sleepy tropical town and began to develop as a major tourist centre, providing a jumping-off point for bush tours into the outback. All of a sudden, the 'outback experience' became a readily marketable commodity, and what had previously been seen as relatively worthless bush was recast as desirable 'wilderness'. The tourist industry seized on the potential of the area, enthusing about its wildlife, its 'pristine quality' and its 'remoteness'.

> In a world in which populations of single cities are reaching over 30 million . . . a virtually untouched area like the Cape York Peninsula . . . must have a very important future for tourism.
>
> (Pacific Asia Travel Association, 1990: i)

With the State's primary industries suffering in a long recession, the government was similarly quick to realize the economic potential of an industry that relied only on Queensland's 'natural assets':

> Tourism has added a further dimension to the North Queensland economy, with the region attracting millions of dollars from visitors and investors . . . North Queensland's natural assets are recognised by the State Government . . .
>
> (Queensland Government, 1992: 5)

The government commissioned several 'resource inventories' sending experts—botanists, biologists, geologists and suchlike—into every corner of the Peninsula to list its contents and assess their potential. In 1992, nine million dollars of State funding was invested in the Cape York Land Use Strategy

(CYPLUS) as the government saw that the Peninsula had more than the occasional bauxite and gold mine to offer:

> The information will give an overview of the region and is an essential component of the land use planning process. It will identify the natural resources and will be useful for looking at how these natural resources might be used and managed.
>
> (CYPLUS, 1993: 1)

Major tourist developments along the east coast were given strong political and financial support, and the industry boomed. People began to pour into Cape York, to hunt wild pigs, to fish, to go bird-spotting and camping. Development burgeoned rapidly and, anxious to protect the local environment, conservation organizations leapt into action, all but throwing themselves in the paths of the bulldozers. Dozens of tour operators appeared, organizing wildlife tours to the rainforests and savannahs. The National Parks and Wildlife Service woke up, and instead of barely administering large tracts of land that they had been given because no one of any influence wanted them, realized that they had a major resource in their hands. They began organizing camp sites and barbecue areas, and trying to control the activities of increasing numbers of visitors. As the land became more heavily used, the whole issue of National Parks became increasingly contentious, being tied to the wider debate about land rights and management. In 1992 the State Government set aside $10.5 million to acquire land for new National Parks.

> The significance of national parks in a Cape York peninsula tourist industry cannot be overstated. The fundamental assets of the peninsula are natural—landscapes forests, reefs, rivers, lakes, birds and animals . . . Where significant natural assets are not yet protected, it is to be hoped that they will be included within the national parks system in future . . .
>
> (Pacific Asia Travel Association, 1992: 46)

Thus, within the space of a few years, the Cape York Peninsula became the focus of intense attention and activity. As the infrastructure improved accordingly, tourists began to penetrate even the most remote areas, finding their way to the cattle stations and the Aboriginal communities on the western coast.

EARLY INTERACTIONS WITH VISITORS

The interactions between the visitors and the Aboriginal groups and cattle farmers have gone through several phases. At first, the tourist influx was mostly unwelcome. Although tour operators, vehicle hire companies and camping suppliers along the east coast were making money, very little of it came into the western communities. Most of the time, all they received was the disadvantages.

For the cattle station inhabitants, these were largely just an annoyance: tourists tended to call at homesteads for help when they got bogged in the river crossings or needed supplies, and since they only came in the dry season, this invariably took place at the height of the busy mustering round. The tourists would break through fences rather than struggle with awkward gates, necessitating repair work and sometimes undoing weeks of careful mustering; they would shoot pigs and wallabies, disturbing the cattle; and they would set fire in the wrong places at the wrong times. In increasing numbers, their vehicles churned up the dusty roads and muddy creek crossings. As one manager commented:

> I don't like [pig] shooters on the property . . . they disturb the cattle, and although some people are one hundred per cent responsible, there's others that aren't. So I say no to everyone.
>
> (David Hughes, 1992)

For the Aboriginal groups, the tourist invasion involved more serious problems. People on fishing and hunting expeditions competed, for fun, for bush foods that they regarded as essential, and the increasing numbers of visitors in the region also meant that the commercial fishing industry expanded rapidly, often overfishing limited resources which the Aboriginal groups considered to be theirs.

> I want to say this about caring for the land. The fishermen . . .I'd like to see every European . . . goes out to shoot pig, wallaby—or even go fish—must bring [the food] back into the community—give it to the people. In that case they are caring for the land all right. No good shooting pig and wallaby and leaving it out there waste . . . We seen dead fish all along the beach. They don't care about us.
>
> (Thomas Bruce, 1993)

> We want the wildlife protected on our land. A lot of the tourist come in with a big gun and . . . we'll have no wildlife here soon. Some of them fellers come [from] overseas and they shooting all them pigs . . .
>
> (Kenny Jimmy, 1993)

On a social level, many people in Kowanyama also felt very uncomfortable about the arrival of groups of strangers in their small, familiar community. The strangers, they said, stared too much, smiled too much, and photographed everything in town. Even more worryingly, tourists blundered about their country without knowledge of its story places, sacred sites and 'poison places', and thus unable to avoid or respect them. This is a matter of grave concern to the Aboriginal people who see the spiritual well-being of the country as their responsibility, and who believe that their well-being is linked to that of their country. (Kolig, 1987; Morphy, 1984, 1988; Myers, 1986; Strang, 1994). As one old man (Figure 4.2) said about keeping tourists away from his own spiritual home or 'story place':

> People come up here this way, I got to put a law against this place. Too many people come here, they make me go down too—make me sick. Because this place I got story—too much footprint on me . . . Sometime they might sneak in here . . . old people go die then.
>
> (Nelson Brumby, 1992)

Figure 4.2 Nelson Brumby, a Kunjen elder

Like the early settlers in Australia, the tourist industry tended to try to deny the existence of the people who live on the peninsula, preferring to see it as untouched wilderness. Tour operators offered 'expeditions', 'safaris', and 'explorations' as if inviting visitors to conquer virgin territory. To the Aboriginal people who have been there 'since the beginning to us' as one elder called it, and to the cattle farmers whose lives have been bound up with the land for generations, this vision of empty bushland is both baffling and insulting. For them, the Gulf country is an intensely humanized landscape, and they are an integral part of it. Neither group accepted this marginalization readily, and with loud protests have forced the tourist industry to acknowledge their existence.

Inevitably this has resulted in the romantic exoticization of both cultural groups, so that they could be 'sold' to tourists as an added part of the 'wilderness experience'. The Aboriginal people are presented as mystical, Stone Age guardians of bush lore and spiritual connection with the land, and the cattle folk are portrayed as salt-of-the earth cowboys who battle the wild animals and elements of their environment, stoically shrugging off injury and hardship. As in so many other tourist areas, these portrayals are a double-edged sword: on the one hand, they distort the culture of both groups, highlighting some aspects of their lives while denying others, making the mundane exotic and invading the privacy of the special. Both groups find themselves called upon to perform a cultural self-parody of their traditions, and discouraged from changing and perhaps improving their lives. On the other hand, this romantic spotlight has proved to be a considerable educational tool, giving Aboriginal people in particular the opportunity to teach people about their culture. And while the young men on the cattle properties may sneer at tourists, they are at a stage of life when an admiring audience for their activities is not, perhaps, entirely unwelcome (Figure 4.3).

REGAINING CONTROL

The higher profile provided by tourist interest in local cultures has given both groups a louder voice, and ensured that they can, increasingly, demand respect for their rights and needs. This has enabled them to gain more control of the situation, and thus to shift the economic equation. Tourist operators are being forced to realize that they cannot merely ride roughshod over local groups, but must instead consult them, gain permission for activities and, ultimately, share the profits.

An increasing say in what goes on has allowed Aboriginal groups and cattle-station owners to consider a number of tourism options, ranging from demanding fees for the use of their land and resources, to setting up tourist operations of their own. Consequently, the number of dude ranches is on the rise, with small herds of tourists being rounded-up, mustered and chivvied along with the cattle. As a helicopter pilot, mustering on one of the stations, conceded:

> There'll always be more tourism, and that's how I'll probably end up myself, with helicopters [offering tourist flights]. I think the mustering is going to get harder and harder . . . more properties are opening up to tourism.
>
> (Don Kuhn, 1992)

In Kowanyama, the community guest house has been refurbished, the production of local crafts is on the increase, and there are plans for a small

Figure 4.3 Buckjumping at the Kowanyama rodeo

museum. Some families are hoping to set up small tourist businesses on their own land, so that they can move out of the mission village and back to their own country. As one woman suggested:

> We could have something built there, and cook for them. Tourist house . . . proper building . . . and plant some lawn and some garden there for them to see. If we have horses, we can let the people go for a ride. Elders might take them out, show them places, wildlife—show them what we have there in that country. That's what I'm thinking of . . . People like to see something, you know . . . I think it would be good for them to just go in and check on it, visit . . . get permission of us first.
>
> (Alma Wason, 1992)

Kowanyama now has an Aboriginal Land and Natural Resources Management Office which negotiates on the community's behalf with the government and the other groups on the Peninsula. Concern for the land has led the community to initiate a joint watershed management organization (the Mitchell River Watershed Management Group) with these various interest groups. The Council has also appointed several Aboriginal Rangers to safeguard the community's spiritual and economic resources, and this role has become increasingly important as a way of controlling tourism and other activities on Aboriginal land.

The key issue here is obviously one of control. Tourists invited in are welcome where casual invaders are not. Numbers can be controlled and, under the wing of the elders, tourists can be protected from the spiritual forces and other potential dangers, and the country and its spiritual and economic resources can be protected from their ignorance. Similarly, for the cattle stations, tourists who come to visit and help muster cattle will not only pay large fees for the privilege of participating, but can also be prevented from harming themselves, the cattle station infrastructure, or the land. Thus, with continued insistence on some control from the minority cultural groups and some cooperation from the government and the tourist industry, there is clearly some potential for a positive exchange in which local cultural groups can solve some of their economic difficulties while also maintaining a decision-making role in the equation.

As with the economic aspects, tourism is also a mixed blessing for the Peninsula on an ecological level. It undoubtedly has some detrimental effects on the land: for example, the heavy use of four-wheel drive vehicles can be quite damaging, in particular to the delicate sand-dune country along the Gulf coast; fish resources are already showing signs of depletion; and providing accommodation for tourists would inevitably place more demand on limited waterholes and the already overused artesian sources (Kowanyama Aboriginal Land and Natural Resources Management Office, 1991, 1992; McKeague, 1992; Pressland et al., 1988; Sinnamon, 1992). But limiting the numbers of visitors, and giving the local people more control about where tourists go and what they do, can alleviate these problems to some extent. In many respects, tourism is a better ecological choice than the more intensive grazing which some cattle station managers see as the industry's only other survival option. Ironically, the increased tourism in the area has encouraged the growth of a powerful environmental lobby group, which is already demanding (and getting) greater protection of the more sensitive areas and encouraging better land use practices within the cattle industry.

But what of the more ephemeral cultural exchanges that tourism has created? The industry has begun to play a major part in educating the wider population about Aboriginal culture and encouraging acceptance of its traditional beliefs and values. In the popular media, the negative stereotype of Aboriginal people as drunken no-hopers has been largely replaced by a much more positive one that casts them as wise and mystical folk who care passionately for their land and have a deep knowledge about the bush. It is a heavily romanticized portrait, but this increased respect for Aboriginal culture has contributed to a social and political climate in which communities can be much more self-directing. After years of suppression and discouragement, many traditional ideas and practices are being revitalized, and there is a new pride in Aboriginality. Greater appreciation of traditional land-management practices and the vast lexicon of Aboriginal bush lore has also led to quite egalitarian collaborations between scientists and elders, and an enthusiasm for recording many kinds of cultural information. Thus, partly through the more appreciative viewpoint of tourism, Aboriginal people have gained status, respect and greater self-determination, which has allowed them to stand firm on their own environmental values and visions of the land.

The cattle-station inhabitants, although they have always benefited from the pioneer image which is so central to the Australian national identity, have also, at times, been sidelined and disparaged as ignorant rural 'myalls' [rednecks]. So they too have gained, albeit in lesser ways, from the tourist industry's kinder portrayal of them as down-to-earth outback characters, with old-fashioned values and lives unsullied by modernity.

NEW PERCEPTIONS

The more positive view of the Cape York Peninsula and its inhabitants engendered by the tourist industry is predictable. The industry is, after all, based on an appreciation and enjoyment of particular places and people. On the old maps of Australia, vast areas of inland country were simply left blank and labelled 'no significant use'; now, with the advent of tourism, these areas have suddenly become 'beautiful . . . heritage areas . . . national treasures'. This has some very interesting implications in terms of the environmental perceptions and values that it has pushed to the fore. Tourism is unique in providing specialized, stylized ways of expressing environmental values and interacting with the land free from the demands of economic necessity. Thus, although the framework of tourism is often cynically commercial, reducing the land and its inhabitants to measurable, marketable things to be 'consumed', it nevertheless tends to generate largely qualitative evaluations of the landscape, actively encouraging positive, subjective responses and a protective and appreciative environmental relationship.

This is one of tourism's less tangible offerings to local communities and to the wider population: a new and different view of the landscape that is based on a qualitative, 'aesthetic' appreciation of its various components. In western Cape York, both Aboriginal and pastoral communities are so intensely involved with the land in their own ways that they find it a little odd, initially, to step back and consider it in largely visual terms. Aboriginal people, closely aware of the use and often complex meaning of every part of the local environment, often express puzzlement that tourists just want to photograph the animals, flowers and landscapes. And the white stock workers, caught up in a highly physical interaction with the landscape, have some aesthetic sense of the style of what they are doing, but rarely pause to frame it in these terms. The tourist vision of the landscape has thus caused both groups to re-evaluate their surroundings in some new ways, and in the case of the pastoralists, to become more open to ideas about protecting the local ecology. It has also helped to promote concern for the environment throughout Australia, creating widespread support for new legislation and protective measures.

The tourist 'gaze' (Urry, 1990) also offers the local inhabitants the chance to see themselves and their activities in a new light. The effects of this greater opportunity for reflexivity are complex, and perhaps beyond the scope of this discussion, but it is an aspect of tourism which should not be ignored, given its potential for encouraging introspection and the re-evaluation of traditional beliefs and values.

CONCLUSIONS: SUSTAINING TOURISM

So far in this chapter I have concentrated on some of the tangible and intangible things that tourism brings into outback communities. However, the interaction is a two-way street, and in this last section I would like to consider what the tourists themselves seek and gain in their cultural and economic exchange with Aboriginal people and pastoralists.

Firstly one might ask what they are looking for. Tourism is generally perceived as a fairly superficial indulgence: a pleasure-seeking outing, and there is no doubt that plain fun and relaxation are high on most tourists' list of priorities. What could be more fun, after all, than the 'Boy's Own' adventures offered by the Cape York Peninsula—camping and fishing in a remote 'wilderness', with dangerous animals, exotic local cultures, and lots of open space. It is easy to be disparaging about grown men driving into the outback in a four-wheel-drive truck laden with high-tech fishing rods, halogen lamps, freezers and large supplies of beer, and calling this 'going bush', to or to poke fun at adults who choose to wriggle around on their bellies hunting wild pigs with a crossbow, but this perhaps fails to acknowledge the more complex needs and desires underlying these cultural activities.

Let us consider what the outback represents for tourists and what they focus on and value when they get there. On the Cape York Peninsula, tourists take part in a variety of activities which range from aggressive 'bush-bashing', which is a kind of cross-country rally driving, to 'twitching' which means sitting quietly in the bush spotting birds. There are, however, some important common themes that run through each of these ways of interacting with the landscape. Firstly, tourism frames the peninsula as a place apart from normal life, unspoiled, and uncorrupted by modernity, and suggests that it is 'rejuvenating' to jaded souls, harried by modern pressures. The concept of 'untouched' wilderness fulfils both of these ideas very nicely, and it is surely no coincidence that there are proposals to rename the road to the tip of the peninsula 'The Cape Escape'.

> The region beckons the adventurer in us all, to rejuvenate our batteries through any one of the exciting encounters with the environment. Whether you seek adventure in the air, on land or under the sea, Cairns and the Far North gives you every opportunity to 'avago' in the real Australian tradition.
>
> (Far North Queensland Promotion Bureau advertising literature, 1993)

> Cape York . . . is a region of great beauty and variety . . . Its vast plains and unvarying woodlands evoke a feeling of freedom and a rawness that is unknown in crowded, civilised south-eastern Australia.
>
> (Moon and Moon, 1989:15)

Tourism's theme of release from responsibility and consequent rejuvenation is powerful, and it is particularly interesting if one considers the true meaning of the term rejuvenation—to become young again. Despite the huge variation in the forms of tourist activity on the peninsula, all are characterized by 'becoming young again': as well as releasing people from 'authority' and grown-up responsibility, all involve 'play', and all contain an intensely physical and direct involvement with the landscape.

Another facet of life on the peninsula that is highly valued by tourists, is the fact that it contains small-scale, face-to-face communities in which everyone is known and familiar (Figure 4.4). It thus represents an 'ideal' way of life that is—at least theoretically—stable, secure, and nurturing. This, like the notion of 'play', could be said to represent the safer world of childhood. Tourist industry promotional literature, and the responses of the tourists themselves, express a nostalgia for the values that these places are believed to represent. People focus on the gentle pace, the manageable scale of social life, and the timeless continuity—all the things that urban Australia has supposedly left behind. There is the assumption that 'going bush' permits a quality of social interaction that can no longer be found elsewhere. This may arise from spending time in the small and cohesive outback communities, sharing a common adventure with family and friends, or communing with nature and thus with other human beings. It may also be generated by contact with Aboriginal people, who are presented to tourists primarily as the guardians of ancient and mystical connections with nature.

This brings us to another of the underlying themes that indicate some of the beliefs and values encouraged by the tourist industry: the idea that escaping from the cities and 'going bush' permits people to 'commune' with nature,

Figure 4.4 Children in Kowanyama

re-establishing—if only temporarily—a particular kind of environmental relationship. In this idealized relationship, humans and nature are no longer at odds, but are symbiotically linked in perfect homeostasis. Is this yet another aspect of a yearning for a safe and childlike communion with the world?

The idea that people in a relaxed state re-connect with their environment is particularly interesting when it is placed alongside the 'aesthetic' response to the landscape I discussed earlier. An 'aesthetic' vision of the landscape is a very western construct (Berger, 1972; Bender, 1993), but I would suggest that it shares considerable common ground with 'religious' visions of the land, for example, the strong spiritual and emotional links to country that Aboriginal people express. To what extent is an 'aesthetic' view only a different, secular idiom for the same kinds of values, a pale western imitation of a much closer environmental relationship? Clearly people who live in a highly mobile culture, in which land is regarded as an alienable commercial resource, cannot hope to create the kinds of attachment to land that Aboriginal people have built over time. But that does not mean that they cannot value this kind of attachment, or wish to recreate it.

Untrammelled by the need to make a physical living from the land, tourism permits people to use the land purely to meet their emotional and spiritual needs. Is this an indulgence or a necessity? It may be that this freedom allows them to focus on needs that are, perhaps, not met in their daily lives. I do not wish to suggest that tourism is solely a 'back to the womb' kind of activity, or that in terms of environmental values, it necessarily attempts to take us 'back to basics'. However, I would argue that most, if not all, forms of tourism are united by a desire for relief from the somewhat harried lifestyle generally experienced by modern westerners, and by a real need for a more balanced and sustaining environmental relationship. It may well be that the aspirations and values emerging from the tourist industry can provide some useful clues about ways to create more stable and habitable urban environments.

Despite its negative effects, tourism in North Queensland—as in other parts of the world—is sustaining in a number of ways: it gives the minority cultural groups in the area greater self-determination, and enables them to maintain or re-establish many of their traditional ways of interacting with the environment. It encourages, both within these local groups and in the wider Australian population, new ways of evaluating the land in qualitative terms, and more protective (and sustainable) environmental values. Perhaps most importantly, it provides a counterbalance to the stresses and inadequacies of urban life and, by highlighting some real needs, points to ways in which this might be made more manageable and enjoyable.

REFERENCES

Bender, B. (ed.), 1993, *Landscape, Politics and Perspectives*, Berg, Oxford.

Berger, J., 1972, *Ways of Seeing*, Penguin, London.

Berndt, R.M. and Berndt, C.H., 1977, *The World of the First Australians*, Ure Smith, Sydney.

Berndt, R.M. and Berndt, C.H., 1987, *End of an Era: Aboriginal Labour in the Northern Territory*, Australian Institute of Aboriginal Studies, Canberra.

Cape York Peninsula Land Use Strategy [CYPLUS], 1993, *Natural Resource Analysis Program*, Government Publishing Service, Queensland, Brisbane.

Chapman, J.W., undated, Kowanyama Mitchell River, Report for Australian Board of Missions (Review Reports for Chief Protector of Aborigines).

Connell Wagner, 1989, *Cape York Peninsula Resource Analysis*, Premier's Department, Cairns.

Dale, A., 1991, *Aboriginal Access to Land Management Funding and Services*, Australian National Parks and Wildlife Service and the Aboriginal and Torres Strait Island Commission, Queensland, Brisbane.

Dale, A., 1992, Planning for Rural Development in Aboriginal Communities: A Community Based Planning Approach, unpublished PhD thesis: Griffiths University.

Done, J., 1987, *Wings Across the Sea*, Boolarong, Brisbane.

Flood, J., 1983, *The Archaeology of the Dreamtime*, Collins Australia, Sydney.

Gibb, C.A., 1971, *Report of the Committee to Review the Situation of Aborigines on Pastoral Properties in the Northern Territory*, Government Publishers, Canberra.

Hill, R., 1992, Models for Aboriginal Involvement in natural Resources Management on Cape York, *National Park Conservation*, Queensland: A.I.R. 008, 19–24.

Kolig, E., 1987, *The Noonkanbah Story*, University of Otago Press, Dunedin.

Kowanyama Aboriginal Land and Natural Resources Management Office (KALNRMO), 1990, Land and Natural Resources Management: Community Awareness Programme, unpublished m.s., Kowanyama.

Kowanyama Aboriginal Land and Natural Resources Management Office (KALNRMO), 1991, Mitchell River Watershed, unpublished m.s., Kowanyama.

Kowanyama Aboriginal Land and Natural Resources Management Office (KALNRMO), 1992, Mitchell River Watershed Conference, unpublished m.s., Kowanyama.

McConnel, U., 1957, *Myths of the Munkan*, Melbourne University Press, London.

McGrath, A., 1987, *Born in the Cattle: Aborigines in Cattle Country*, Allen and Unwin, Sydney.

McKeague, P.J., 1992, *The Cattle Industry of Cape York Peninsula*, Government Publishing Service, Queensland, Brisbane.

Merlan, F., 1978, 'Making People Quiet' in the Pastoral North: Reminiscenses of Elsey Station, *Aboriginal History*, 2, 70–106.

Moon, R. and Moon, V., 1989, *Cape York: An Adventurer's Guide*, Kakirra Adventure Publications, Victoria.

Morphy, H., 1984, *Journey into the Crocodile's Nest*, Australian Institute of Aboriginal Studies, Canberra.

Morphy, H., 1988, Maintaining Cosmic Unity, in T. Ingold, J. Riches and J. Woodburn (eds), *Hunters and Gatherers: Politics, Power and Ideology*, Berg, Oxford, 249–271.

Mulvaney, D.J. and White, J.P., (eds), 1987, *Australians to 1788*, Fairfax, Syme and Weldon, Sydney.

Myers, F.R., 1986, *Pintupi Country, Pintupi Self*, Smithsonian Institute, Washington DC, and Australian Institute of Aboriginal Studies, Canberra.

Pacific Asia Travel Association [PATA], 1992, *Cape York Peninsula: Tourism Issues and Opportunities*, PATA, Wooloomooloo.

Peterson, N., 1972, Totemism Yesterday: Sentiment and Local Organisation Among the Australian Aborigines, *Man*, 7, 12–32.

Pressland, A.J., Mills, J.R. and Cummins, V.G., 1988, Landscape Degradation in Native Pasture, in *Native Pastures in Queensland: Their Resources and Management*, Queensland Department of Primary Industries, Brisbane.

Queensland Government, 1992, *North Queensland: Tourism, Exports and Growth*, Government Publishing Service, Queensland, Brisbane.

Reynolds, H., 1987, *The Law of the Land*, Penguin, London.

Rose, D., 1984, The Saga of Captain Cook: Morality in Aboriginal and European Law, *Australian Aboriginal Studies*, 2, 24–39.

Sharp, L., 1933, Map of Yir Yoront Clan Land. unpublished m.s., Kowanyama.

Sharp, L., 1937, The Social Anthropology of a Totemic System of North Queensland, unpublished PhD Thesis, Harvard University.

Sharp, L., 1939, Tribes and Totemism in North-East Australia, in *Oceania*, 9, 3, 254–275 and 4, 439–461.

Sharp, L., 1952, Steel Axes for Stone Age Australians, in E. Spicer (ed.), *Human Problems in Technological Change: A Casebook*, The Russell Sage Foundation, New York.

Sinnamon, V., 1992, Gulf of Carpentaria Coast and River Management, unpublished m.s., Kowanyama.

Stevens, F., 1974, *Aborigines in the Northern Cattle Industry*, Australian National University Press, Canberra.

Strang, V., 1994, Uncommon Ground: Concepts of Landscape and Human Environmental Relations in Far North Queensland, unpublished D.Phil thesis, Oxford University.

Taylor, J., 1984, Of Acts and Axes: An Ethnography of Socio-Cultural Change in an Aboriginal Community, Cape York Peninsula, unpublished PhD thesis, James Cook University.

Urry, J., 1990, *The Tourist Gaze: Leisure and Travel in Contemporary Societies*, Sage, London.

Von Sturmer, J., 1982, Aborigines in the Uranium Industry: Towards Self-Management in the Alligator River Region, in R.M. Berndt (ed.), *Aboriginal Sites and Resource Development*, University of Western Australia Press, Perth.

Willshire, W.H., 1896, *The Land of the Dawning: Being Facts Gleaned from Cannibals in the Australian Stone Age*, W.K. Thomas and Co., Adelaide.

5 From Sami Nomadism to Global Tourism

KIRSTI PEDERSEN AND ARVID VIKEN

INTRODUCTION

The indigenous Sami people have lived in Northern Fennoscandia for thousands of years, and are spread across four countries: Norway, Finland, Sweden, and Russia (Figure 5.1). The majority live in Finnmark, Norway's northernmost county. Formerly known as Lapland, most Sami now prefer to call their homeland Sapmi. Yet Sapmi is no longer only the homeland of the Sami, but also a playground for people from all over the world; a reality, however harsh, that many of the indigenous population must face. In a recent television documentary, one Sami expressed the tension between his people's traditional use of the land and modern recreation and tourism as follows:

> This is our land. We live and work here, we own this . . . I hope those who come after us will also feel the same way . . . Only the Sami used this land. But today more and more Norwegians come here.
>
> (NRK TV December 26 1994)

According to Giddens (1994: 62), tradition is 'an orientation to the past, such that the past has a heavy influence . . . over the present . . . traditions have an organic character: they develop and mature, or weaken and "die"'. Traditions represent truths and rituals protected by guardians, be it 'elders, healers, magicians or religious functionaries, . . . believed to be agents, or essential mediators of its causal power' (Giddens, 1994: 65). For most people, traditions represent 'taken-for-granted' knowledge and attitudes, including moral guidelines. Traditions discriminate between insiders and others, thus shaping people's identities; they are 'the glue that holds premodern social orders together' (Giddens, 1994: 62). Today, traditions are believed to be losing their hold on people's everyday life, and in modern societies they are replaced by rational enquiry, scientific knowledge and expertise. At the same time as recreation and tourism challenge traditional Sami society, they represent new opportunities. In this chapter, we discuss the challenges and paradoxes that are inherent in ethnic and

People and Tourism in Fragile Environments. Edited by M. F. Price.

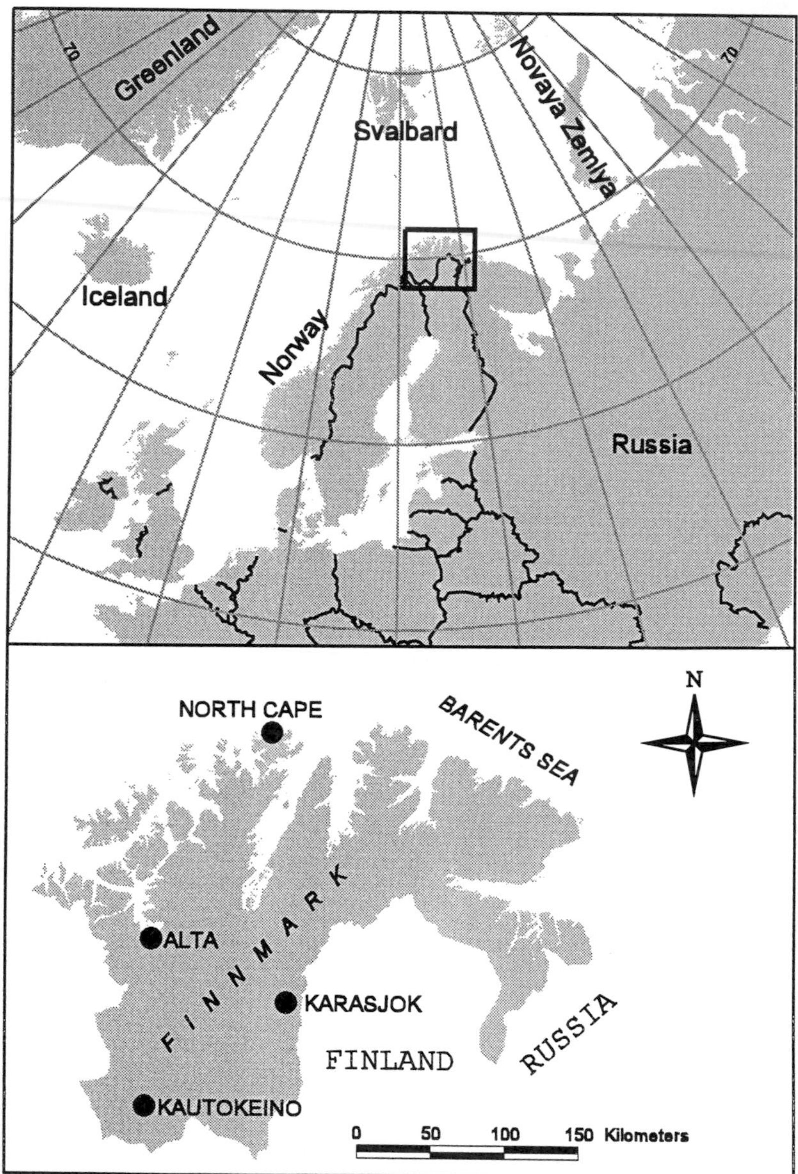

Figure 5.1 Location map of Sapmi

adventure tourism, and how the growing recreation and tourism industry contributes to the development of a vigorous Sami society.

FINNMARK—THE LAND OF THE SAMI

Several thousand years ago, the Sami most probably arrived in Sapmi from the southeast. Sami is a Uralic language, similar to Finnish, Hungarian and the languages of several ethnic groups in Russia. The official name Finnmark, which means the land of the 'Finns', indicates a broad acceptance of the area as the land of the Sami, and Norway was the first country to ratify the International Labour Organisation's Convention on Indigenous Peoples in 1990. In Finnmark, nature, not human settlement, dominates the landscape; 75 000 people are scattered unevenly across 48 600 square kilometres of open, inland mountains, forested valleys, fjords, and a long, rugged coastline towards the Barents Sea.

Although Finnmark stretches as far north as Alaska's Point Barrow, the Gulf Stream moderates the climate and even allows agriculture to flourish. Far north of the Arctic Circle, two months of midnight sun make the summer an intensely productive season. Rich coastal fisheries, hunting, and possibilities to harvest natural resources have created a basis for human livelihoods for at least ten thousand years. Along the rugged coastline and on the mountain plateau, people living in small, isolated communities subsisted on a combination of fishing, hunting, and farming. Although the conditions were harsh, the rich fisheries attracted Norwegian and Finnish immigrants. Finnmark today is a mixture of traditions and modernity, deeply rooted in three cultures: Sami, Norwegian, and Finnish. Finnmark's remoteness, its mythical landscape, and the midnight sun make the region exotic for other people. Today, even local people are becoming aware of this 'uniqueness'.

THE COLONIZATION OF SAPMI

In tourist brochures, Finnmark is often presented as the last wilderness of Europe. For people coming from the 'outside' it may seem like a wilderness: a *terra incognita* or a blank space on a map (Nash, 1981). For the Sami, however, the land carries memories of their ancestors, their whole culture. According to a local newspaper (*Nordlys,* September 27, 1993), the President of the Sami Parliament in his introductory speech to the Fifth World Wilderness Congress, held in Tromsø, claimed that 'wilderness' is an imperialistic term which defines Sapmi as uninhabited land, giving the outside world legitimacy for whatever action it might take in the area. To define areas that one would like to conquer as 'wild' was a well-known strategy when Europeans colonized America (Nash, 1967) and Africa.

The Sami past is one of exploitation, suppression and suffering (Lorenz, 1991). The Norwegian colonization of Sapmi had three stages: taking over the fisheries in the thirteenth century; the regulation of trade; and taking over the land for traditional farming. In the Middle Ages, the Sami came to know the region's nation-states through taxation and commercial restrictions. When borders were drawn between Norway and Finland and Sweden in 1751, and between Norway and Russia in 1826, the Sami were divided. No serious efforts have ever been made to establish Sapmi as a national state, although national symbols, such as the Sami flag, have been frequently used in recent years. At the end of the nineteenth century, the Norwegian state gave land only to Norwegian-speaking farmers as a part of the assimilation policy, and registered the rest of the land (about 95 per cent) as state property (Pedersen, S., 1994).

During the twentieth century, the Sami have become a minority in their own land. Many Sami have been 'successfully' assimilated into Norwegian society. In the late nineteenth century and the first half of the twentieth century, Norwegian policy, influenced by social Darwinism, claimed Sami inferiority. The establishment of Norwegian institutions, such as schools, and the introduction of the Norwegian language also happened in this period. The assimilation process has also been encouraged from people inside Sami society (Stordahl, 1994). The history of the inter-ethnic relationship between the Sami and the Norwegians shows us that 'ethnic distinctions do not depend on an absence of social interaction and acceptance; but are quite to the contrary often the very foundations on which embracing social systems are built' (Barth, 1969: 10). Yet the Sami culture and language survived due to, among other things, Sami lifestyles, a strong religious belief, and the ability to incorporate new technology into traditional ways of life (Bjørklund, 1985).

Around 1960, a new era began, with the revitalization of Sami culture and language. This was also a period of democratization and the building of autonomous institutions, such as the Nordic Sami Institute (1974), the Sami Educational Board (1975), the Sami College (1989), and the Sami Parliament (1989). Around 1980, the Alta River case, which concerned the construction of a hydro-electric power plant, put the Sami issue on the national agenda. This case functioned as a tremendous consciousness-raising process, both among the Sami and in wider Norwegian society. Since then, a government commission has been working to clarify the Sami people's legal rights to the land and the natural resources of Finnmark.

The incorporation of the Sami society into the Norwegian welfare state with its market-oriented economy means that most Sami are challenged by modernity. New technologies, models, concepts, and knowledge, all developed elsewhere, are replacing traditional ways of living, knowledge, tools, and materials. Today most Sami live modern lives; less than ten per cent are the reindeer herders still perceived as the 'real' Sami by the outside world. However, these semi-nomads are also modernized and have become part of a cash economy. The snowmobile was introduced in reindeer herding in 1964, and had replaced the reindeer for transportation within a few years (Pelto, 1973).

Before the 'snowmobile revolution', it was possible for one family to make a livelihood from a herd of 100 reindeer (Figure 5.2). Today this is just enough to buy one snowmobile. Consequently, modernization has made ever larger herds necessary, so that the mountains of Finnmark are overcrowded and heavily overgrazed, and the government has started a restructuring programme in order to reduce the number of reindeer and get people out of the herding industry. The social effects of this modernization are tremendous. Education and housing programmes in the 1960s forced many women and children to stay in the villages,

Figure 5.2 Autumn migration of reindeer
(Bjønar Johansen)

Figure 5.3 Summer tourists buying handicrafts by a *lavvu*
(Bjønar Johansen)

while herding became the men's responsibility. The modern reindeer herder no longer migrates with his herd in an eight-season cycle, but commutes between the mountains and his home with a motorized vehicle (Nilsen and Mosli, 1994). New occupations have emerged, but at the same time unemployment has increased. The growing tourism industry has, however, strengthened women's contributions to the family income. Tourism represents a significant market for their home-made handicrafts, and some tourists are given genuine ethnic experiences in the traditional Sami home—the Sami tent or *lavvu* (Figure 5.3). Modernization has also produced a Sami elite which consists mostly of bureaucrats, professionals, educators, and scholars.

Another result of modernization is that the Sami have become part of the modern leisure society. Soccer and snowmobile racing are the most common sports among young men in Sami communities. The Sami organize their own sports clubs, arrange Sami championships, and play 'national' soccer games against other 'small nations' in Europe (Pedersen and Rafoss, 1989). In the 1990s, reindeer racing has been organized as a World Championship, an event which attracts hundreds of tourists every Easter. The modern Sami's relationship with nature is as for other modern people: a place for work for the few, and an arena for recreation, sport, and leisure for the majority.

NEGOTIATING SAMI IDENTITIES

Until recently, the Sami have been a people without any faith in the future of their own culture. In the 1960s, Sami were socially stigmatized (Eidheim, 1969) and, as late as the 1980s, many denied having any past and did not regard their identity as being tied to history (Bjørklund, 1985). According to Friedman (1994) 'people without history . . . are the people who have been prevented from identifying themselves for others'. For almost a century, images of the Sami as inferior were presented through public documents and popular narratives. Today, the Sami present their own experiences, telling about generations of suffering. Richardson (1990: 131) maintains that 'Telling collective stories is an effective way . . . to reveal personal problems as public issues, to make possible collective identity and collective solutions'. The narrative about the past has an acknowledged function as therapy, and is a key function in rewriting history (Nergård, 1994). In rewriting the past, the complexity and diversity of the Sami culture is made visible, creating a plurality which also gives room for the construction of, and negotiation between, different Sami identities: for instance, between an official and political, or a subjective and a locally constructed Sami identity; between the identity of the nomads and the settled.

The definition of what it means to be a Sami today is a question of how knowledge is constituted, people's socio-cultural contexts, and to some extent how the individual chooses to construct his or her identity. The emphasis put on one's Sami identity may change from one situation to another. The most prominent members of the Sami elite have largely learnt their Sami culture and identity in boarding schools and universities from teachers who, until recently, were mostly Norwegians. Away from home since the first day of school, Sami academics have become visitors in their parent culture (Stordahl, 1994). Back in their original communities, they apply what they were taught, as a kind of social engineering (Eidheim, 1993). Their Sami identity does not always coincide with that of their parents or people who were brought up within a local context (Stordahl, 1994). This antagonism between the traditional ways of living, and the agents of modernity with their academic discourse, represent potential for local frustration and conflicts. What a reindeer herder or souvenir trader may offer on the tourist market may be regarded as cultural betrayal by others. Yet the new elite also sees tourism as one way in which the Sami culture can survive. Through tourism, the Sami culture is made visible to the world as, for instance, at the Olympic Winter Games at Lillehammer in 1994.

FROM HARVEST LAND TO PLAYGROUND

Due to its strategic geographical position, Finnmark played an important role as a frontier between Germany and Russia during World War II. During the German retreat in 1944, all buildings except some churches were burnt, and the population was forced to evacuate. After the war, an intense rebuilding and modernization programme took place. The planners wanted to gather the population in new towns, but people rejected this and moved back to the places where they had lived before. Yet they did not escape modernity and the associated changes in society, culture, economics, and communications. In 1970, twice as many were employed in fishing as in education and knowledge production. Today, fishing only employs a third as many people as the education, research, and consulting sector. Along with reindeer herding, fishing has been transformed from a traditional lifestyle to a modern industry (Tjelmeland, 1994). Fishing, reindeer herding, and tourism vocations are now taught at school. New means of transportation have broken down old regional and ethnic divisions. People cross ethnic borders, mix socially, and intermarry more often than before. There is a constant search for new ways of living, and renewal is the key policy-making word. Since the mid-1980s, the development of tourism in the north has been a national effort—and for many a hope for the future.

A major result of the modernization processes is that the organization and content of people's work have changed. Industrialization and possibilities for paid work have resulted in a sharp division between work and leisure, between work and family life. These changes influence people's relationships with nature. Yet fishing, hunting, and berrypicking still play an important role, both as a part of the household economy, and more often as a symbol of local identity, competence and belonging. Today, these activities are often combined with the use of motorized vehicles. To hike just for pleasure, which is the dominant understanding of outdoor life in Norway, and can be interpreted as a key symbol of a Norwegian national identity (Nedrelid, 1991), is something new for most people in Finnmark. Until recently, this was an exclusive activity for well-educated civil servants and professionals, often from the 'south'.

Figure 5.4 Gazing at modernity: sleighs and snowmobiles
(Kirsti Pedersen)

Figure 5.5 Gazing at tradition: a girls' reindeer-sled race
(Bjønar Johansen)

For about half of the population, snowmobiling is the most popular leisure activity during the almost eight months of winter. There is a web of tracks all over the mountains, and between the many lakes which are attractive for ice-fishing. Areas that were inaccessible a generation ago can be reached in a few hours. Thus the snowmobile makes it possible for men to continue their traditional harvesting activities despite the constraints of employment (Figure 5.4). Nevertheless, the 'snowmobile revolution' has caused a deep emotional and political conflict between contrasting views on nature, between a national and a local understanding of outdoor life. It involves questions such as who has the right and the competence to manage local natural resources, and reflects the deep antagonism between the 'centre' and the 'periphery', between the 'north' and the 'south' (Pedersen, 1993).

Earlier definitions saw leisure as the antithesis of 'work'—which implicitly meant 'paid work'—and it was the white working-man's leisure patterns and work experiences that were taken as a norm. This definition suggests that the division between leisure and other aspects of life is clear-cut; that domestic obligations and leisure cannot happen concurrently. Leisure is supposed to be free and uncommitted, a definition which does not capture most women's lives and experiences. What most women appreciate in connection with outdoor life is the social togetherness with family and friends. Women use their neighbourhood more often than men, and spend less time in the mountains. Women do not emphasize the risky challenges, the excitement or the 'toughness'. Some claim that the snowmobile is a liberating force; it has made it possible for women to participate in the outdoor activities. Equally, many men seem to be proud of being able to bring their wives and children into the mountains this way. Until recently, however, traditional gender roles in adventure recreation have been taken for granted by both women and men, as well as in research. Today an increasing number of women challenge the male hegemony, for instance by arranging exclusively female events, such as dog-sled races and ski races (Figure 5.5). In these events, feminine values such as social togetherness, not competition, are strongly emphasized (Pedersen, 1993; 1994).

Today one can identify three main forms of outdoor recreation among the inhabitants of Finnmark; 'traditionalists' for whom harvesting nature is the prime motive; 'classical trekkers'—hiking and skiing just for pleasure and health; and 'special interest recreationists'—salmon anglers, hunters, dog-sledders, kayakers and other adventurers (Figure 5.6). A common denominator for the last, rather heterogeneous, group is that their activities are technology-based and commercialized, globalized, media-focused and, to some degree, imported. In addition, these activities play an important role in constituting masculine identities. The three types overlap and challenge each other, but the dominant national understanding of outdoor life has never had the power to dominate the local culture. The traditional local culture has lost some of its status, while the globalized and technology-based activities have become the 'winners'.

TOURISM IN LAPLAND AND TO THE NORTH CAPE

Different kinds of people from all over Europe have travelled to and through Sapmi since the Middle Ages: explorers, missionaries, traders, and fishermen.

Figure 5.6 The campfire, an important social arena for recreationists
(Kirsti Pedersen)

Figure 5.7 Madame Bongo preparing a traditional meal for tourists
(Ole Rapp)

In the search for a northern sea passage to China, Scottish sea captain Richard Chancellor (1553) named the northernmost point of Europe North Cape, while Wilhelm Barentz (1594) gave his name to the surrounding ocean. Royal visitors included Prince Louis Philippe of France (1795), King Oscar of Sweden and Norway (1873), and King Haakon VII of Norway on his first journey through his recently independent nation (1907).

The exploration of the Arctic resulted in a rich travel literature (Schiötz, 1970). In the beginning of the nineteenth century, most writers described nature as harsh and dangerous, and the Sami as small, dirty, inferior, and without dignity (Mathisen, 1994). The Romantic period changed this view: the 'wild land without civilization' became beautiful and majestic. People searched beyond the Arctic Circle for the midnight sun, Lapland, and the mythical Ultima Thule. North Cape became a major destination for commercial tourism. Cruise ships have visited since the 1870s, and a coastal steamer has sailed a regular route between Bergen and Finnmark since 1893. Travellers visited Sami camps more or less as tourists do today. The Sami had been trading for centuries, and it was natural for them to look upon the visitors as potential customers. Their interaction with other cultures also took place in other settings. Some Sami were 'exhibited' at the World Fair in Paris in 1900, and as late as 1930 others were 'exhibited' in several German towns (Hætta, 1994). Yet modern mass tourism in Finnmark did not begin until the road to North Cape was completed in 1957. Since then, the roadside has been a place for inter-ethnic contact and for souvenir trade. In 1994, there were 263 000 tourists to North Cape, of whom 79 per cent came through Sapmi by car or bus (Viken and Krogh, 1995).

Two centuries ago, the state built mountain lodges in the interior as part of a transportation system that served traders, tax collectors, postmen, and the clergy who regularly travelled through Finnmark. Later a whole chain of lodges was built, and rebuilt after the war. Despite this infrastructure, and several attempts to promote the area for do-it-yourself wilderness travellers, mountaineering in Finnmark has been very modest compared to Southern Norway. Finnmark could not give the hikers the dramatic scenery and the challenges they sought, and in the summer the mosquitoes effectively protected the area! In pre-motorized times, only occasional hikers and people on official business found their way along the old routes. The landscape itself does not demand particular skills, but the climate is tough. The travellers had to be well informed and self-sufficient, and they had to have time. Visiting these mountains has always been regarded as an expedition for the more advanced: for people seeking primitive conditions, or for ardent hunters and anglers. There are, however, two exceptions. The ptarmigan hunt, when autumn displays its spectacular colours, has long been a highly reputed tourism niche. Even more important is salmon fishing along the rivers. Accommodating and serving the anglers—'rowing' for the 'salmon lords'—is a prestigious local occupation.

During the 1980s, the introduction of the snowmobile led to a considerable increase in recreational travel in the mountains in the winter. Visitor statistics from the mountain lodges now show that there are about twice as many guests during the winter as in the summer. Most are locals, and the short tourist seasons are a problem for the industry, here as elsewhere. Organized adventure tourism has been limited, with the Norwegian Tourist Association organizing one or two annual skiing trips. During recent years, these have been in cooperation with a local dog-sled musher; earlier also together with a Sami herder who arranged reindeer sleigh rides. The challenge, according to tourism planners, is to make the two months of darkness, the Aurora Borealis, and the snowy, cold weather into an interesting tourist attraction for an international market (Finnmark Opplevelser, 1995).

SAPMI—A PLAYGROUND FOR THE WHOLE WORLD

The basis for Norwegian outdoor life is the principle of free access to the countryside for all Norwegian inhabitants. This privilege to move freely and harvest natural resources with only minor restrictions was established through the Right to Access Act in 1957 (Miljøverndepartementet, 1993). The many opportunities to go hunting, fishing and snowmobiling for recreational purposes are often said to be the major reason why people stay in Finnmark or move there. Everyday life is regulated according to the recreational opportunities that nature offers in each season. Yet many Sami have experienced a major change: from being the only ones who utilized these resources, many others now compete for them. New roads and longer vacations have resulted in a stream of people from the coastal towns and fishing villages to the inland. The principle of common access to the countryside has become not only a theory but a reality for thousands of people. This has resulted in a race for the best fishing areas and hunting grounds, and pressure on, or even suppression of, the old Sami rights to harvest according to kin-group (*siida*) agreements. Sami protests against this encroachment of their old rights were not heard, and as a minority they had no power to defend their old common rights (Pavel, 1979). In general, foreigners have almost the same rights as Norwegians. Only cloudberry picking is an exclusive right for the inhabitants of Finnmark.

Until recently, the tourism industry was modest in its use of the Right to Access Act in product development and marketing, most probably because there was no market. During the last decade, an increasing number of guides have offered specially designed nature and adventure tours: snowmobile safaris, horseback riding, hunting, angling, kayaking, and dog sledding. In the coastal areas, deep-sea fishing is about to become a tourist business. Most of these 'products' are built on local traditions, but 'packed' in modern equipment and a globalized language. The right of common access to the wilderness for everyone is more frequently emphasized in marketing. That the law is not just an individual right, but also a general obligation to be considerate, is something most tourists have to be taught. In the 1990s, a new trend can be seen: the development of an intimate ethnic tourism. Reindeer sleigh rides, including a visit to an 'authentic' Sami camp in the mountains, eating a local meal and listening to traditional folk song (*joik*), are frequently offered (Figure 5.7).

To start a tourist business there is no need for a specific concession or formal education. Yet, while relatively few tourists make use of the 'new' 'tourism in close contact with unspoiled nature', the potential in the international market is considerable (Weiler and Hall, 1992). There is no doubt that increasing pressure on natural resources is a result of the general growth in the tourist industry. So far, the potential problems connected to this development have not been on the agenda, whether in public debate or research. Instead, expectations about profits and employment from tourism are tremendous. Some critics can be heard; local people now not only have to fight for local resources with people from the growing urban centres and other parts of Norway, but also with the needs of people from all over the world. In such a perspective, the development of adventure tourism can be seen as another step in the colonization of Sapmi.

In the future, great changes in the management of the natural resources in Finnmark may occur. The discussions about Sami land claims, and whether the land should be managed according to exclusive ethnic rights, are just beginning. The government commission which was constituted after the Alta River case in 1980 should deliver its proposal in 1995. A preliminary report (Norges Offentlige Utredninger, 1993) resulted in an emotional local debate, with critics saying that the report built on a Norwegian perspective, giving legitimacy to the State's property rights. Consequently, a presentation of the issues from a Sami point of view was prepared (Norges Offentlige Utredninger, 1994). The implications of this debate for the Sami, for local recreation, and the development of the tourism industry are impossible to predict.

FINNMARK—A SHOWCASE FOR THE INTERPLAY BETWEEN TRADITIONS AND MODERNITY

Recreation and tourism are modern phenomena but, as we have seen in Sapmi, have a strong affiliation to the past. Tourism depends on differences between places and cultures, and people's desire for otherness. The Sami otherness is, or is believed to be, preserved in tradition. Two aspects of the interplay between tradition and modernity have to be discussed: first, the character and meaning of ethnic and adventure tourism from a tourist's point of view and, second, the role of these types of tourism in an ethnic society like Sapmi.

There are many interpretations that explain why Finnmark and Sapmi have become popular tourist destinations. People's motives are definitely varied, and some even visit the area without any special motive, participating in a package tour of Scandinavia or Europe (Viken, 1991), just following a fad. Most of the tourists who visit Sapmi probably come as 'conquerors'. For some, this conquest is merely one more 'item' in their collection of places; for others, the remoteness of the area symbolizes their personal conquest of the world. To go to foreign and remote places, regarded as unusual and exclusive in their own culture, is of high symbolic value and significance in the constitution of the tourists' identities. However, commentators do not agree on the meaning and context of ethnic tourism. One perspective is that it fills modern human beings' needs to be convinced about their cultural superiority, and has been a major motive for western travel to the third world (Buzard, 1993). Others contest this, and even claim the opposite. Possibly, ethnic tourism may permit 'superior' groups to show solidarity with 'inferior' ones. MacCannell (1992: 167), however, sees ethnic tourism as 'the final ratification of the results of a white cultural totalization'—a gesture the majority can afford when its superiority is no longer threatened.

Most ethnic and adventure tourists do not look upon themselves as tourists, but as travellers or participants, a distinction which is often of great importance (Levi-Strauss, 1972; Buzard, 1993). To 'go native' or 'back to nature' is motivated primarily by the tourists' search for first-hand, authentic and intimate contact with people whose ethnic or cultural background is different, and to come in touch with pure nature. Such tourists really want to be 'decivilized' (Nash, 1981): to experience and learn 'natural' or alternative ways of life. A parallel can be found in Norwegian outdoor life. The do-it-yourself hikers definitely do not like to be categorized as tourists. They prefer to be looked upon as pioneers, performing a 'pure', well-skilled, simplistic, and ecological life in close contact with nature, an understanding inherited from polar explorer Fridtjof Nansen, and in recent years heavily influenced by the deep ecology movement (Naess, 1989). This gives another story to tell, one that is more heroic or highly valued. Such an image and identity places these people in the new middle class, a class constituted by a special taste and lifestyle which differs from that of the masses. Among the signifiers of distinctive identities in late modernity are the consumption of recreational activities and tourism (Bourdieu, 1984; Rojek, 1992; Munt, 1994).

One example of the complex relationships that are inherent in modern ethnic and adventure tourism is the development of the Easter festival in the Sami heartland. Many people who visit Sapmi do not have the feeling of being in the middle of an indigenous culture. Most Sami wear modern clothes, drive modern cars, and live in pre-fabricated houses. To get a taste of an 'authentic otherness' tourists have to buy pre-arranged tours, where the Sami culture is staged. Easter is different, with ten days of religious ceremonies, plays and shows, Sami music and *joik* contests, reindeer sled races, and people wearing their traditional costumes. A mixture of old and new cultural expressions are on display. One interesting example is how the traditional skill of reindeer sledding has been transformed into a World Championship and thus adapted to globalized and competitive sports values. Yet it is not clear whether this leads to tourism playing a positive role in the revitalization of Sami culture.

Changing social patterns have given rise to new patterns in holiday-making, notably activity holidays for those whose sedentary occupations encourage more energetic forms of travel. The postmodern tourist is, according to Urry (1990), searching for adventure, fun, prestige, the collection of unique experiences and artefacts, and the feeling of being unique and different from most travellers. The development of tourism in Finnmark follows the international trends. On the one hand, more and more is arranged for the tourists, pre-packaged and displayed in handsome visitor centres. On the other hand, a more flexible tourist supply is able to offer unique, personally designed experiences.

In Finnmark, intimate ethnic and nature tourism take place side by side and are mixed with the most technological advanced tourism the world can offer. Thus, Finnmark is not only a meeting place for traditions and modernity, but a showcase of the interplay between the two. One day, the tourist can do traditional trekking or skiing, and experience traditional 'primitive' ways of living in a *lavvu*. The next day, he or she can speed across the mountains on a snowmobile, exposed to the elements of nature, the harsh climate, the wind, the cold, and the snow, challenging his or her own and the 'natural' boundaries or feeling the risky life of premodern times wrapped in secure modern technology. Put another way, the ethnic experience is served with a garnish of aestheticism, adventure, and fun.

Thus, Finnmark is an arena for the self-realization and fulfilment of hedonist needs and motives, and at the same time for learning about the Sami way of life, the vulnerability of nature, modern technology, and sustainable development. Running out of time, a tourist can also get a compressed version of all this by visiting a nature interpretation centre or experiencing the wilderness in a widescreen theatre. Finnmark also offers opportunities for urban life and shopping; almost everything a modern human being can demand. The tourist industry in Finnmark seems to adapt to what Urry (1990: 92) calls 'the three-minute (or five-minute!) culture'. The tourist can switch between tradition and modernity, like zapping TV-channels. This 'zap-tourism' satisfies the postmodern tourists' needs for constantly new, 'authentic' experiences. The postmodern tourist is met by a tourism industry well aware of his or her preferences. At the same time, the industry satisfies local people's needs to be regarded as part of the modern world—not as a backward periphery. Some local people, however, feel alienated from the image of 'real' culture that is constructed for the tourists.

The other aspect of the tradition–modernity relationship in tourism concerns the role of ethnic and adventure tourism in Sapmi: how, and by whom, should Sami culture be exposed to tourists? Together with municipal authorities, the tourism industry has been the main force behind the organization of the modern Easter festival based on long-standing local traditions. The people involved have mostly been Sami, but in general, the development of tourism in Sapmi has been managed by Norwegians. None of the bigger hotels are run by Sami. Yet, while Sami are not given preference in the regional tourist board or specific rights in tourism development, one criterion for government project funding is to be Sami. Both Sami and Norwegians operate adventure tourism, mainly as small-scale business. The first initiative was taken by an international hotel chain as a strategy to fill its empty rooms during the winter season (Viken and Krogh, 1995). This hotel chain has also used Sami models in their development of restaurants and uniforms.

The only area where Sami seem to have developed a tourism business on their own is the souvenir trade. Norwegians have not done much in using authentic Sami culture in product development and marketing. Finland, on the other hand, has developed products where Sami culture is mixed with myths about the Sami, with traits from other ethnic cultures (Santa Claus, for example), and whatever else may be fun for the visitors. Such products are even not necessarily mediated by Sami; it is a culture where fake and real elements are intermingled, and where neither the hosts or the visitors know the difference—what Eco (1986) calls hyperreality. A Norwegian Sami tourist operator has claimed: ‘our aim is to show authentic Sami culture, not a Sami Disney World with Santa Claus’. The problem is that the tourists cannot distinguish a constructed culture from reality. Finland has had much more business success, and the fake Sami image is probably about to be settled in the market.

When used in tourism, the significance of cultural symbols changes. The Sami knife is now produced in smaller sizes, more suitable for transportation than the original, and with ornaments to make it nicer and more suitable for tourism. It is not a solid tool any more. The *lavvu* has also undergone a revolution. A local producer created a smaller, more easily transportable one, primarily for leisure use. Today this ‘light’ version is used by reindeer herders, and bigger *lavvus* are made to serve as restaurants for groups up to 40. The souvenir trade has developed new products which have never been anything but souvenirs: dolls, paper knives and key rings.

Again, the production of souvenirs leads to a dichotomy. When a traditional Sami product, or Sami-inspired product, is used in connection with tourism, thus creating employment, tourism functions as a cultural preserve, at least as long as the Sami look upon the production as authentic, thus confirming their identity. In contrast, if the production is industrialized and moved out of Sapmi, most Sami will feel exploited. Performed and controlled by the Sami themselves, tourism may give new meaning to old cultural expressions, something that Giddens (1991) calls reembedding. Whether this will preserve traditions is another question. Performed by professional artists, the cultural display has become a matter of expertise, and a kind of relic (Giddens, 1994) with reduced value as tradition. If the Sami culture becomes a mere surface, a demonstration of ‘otherness’, ethnicity is reduced to rhetoric. As MacCannell (1992: 168) notes, when ethnic reconstruction happens as a result of a ‘global network of commercial transactions’, ethnicities ‘begin to use former colourful ways both as commodities to be bought and sold, and as rhetorical weaponry in their dealing with one another’.

Mediating the suppressed history and traditions of the Sami may function as a reminder of what the region and the Sami culture once were, and as a way of keeping that past alive in the present; for instance, the skill of using reindeer for transportation. Performed by the Sami, focusing Sami culture, tourism may contribute to regained status and strengthened Sami identities. According to Lash and Urry (1994: 275), tourists from foreign countries ‘contribute to the partially conscious evaluation of its future trajectory'. Tourism will obviously have a central place in the trajectory of Sapmi. Tourists are unreliable friends, however, especially those who are pioneers (Smith, 1992), inclined to disappear once a destination becomes well known.

To avoid these circumstances, tourism should only be one of several development trajectories given priority in Sapmi. Tourism in Sapmi depends on its differences from the rest of the nation and the world, and its image of wildness. These, in turn, demand the maintenance of both wilderness and the Sami culture. The paradox is that both the Sami culture and nature can be loved to death. Thus, the challenge for tourism is to maintain a difficult balance: to present wilderness and Sami culture without exploiting or destroying either.

CONCLUSION

'The difficulty of finding new ground for travel is increasing every year for those who, with but limited time at their disposal, are yet tired of the beaten paths . . . ', wrote Alexander Hutchinson in 1870. As a solution he recommended 'Try Lapland. A fresh field for summer tourists'. In analysing Alaskan tourism, which has many parallels to the development of tourism in Northern Fennoscandia, Nash (1981) claims that the mystique has to do with the notion of being at the edge of civilization: 'the end of the earth idea' which, in the tourist's mind, is to have done something special and unusual. Even those who only go to the edge of the wilderness on a cruise ship or in a tourist bus can get the feeling of the 'wild'. Sami travel in the 1990s is built on a transformation of the 'fresh fields of Lapland' into a romanticized Last Wilderness of Europe. In order to attract tourists, many Sami are willing to redefine their ancestral homeland as wilderness, for ' the wilderness experience has much more to do with the attitude of the visitor than with the realities of history and geography' (Nash, 1981: 16).

The history of tourism and recreation in Finnmark is an image of local, national, and transnational relations and travel. In the 1950s and 1960s, development in Finnmark meant adaptation to traditional industries. In the 1990s, in the 'late-modernity of Finnmark', industrial development means adaptation to global tourism (Tjelmeland, 1994). The development of tourism in Sapmi has an important function in preserving Sami culture. It both represents new ways of living and contributes to building local identities that fit into modernization and globalization processes. If it is successful, it may be accepted as a contribution to the revitalization of Sami culture. If it fails, the tourism industry may be blamed. This buffer position seems to give tourism the freedom to function as a laboratory for cultural inventions.

To capture the complex processes where people move between traditions and modernity, 'primitivism' and 'civilization', the past and the present, 'nature' and 'culture', creating and recreating a mixture of realities, the 'travelling cultures' paradigm (Clifford, 1992) could be appropriate. As Slowikowski (1993) has pointed out, this paradigm opens up a dialogue concerning travel as a reflection of humanity's condition. This paradigm goes far beyond the study of tourism; all cultural movement is broadly and inexactly conceived of as travel.

In the history of Finnmark, mobility seems to be a central experience; it is a region of departures, arrivals, and transits. In recent years, Sami have been actively involved in the work of international organizations for indigenous peoples and environmental issues. The Sami President has played an important role as peace negotiator in Guatemala, and the Dalai Lama has visited Sapmi. This modern 'nomadism' performed by a Sami elite has probably significantly strengthened the status of the Sami, at least in the eyes of many Norwegians. For people in northern Norway, Mediterranean resorts have long been the most popular holiday destination. Today, the new middle class travels world-wide from their home base in Finnmark. The Sami are participating in indigenous affairs as well as international business. In the local arena, people are used to travel, with airplanes being the local 'tram'. People still travel to the Canary Islands, but also to the Bahamas, Bali, London, and New York; and some even take part in expeditions to the Himalaya or across the Greenland Ice Cap. One could say that Finnmark, as the heading of this chapter rhetorically indicates, is an example of an emerging 'culture as travel' (Clifford, 1992). The people of Finnmark, like the visitors, switch between local and global roles, identities, and cultures. This interplay, however, presents a challenge: how to preserve local uniqueness and remaining wilderness?

REFERENCES

Barth, F., 1969, Introduction, in F. Barth (ed.), *Ethnic Groups and Boundaries*, Universitetsforlaget, Oslo, 9–38.

Bjørklund, I., 1985, *Fjordfolket i Kvænangen: fra Samisk samfunn til norsk utkant 1500–1980*, Universitetsforlaget, Tromsø

Bourdieu, P., 1984, *Distinction*, Routledge and Kegan Paul, London.

Butler, R.W., 1994, Seasonality in tourism: issues and problems, in Seaton, A.V. (ed.) *Tourism: The State of Art, Wiley*, London, 333–339.

Buzard, J., 1993, *The Beaten Track*, Clarendon Press, Oxford.

Clifford, J., 1992, Traveling cultures, in Grossberg, L., Nelson, C., Treichler, P. (eds) *Cultural Studies*, Routledge, London, 96–116.

Eco, U., 1986, *Travels in Hyper Reality*, Picador, London.

Eidheim, H., 1969, When ethnic identity is a social stigma, in F. Barth (ed.), *Ethnic Groups and Boundaries*, Universitetsforlaget, Oslo, 39–57.

Eidheim, H., 1993, Bricolage og ingeniørverksemd i Sapmi, *Norsk sosialantropologi 1993—Et utsnitt*, Norges forskningsråd, Oslo, 225–265.

Finnmark Opplevelser, 1995, *Nordnorsk markedsplan*, Finnmark Opplevelser S.A., Alta.

Friedman, J., 1994, The past in the future: History and the politics of identity, *American Anthropologist*, 94(4), 837–859.

Giddens, A., 1991, Modernity and Self-identity, Polity Press, London.

Giddens, A., 1994, Living in a Post-Traditional Society, in U. Beck, A. Giddens and S.O. Lash (eds) *Reflexive Modernization*, Polity Press, Cambridge, 56–109.

Harron, S., and Weiler, B., 1992, Ethnic tourism, in Weiler, B. and Hall, C.M. (eds) *Special Interest Tourism*, Belhaven Halsted, Toronto, 83–94.
Hutchinson, A., 1870, *Try Lapland. A Fresh Field for Summer Tourists*, Chapman and Hall, London.
Hætta, O.M., 1994, *Samene. Historie, kultur, samfunn*, Grøndahl Dreyer, Oslo.
Lash, S. and Urry, J., 1994, *Economies of Signs & Space*, Sage, London.
Levi-Strauss, C., 1972, *The Savage Mind*, Wiedenfeld and Nicolson, London.
Lorenz, E., 1991, *Samefolket i historien*, Pax, Oslo.
MacCannell, D., 1992, *Empty Meeting Grounds*, Routledge, London.
Mathisen, S.R., 1994, Modernitet og etnisk identitet i Nord-Norge, *Nord Nytt*, 54, 33–44.
Miljøverndepartementet, 1993, *Friluftsloven* (Ajourført utgave), T–981, Miljøverndepartementet, Oslo.
Munt, I., 1994, The 'other' postmodern tourism: Culture, travel and the new middle classes, in Theory, *Culture & Society*, 11, 101–123.
Naess, A., 1989, *Ecology, Community and Lifestyle*, Cambridge University Press, Cambridge.
Nash, R., 1967, *Wilderness and the American Mind*, Yale University Press, New Haven.
Nash, R., 1981, Tourism, Parks and the wilderness idea in the history of Alaska, *Alaska in Perspective*, 4(1), 1–27.
Nedrelid, T., 1991, Use of Nature as a Norwegian Characteristic, *Ethnologica Scandinavia*, 21, 20–33.
Nergård, J-I., 1994, *Det skjulte Nord-Norge*, Ad Notam, Oslo.
Nilsen, R. and Mosli, J.H., 1994, *Inn fra vidda. Hushold og økonomisk tilpasning i reindrifta i Gouvdageaidnu 1960–1993*, NORUT Samfunnsforskning, Tromsø.
Norges Offentlige Utredninger, 1993, *Rett til og forvaltning av land og vann i Finnmark*, Justis- og politidepartementet, Oslo.
Norges Offentlige Utredninger, 1994, *Bruk av land og vann i Finnmark i historisk perspektiv*, Justis- og politidepartementet, Oslo.
Pavel, H., 1979, Jakt, fangst og innlandsfiske, in Hirsti, R. (ed.), *Finnmark. By og bygd i Norge*, Gyldendal, Oslo, 367–371.
Pedersen, K., 1993, Gender, nature and technology: Changing trends in 'wilderness life' in northern Norway, in R. Riewe and J. Oakes (eds), *Human Ecology: Issues in the North*, volume II, University of Alberta, Edmonton, 53–66.
Pedersen, K., 1994, Outdoor Life in Women's Lives, in *Kvinner—en utfordring til idretten?*, Norges forskningsråd, Oslo, 139–142.
Pedersen, K. and Rafoss, K., 1989, Sports in Finnmark and Saami districts, *Scandinavian Journal of Sports Science* 11(1), 35–42.
Pedersen, S., 1994, Bruken av land og vann i Finnmark inntil første verdenskrig, *Bruk av land og vann i Finnmark i historisk perspektiv*, Norges Offentlige Utredninger, Oslo, 13–134.
Pelto, P.J., 1973, *The Snowmobile Revolution: Technology and Social Change in the Arctic*, Cumming Publications, Menlo Park, California.
Richardson, L., 1990, Narrative and sociology, *Journal of Contemporary Ethnography*, 19(1), 116–135.
Rojek, C., 1992, *Ways of Escape*, Macmillan, London.
Schiötz, E.H., 1970, *Utlendingers reiser i Norge. En bibliografi*. Universitetsforlaget, Oslo.
Slowikowski, S.S., 1993, On 'primitive' physical culture in 'civilized' places, in Laine, L. (ed.), *On the Fringes of Sport*, Academia, Sankt Augustin, 181–188.
Smith, V., 1992, Borocay, Philippines: A case study in 'alternative' tourism, in V. Smith and W. Eadington (eds) *Tourism Alternatives*, University of Pennsylvania Press, Philadelphia, 135–157.
Stordahl, V., 1994, Same i den moderne verden, Universitetet i Tromsø, Tromsø.

Tjelmeland, H., 1994, Det sen-moderne Nord-Norge. Om tenesteyting, tettstader og tusseladdar, in Drivenes, E-A, Hauan, M.A., and Wold, H.A. (eds), *Nordnorsk kulturhistorie*, Gyldendal, Oslo, 346–387.

Urry, J., 1990, *The Tourist Gaze*, Sage, London.

Viken, A. 1991, *Nordkalotturismen*, Report 5, Finnmark Regional College, Alta.

Viken, A. and Krogh, L., 1995, *Et konkurransedyktig Nord-Norge: Reiselivsnæringen*, Finnmark Research Centre, Alta.

Weiler, B., and Hall, C.M. (eds), 1992, *Special Interest Tourism*, Belhaven Halsted, Toronto.

6 Tourism in Svalbard: Planned Management or the Art of Stumbling Through?

BJØRN P. KALTENBORN

A FRAGILE PLAYGROUND

Four centuries ago, the Dutch explorer Wilhelm Barents sighted a mountainous coast after a long and arduous journey through arctic waters in search of the Northwest Passage. The encounter was welcome as Barents and his crew had been sailing for weeks hardly knowing where they were, and were fast running out of supplies. The virgin arctic island offered respite from the stormy seas and bountiful wildlife to replenish their stocks. Although the Icelandic sagas mention Svalbard as early as 1194, its rediscovery in 1596 paved the way for extensive exploitation of the Norwegian High Arctic with its vast natural resources. The era since Barents' trip has transformed the archipelago of Svalbard from an unknown polar region to an internationally known wilderness tourism destination visited by people from most continents.

Svalbard is an Icelandic word meaning the 'land of the cold coast', a term aptly applied by early explorers, whalers, and fur traders who roamed the shores. The islands constitute a vulnerable high arctic environment, experiencing increasing pressures from the mineral and petroleum industries as well as international tourism. Yet the archipelago still enjoys the status of Europe's last wilderness, offering the visitor outstanding experiences of the relatively untrammelled arctic environment.

As a tourist destination in a marginal environment, Svalbard faces many issues and challenges. Tourism has slowly grown to an intensity and extent where it potentially affects the ecological conditions of the islands. Wilderness and unspoiled nature are the key attractions of the tourism sector, and must be managed carefully in order to maintain a tourism product and protect the ecology of the region. The interests of tourism are also challenged or threatened by other types of resource uses, such as the oil and gas industry, creating considerable policy debates around the priorities of resource uses.

People and Tourism in Fragile Environments. Edited by M. F. Price.

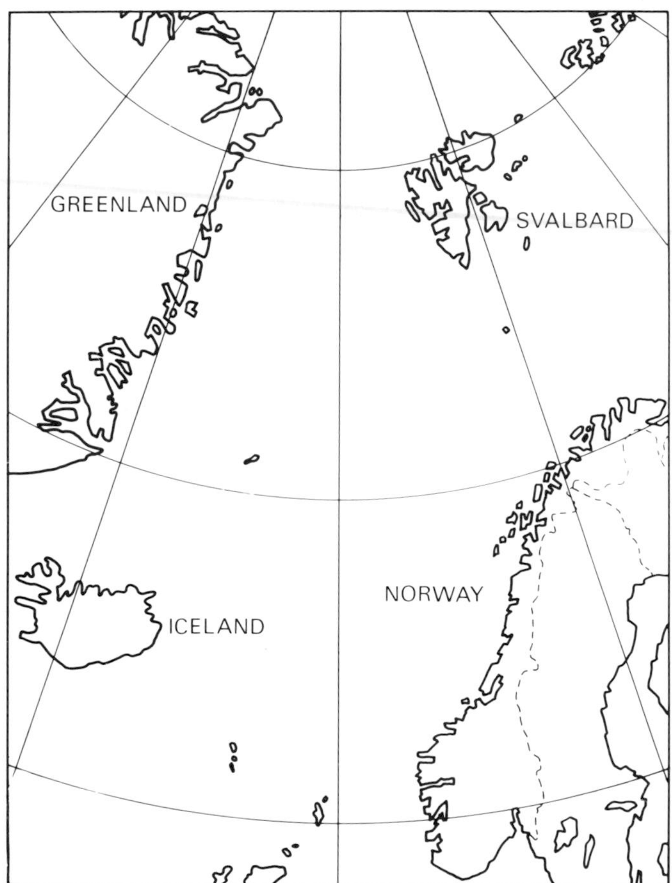

Figure 6.1 Location of Svalbard in the Northern Barents Sea
(Norwegian Polar Institute)

The communities of Svalbard have single-industry economies based primarily on coal mining, heavily subsidized by the state to keep the industry and communities alive. Their economic base suffers from low coal prices in the international economy, and tourism is seen as a future avenue to strengthen the local economies. Consequently, tourism has changed from being a small and mostly unwelcome actor, at least in the eyes of environmental managers, into a large and complex player in the game of Svalbard's future. This player has come to raise the concern of managers and policy-makers to a level where improved knowledge, planning, and practical management have become essential.

To provide data for a management plan for recreation and tourism, several research projects on recreation and tourism have been conducted in Svalbard in

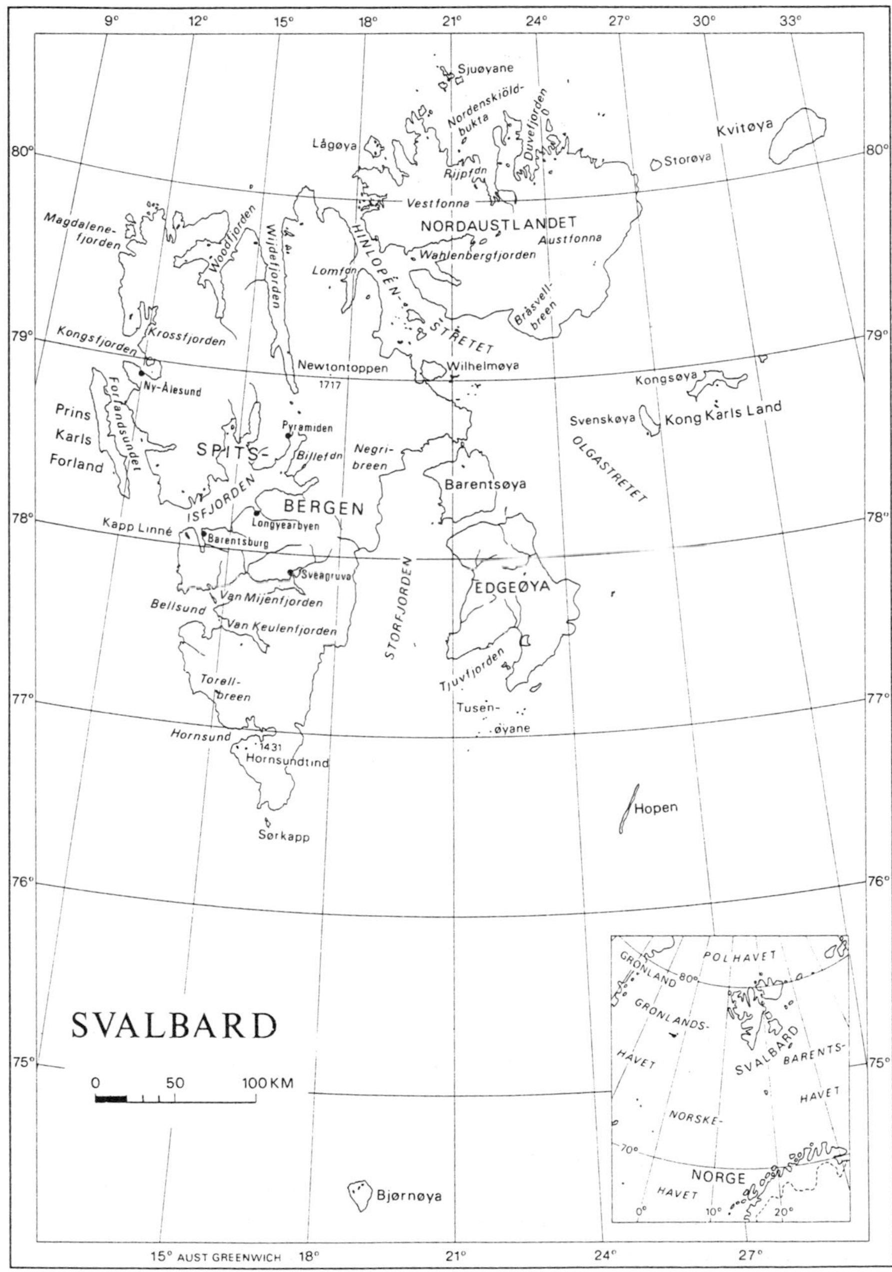

Figure 6.2 The archipelago of Svalbard
(Norwegian Polar Institute)

recent years. This process has accentuated the interface between ecosystem management and tourism development, forcing the question of whether the tourism industry and the management sectors are partners or adversaries. Other salient questions also surfaced: can tourism development in large, remote settings be controlled; what constitutes a suitable scientific paradigm for tourism management in marginal regions; and what benefits may derive from tourism in a pristine arctic wilderness setting?

THE LAST EUROPEAN WILDERNESS

Svalbard is located in the Norwegian Arctic, roughly halfway between Northern Norway and the North Pole (Figure 6.1) between latitudes 74 and 81 degrees North. The archipelago consists of five large islands and a number of smaller ones (Figure 6.2), with a total area of approximately 64 000 km^2. Due to a favourable combination of sea currents and wind patterns, the climate is surprisingly mild for a location this far north (Barr, 1987). Roughly two-thirds of the land area is covered by snow and ice. Almost all biological life and human activity is concentrated in the remaining areas along the coasts and central valleys of the largest island of Spitsbergen. The landscape ranges from the rugged and alpine west coast of Spitsbergen to broad valleys, immense ice plateaux, and the broad flat-topped mountains characteristic of sedimentary rocks in the eastern parts of the archipelago. The bedrock and landforms of the islands have long attracted scientists, since every epoch of the Earth's geologic history, culminating in the present landscape, can be studied here.

Both the terrestrial and the marine life are relatively diverse by arctic standards. Three species of terrestrial mammals—polar bear, Svalbard reindeer, and polar fox—inhabit the islands, together with seals, walrus, and numerous species of seabirds. The breeding bird populations are some of the largest seabird colonies in the North Atlantic. The masses of pelagic birds feeding in the oceans and bringing nutrition to these colonies form the vital link between the marine and the terrestrial parts of the ecosystem. The vegetation ranges from polar desert to lush tundra, with 160 species of higher plants (Rønning, 1979, Mæhlum, 1989). Svalbard is, by almost any definition, a vulnerable ecological environment, but it is also a biologically diverse and, in some respects, resilient ecosystem by high-arctic standards.

Svalbard is often labelled the last European wilderness. As Oelschlager (1991) and many others have pointed out, 'wilderness' is a cultural and relative term, and some might claim that the world no longer contains wilderness. However, in a comparative geographic sense, and certainly from the point of view of recreational experience, Svalbard does indeed represent one of the last largely untrammelled areas of some size left in Europe. About fifty per cent of the archipelago is protected as nature reserves, national parks, Ramsar reserves and international biosphere reserves. The official Svalbard policy contains explicit goals of sustainable development, stating that the wilderness character of the natural environment must be maintained in a long-term perspective. Natural resources use must develop within the carrying capacities of the environment (Ministry of Environment, 1995). Norway also participates in the circumpolar Arctic Environmental Protection Strategy (AEPS), an international effort to improve the monitoring and management of arctic environments. Svalbard is included in the system of Arctic protected areas defined in the AEPS programme on the Conservation of Arctic Flora and Fauna (Directorate for Nature Management, 1994), giving Norway international responsibility for sound stewardship of the islands. Not only tourism, but also other industrial activities, must be integrated with the long-term perspectives of ecological management.

THE SOCIO-ECONOMIC ENVIRONMENT

As far as we know, Svalbard has never been home to an indigenous population. Considering the ubiquity of indigenous populations throughout the circumpolar Arctic this is surprising. Scientists have not been able to answer why these particular islands remained unsettled until modern times, although a plausible reason may be their geographic location and isolation.

The time since Barents landed on the barren shores spans a turbulent history of intensive resource exploitation and international debates about the jurisdiction over the islands. For about three hundred years, from the sixteenth to the nineteenth centuries, commercial whaling and fur-trapping dominated. Coal was not found until the early years of the twentieth century. People from several European nations, especially Dutch, British, and Scandinavians, frequented the islands and established temporary settlements (Greve, 1975).

Svalbard was one of the last no-man's-lands on Earth to come under national jurisdiction. In 1920, an international treaty was signed in Versailles by 41 countries, giving Norway sovereign power over the islands. The practical implications of the treaty include the equal rights of all the signatory countries to prospect and exploit natural resources within the limits of the treaty and the Norwegian legislation pertaining to the archipelago. It also includes the right to establish settlements as required for the extraction of natural resources. To date, this has not resulted in a proliferation of international communities beyond two Russian settlements and, although several nations have invested in extensive prospecting for minerals, oil, and gas, only minor gas finds have resulted. Yet the industrial scene could change rapidly. The present, but very controversial, plans to build a road through central parts of Spitsbergen to open up new coal fields, or an oil strike—whether onshore or in the waters surrounding Svalbard—could drastically alter the local context.

Today, the permanent population of Svalbard lives in five settlements. Longyearbyen in central Spitsbergen is the main Norwegian settlement, with mining activities and the entire private and public administration. Sveagruva, somewhat further south, is a smaller Norwegian coal mining community. To the northwest, the former mining town of Ny Ålesund is the main Norwegian research centre in Svalbard. While it is run by a small permanent population of Norwegians, several nations have established research facilities here, of which some are used year-round and others seasonally. The Russians have established permanent communities in Barentsburg and Pyramiden in central Spitsbergen, both based on coal mining, with a combined population of about three thousand. They comprise about half of the total permanent population of about five thousand, which is boosted in summer by a large influx of tourists, scientists, and various enterprises engaged in field activities. No roads or facilities except a couple of field research stations exist outside the settlements.

Longyearbyen is currently going through rampant modernization and diversification. As mining loses its stronghold, the need to develop a better economic base stimulates creativity. Disparate types of jobs gain a foothold, new roles are becoming established among locals, and the community is slowly transforming its identity. A strong position for commercial wilderness tourism is part of this context. Extensive debates in Longyearbyen have raised consciousness about the various benefits and potentials of tourism to the community. This has stimulated local initiative, and a considerable number of people have moved into the tourism business as administrators, marketers, and guides. From being a peripheral and somewhat alienated phenomenon, tourism development has become one of the central management and business opportunity issues in Svalbard, and currently provides around a hundred full-time jobs.

IN THE FOOTSTEPS OF EARLY EXPLORERS

Tourism is no newcomer to Svalbard. Organized cruise-ship and adventure travel go back around one hundred years. Svalbard had been important throughout the history of polar explorations as a base for expeditions towards the North Pole basin, and the first tourists followed suit. The first, affluent, adventure travellers literally followed in the footsteps of polar explorers and scientists. The pioneering tourists were soon succeeded by organized pleasure traffic by ship to the islands. Individual tourism slowly increased through this century, but long remained at very modest numbers since facilities and provisions were only accessible to permanent residents. With the opening of a new airport in 1975 and the gradual acceptance of tourists as something more than a menace, the numbers of tourists grew gradually.

At present, twenty to thirty thousand persons visit by cruise ship every summer, but they spend very little, if any, time on shore (Figure 6.3). In contrast, the last decade or so has seen an increase in both adventure travel companies and individual tourists organizing their own trips and travelling without a guide or commercial organization. A few thousand people participate in guided trips travelling by foot and small vessels along the coasts, seeking safe adventure

Figure 6.3 Cruise ship tourists visiting Spitsbergen

through a packaged tour. A comparable number also prepare their own trips, ranging from short day-hikes based in Longyearbyen to expeditionary climbs, hikes, ski trips or kayak trips lasting up to several weeks (Kaltenborn, 1991) (Figure 6.4).

Figure 6.4 Hikers on the arctic tundra, Svalbard

The recreational opportunities are numerous and diverse, matching the wide range of mountain, glacier, plateau, and coastal landscapes, teeming with wildlife during the summer months in particular. Travel is permitted in all of the areas protected as national parks and nature reserves, except for two reserves where travel is prohibited in order to protect denning and resting areas for polar bears and walrus (Ministry of Environment, 1989).

While the management agencies have certain needs to limit and control the use of the natural environment, the tourism industry also has needs in order to operate commercially. Tour operators must have reasonable access to a diversity of areas. They cannot market and sell Svalbard by using only the most impacted and least attractive areas. In order to plan and invest over time, they also need a predictable management system, with clear rules and regulations, stability in policies, and a good dialogue with decision-makers. Until recently, such a system has been lacking, causing great difficulties for the tourism industry.

During the past couple of decades, a series of factors combined to elevate political consciousness around the complex interactions of tourism management, wilderness protection, and economic development. The international adventure travel market increased, especially with a focus on exotic, 'green' destinations. Local infrastructure improved. The local economic base became ever more depressed. Svalbard lost some of its strategic military and geographic importance in the North Atlantic with the demise of the Soviet Union. In addition, awareness of environmental protection increased greatly among the general public. It became increasingly evident that the phenomenon of tourism in Svalbard called for improved knowledge and management.

Contrary to the usual situation in Scandinavia, the government produced several noteworthy statements in white papers in 1982 and 1986 (Ministry of Environment, 1982; Ministry of Commerce, 1986). These include the need to protect the wilderness character of the Svalbard environment, integrate economic development with environmental protection, pay special heed to the vulnerability of the arctic environment, and produce a management plan for tourism and recreation. Thus an unquestionable mandate existed for managing and, if necessary, regulating tourism.

UNDERSTANDING THE MODERN TOURIST

The development and implementation of a management plan for tourism and recreation are now underway. This process attempts to fulfil several goals. As a management tool, the plan will both develop and apply a research-based framework for management of recreational resources. It must also establish a research-based paradigm to deal with the interactions between tourism, the environment, and the local community. The plan describes recreational opportunities, environmental qualities, and levels of environmental changes and impacts, as well as necessary management actions for different parts of the islands. It must also be able to give specific directions for management actions in both short- and long-term perspectives. Consequently, it contributes actively in formulating policy for tourism and environmental management.

For quite some time, tourism was perceived negatively by many people living on Svalbard and elsewhere. Public management agencies frequently expressed concern about the possible effects of tourism throughout the 1970s and 1980s, by which time the notion of Svalbard as vulnerable wilderness had become well embedded in the general public. Lack of empirical knowledge about tourism in Svalbard further facilitated the negative image of tourists as irresponsible actors capable of causing widespread damage to the environment. This image of tourists is seldom visible in public documents, but is all the more evident in discussion and meetings with officials.

Tourism in Svalbard no doubt has the potential to cause harm to the environment, but to date very few significant impacts or problems have been documented. The official attitude towards tourism in Svalbard during the past two decades can be described as changing from clear resistance, to reluctance, to the present conditional acceptance of the inevitable. Slowly, a more widespread understanding of the complex role of tourism is emerging. Tourism in Svalbard has come to stay, regardless of the views of environmental managers in government offices. Also, increasing numbers of public officials are realizing the societal benefits of tourism, as well as the potentially useful alliance between nature conservation interests and the tourism industry.

With this background, a partnership was developed between managers and researchers to achieve the immediate goals of tourism management. Over a period of two years, five studies were conducted to thoroughly study the tourism system (Kaltenborn and Emmelin, 1993). Visiting tourists from around the world were surveyed over two summer seasons using both in-depth field interviews and mail surveys. The resident population in Longyearbyen was included in a survey of all households. Since virtually no previous data existed on recreation and tourism, the surveys had to cover a fairly broad range of topics including characteristics of the recreational users; recreation behaviour and user patterns in time and space; motives and reasons for visiting Svalbard; planning and expectations; skills; knowledge about the environment; sensitivity to impacts; and attitudes, as well as preferences, towards attributes of recreational settings. A study was also made of existing impacts in some of the most used regions of Svalbard, mapping traces of campsites, fire rings, and litter. Such data are necessary to monitor physical changes due to tourism activities over the years.

RECREATION USE AND CHARACTERISTICS

The studies yielded a fairly comprehensive picture of Svalbard's tourism system (Kaltenborn, 1991; Kaltenborn and Emmelin, 1993). Visitors to Svalbard comprise a heterogeneous population, with about a third from Norway, and the rest mostly from other European countries, with a few from other continents. The visitors have a wide variety of education, professional backgrounds, and previous recreational experience. In other words, it is meaningless to speak of tourists to Svalbard as one type of actor.

Much of the data collection was fashioned to suit the needs of the planning process. This applied particularly to travel patterns, as well as preferences and attitudes for various aspects of management and the natural environment. While tourists travel over much of the archipelago during a summer season, this traffic follows distinct patterns. Certain corridors, particularly along the west coast, receive the bulk of the traffic, leaving large regions virtually devoid of humans for long periods. The traffic patterns are determined both by access and infrastructure and by natural attractions such as the spectacular scenery of the west coast. The necessary information included identification of the main travel corridors, access points, locations where travel seemed to concentrate around particular attractions, popular camping spots, and length and duration of trips. The recreation use patterns were recorded in a geographic information system where different types of traffic could be analysed and compared.

PERCEPTIONS OF THE SETTING

Even though the population of tourists was quite heterogeneous in some respects, they also shared important views on many aspects of the environment. An extensive analysis on attitudes and preferences toward attributes of the environment showed that certain dimensions appeared particularly salient. These findings were partly a product of statistical analyses of a large number of items relating to the biophysical environment, the social environment, and the managerial aspects of the setting. The analysis showed that the recreators perceive the environment, in a broad sense of the word, as a complex, multi-dimensional phenomenon. It is experienced as an arena comprised of different complementary qualities. However, the way that visitors experience one aspect of the environment, for instance the desirability of remoteness, is clearly related to how they experience the other dimensions of the same environment. In other words, the arctic setting is not just a collection of independent attributes, but a puzzle of images which the visitors put together in mental maps.

The experience of the physical environment as a vast, pristine setting is quite prominent among the tourists. The Arctic has traditionally conveyed an image of immense expanses of untrammelled, clean nature. The desire to experience a high degree of *naturalness*—an absence of impacts and disturbance and plentiful views of scenic mountains, glaciers and sea—is widely expressed among visitors to Svalbard. *Remoteness* is another salient characteristic valued highly by many. There are few places left in the world where one can experience a natural environment virtually devoid of human traces such as roads, settlements, and other human artefacts. Parts of Svalbard offer remoteness in an

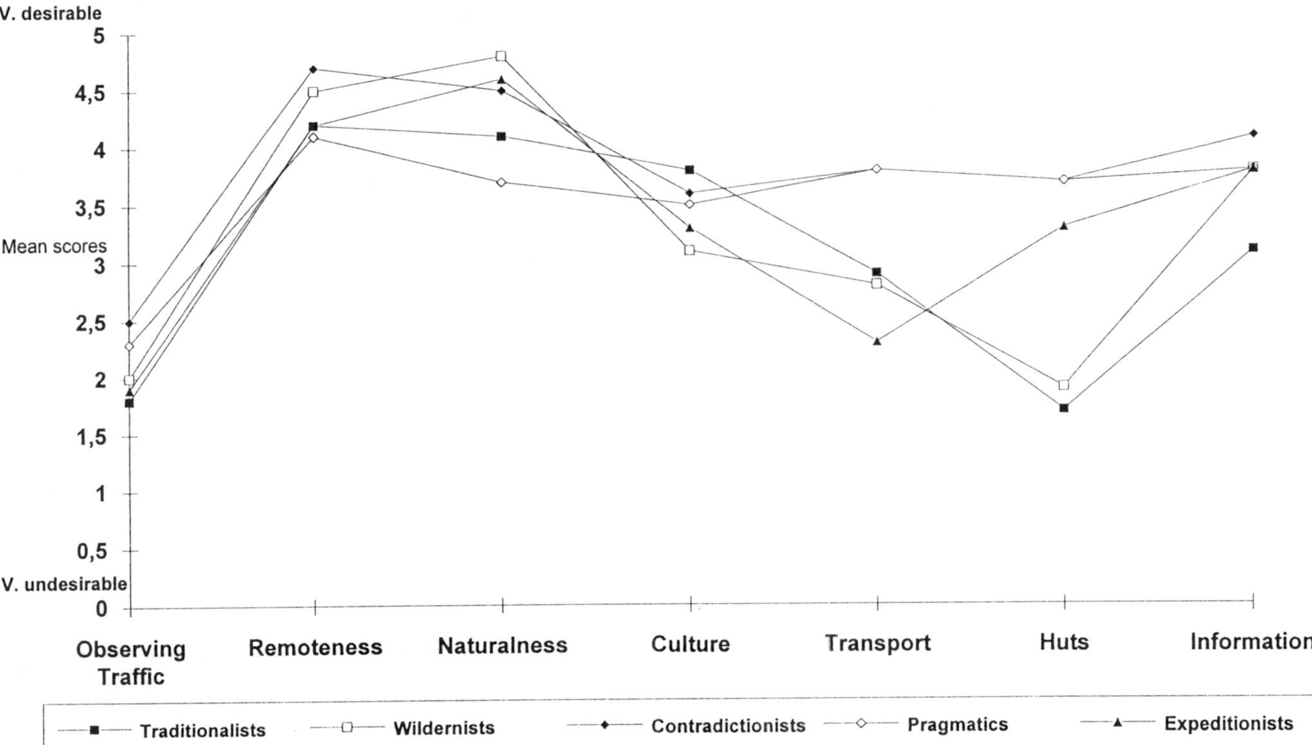

Figure 6.5 The attitudes of recreational user groups towards different dimensions of the Svalbard environment (a high score indicates a positive attitude towards, or a desire for, that aspect of the environment)

absolute sense, much as a visitor a hundred or more years ago must have encountered the islands. On the whole, the environment conveys a great sense of remoteness, at least outside the sparse settlements. Conversely, even though most tourists depend on some amount of transportation, their encounters with motorized traffic—whether at sea, in the air, or on shore—generally elicit negative responses.

Culture was identified as another central dimension of the environment, reflecting a strong interest in the history of Svalbard as well as current trapping activities. This indicates that visitors do not see the islands merely as pure wilderness, totally devoid of human traces, but that they also accept and appreciate Svalbard's human history. Three types of management-setting dimensions were also identified. *Transport* mirrors the obvious need for some infrastructure to facilitate movement and access in the islands. The expressed interest in *huts* indicates that most visitors attach some importance to accommodation facilities. *Information* also emerged as a salient issue, as it generally does in wilderness settings subject to recreational use.

These research results were used to segment the visitor population into distinct groups depending on individuals' attitudes towards these seven key aspects of the Svalbard setting (Figure 6.5). This segmentation of users according to their attitudes, rather than their activities, was the basis of the type of planning model being used. In this model, desired experiences are linked to environmental attributes and recreational opportunities; activities are less suited to discriminate among recreational opportunities than setting-dependent experiences.

Five types of visitors were identified. These can be seen as archetypes of current tourists to Svalbard. One way to obtain an image of these types is to sketch a picture of a 'typical' person in each group. It must be noted, however, that average people do not exist, and that considerable diversity is found within each group. Probably no persons are exactly like the five central figures depicted here, but most individuals in each group resemble their group exponent more than they resemble people in the other groups. The five types of recreational users have been labelled: *traditionalists*, *wildernists*, *expeditionists*, *contradictionists*, and *pragmatists*.

A *traditionalist* is an exponent of the traditional form of dispersed non-motorized Nordic recreation. This is an experienced user who is fairly self-reliant and seeks an untrammelled wilderness environment with a low level of visible management. He or she usually comes from a Nordic country, and is probably somewhat familiar with the image of Svalbard through its relative proximity to mainland Scandinavia.

A *wildernist* commonly resides in a European country outside the Nordic countries. This is a person with a highly aesthetic, and perhaps romantic relationship to Svalbard. The wildernist sees Svalbard as a wilderness antithesis to his or her home environment. Nature and remoteness are the driving attractions, but the wildernist often seeks the comfort and security of participating on a guided trip.

The *expeditionist* resembles the wildernist in many ways, but has, perhaps, a more functional view of recreation. The expeditionist places slightly less emphasis on naturalness and remoteness and is much more in favour of huts in the field. Like the wildernists, this person explores large and remote parts of Svalbard, but is also more accepting of facilities in the field.

The *contradictionist* would like a little of everything. This is a person with limited recreational experience, and probably limited knowledge about Svalbard. He or she wants to experience as much untrammelled nature and remoteness as possible and, at the same time, to increase the general accessibility and support services. This type of user is not particularly concerned with the fundamental contradiction of increasing access to remote and unimpacted areas and simultaneously keeping their resource and social conditions unchanged.

The *pragmatist* is by far the most common recreational user of Svalbard, and has a generally favourable and relatively relaxed attitude toward the overall environment. The pragmatist wants to experience naturalness and remoteness, but is not quite as eager about these topics as the other groups. He or she views a certain level of facilities and services as necessary functions to enjoy the natural environment, but is a flexible type of visitor adapting well to existing conditions. The pragmatist represents the large 'middle' group of users with attitudes close to average with regard to most aspects of the environment.

Segmenting the visitor population gave valuable information for planning and management. First, it highlighted the diversity of attitudes and desires among the visitors, supporting the idea of differentiated recreational management through zoning or comparable measures. Second, the segmentation clearly shows which aspects of the environment elicit a diversity of attitudes. It is noteworthy that all five types of tourists share fairly similar views of the desirability of certain dimensions of the environment to their overall experiences, such as perceptions of naturalness, remoteness, and culture, and observing traffic. Conversely, the five groups express much more diversity towards the managerial aspects of the environment, such as transport, huts, and information. This is what makes the segmentation meaningful, in the sense that the groups actually differ in terms of salient variables. This was a particularly useful finding since it is only the managerial aspects of the environment that can be influenced to any extent through a planning process. The levels of transportation, accommodation and information can be manipulated according to management goals and strategies. However, the degree of naturalness or remoteness, for example, is not subject to the same degree of management control.

DEVELOPING A PLAN

THE PLANNING MODEL

Data about visitors helped to define the main goals and the structure of the plan.

Since a first draft was produced in 1991, two revisions have been made to accommodate further input from other public and private institutions, as well as the local population. The plan will be effective from summer 1995, and revision every three years is planned. It builds on the concepts of the Recreation Opportunity Spectrum (ROS) (Driver and Brown, 1978; Clark and Stankey, 1979; Driver et al., 1987) and the Limits of Acceptable Change System for Wilderness Planning (LAC) (Stankey et al., 1985; McCool; 1989). The basic structure of these frameworks was applied in the conceptual phase of the planning, but the actual planning document was strongly modified to suit Norwegian conditions.

The plan's basic premise is to describe a spectrum of recreational opportunities defined in three dimensions—the physical, social, and managerial environment—and to allocate opportunities, based on differences in these dimensions, to different areas using a zoning system. In theoretical terms, recreational opportunities are seen as the means to realize desired experiences through recreational activities in suitable locations or settings (Driver et al., 1991; Kaltenborn, 1991). Thus, the ROS framework allows the development of a spectrum or continuum of recreation opportunity classes with different levels of access, remoteness, impacts, interactions with other users and managerial regimentation, providing a diversity of activity and experience opportunities.

Since tourists to Svalbard, as in other wilderness settings, are a heterogeneous group, they seek a variety of experiences. Consequently, managers need to provide a diversity of recreational opportunities to satisfy the visitors' varying tastes. The ROS concept focuses on experiences that are setting-dependent, ie, psychological states such as experiencing silence and remoteness or a pristine untrammelled landscape, since these are assumed to vary across different types of settings and recreational opportunities. Other types of experiences, such as family togetherness or getting in better physical or emotional shape, are less suited for discriminating between particular geographical areas.

Rather than attempting to define carrying capacities or absolute limits to use or impacts, the plan treats the issue of environmental change as one of defining desirable environmental conditions. Probing for acceptable levels of use and impacts is as much a policy and normative question as it is a scientific undertaking. Within each opportunity class, standards are developed for acceptable levels of change for each of the characteristics defining the opportunity class, and these standards must be revised over time.

THE IMPLEMENTATION OF THE SVALBARD PLAN

The management plan developed in Svalbard is a macro-level plan involving a framework with guidelines for tourism management. The three main functions are to describe recreational opportunities throughout the archipelago, document environmental qualities perceived as salient by recreation interests, and prescribe sets of short- and long-term management actions considered necessary to achieve the goals of the plan.

After four types of recreation opportunity classes were developed as the plan's basic structure, twelve management areas were designated so that each recreation opportunity class is represented through several management areas. A greater subdivision into management areas was necessary due to the archipelago's size. Even though the recreation opportunity classes differentiate well between areas, certain types of management actions can vary within the same class. Generally, the plan lays out an axis or gradient from more developed and used areas to less developed and impacted areas: from Longyearbyen and central Spitsbergen to the remote outer parts of the archipelago. However, a fundamental premise is the need to provide opportunities for true wilderness-type experiences relatively close to the settlements. Previously, seeking a truly quiet and remote destination in Svalbard meant travelling far from Longyearbyen and other settlements, a journey which incurred great time end expense. While this is still much the case, a relatively simple management measure can considerably improve the conditions for recreationists. During the summer, high-quality wilderness recreation environments are accessible close to the settlements as no roads exist, and virtually all off-road traffic is prohibited during the thaw season. However, during the winter, the main deterrent to a true wilderness experience is the snowmobile traffic (Figure 6.6).

The plan proposes the designation of at least two 'snowmobile-free' areas close to the settlements. These areas must be sufficiently large to accommodate the needs of skiers and dog sledders for short- to medium-length trips. However, whereas all the other management areas are precisely defined in the plan, the exact location and extent of the snowmobile-free areas have not yet been established; they so far only exist as a management goal. Currently a

Figure 6.6 A snowmobiler beneath glacier seracs in Svalbard

group composed of managers, interest groups, and the tourism industry has the mandate to work out the borders for these areas; an approach chosen to ensure local acceptance of the concept.

The intention to introduce zones to be kept free from motorized traffic accentuates latent conflicts among the local population and a centralized management agency, testing the strengths and weaknesses of the planning approach. The planning model is a mixture of a rational comprehensive and a transactive planning approach. It combines the traditional top-down, expert-dominated planning with substantial input and some sharing in decision-making by the grassroot-level interests. The Svalbard community has over the years become quite sensitive and opposed to centralized decision-making, which they at times experience as coercion to meet public goals they do not understand or in which they have no interest.

The success of any management plan which allocates resources hinges precariously on the consent of the various interest groups in the area. While the power and usefulness of local participation is often underestimated, scientific and professional planning expertise is nearly always also required in a good planning exercise. The crux of the problem was to find the appropriate combination so that long-term societal and ecological imperatives beyond the immediate interests of the local community were secured, while at the same time recognizing local knowledge and interest, so as to give interest groups a feeling of ownership in the plan. Considering the numerous previous conflicts over resource use in Svalbard, the management plan will have limited chances of any success unless it is understood, perceived as legitimate, and seen as useful also to local interests. The basic philosophy in transactive or participatory planning is that people will not understand that which they do not engage in, and will not support that which they do not understand (Friedman, 1972).

The plan provides overall guidelines for tourism management. Site-level planning must now be conducted for new tourist facilities such as improved information provision, development of transportation and accommodation facilities, and protection of cultural relicts and monuments. In addition, the local tourism industry, consisting of companies based in Longyearbyen, is in the process of developing a strategic plan within the framework of the plan.

POST-MODERN CHALLENGES

Developing a plan is the traditional response of the public sector to natural resource issues. But is it always an appropriate and adequate response? Will the Svalbard plan work, and what does it mean for a management plan to be effective in a fragile environment? Whose needs are being served, and what costs and benefits are involved in the process?

Tourism management, like a number of other human affairs, is fundamentally a competition over control and allocation of values as well as resources. To evaluate the prospects and efficacy of the management plan, and to decide whether management is a planned and controlled exercise or simply an exercise of stumbling through a complex world of forces, we need to consider future tourism in Svalbard in a larger socio-political context.

Svalbard gradually became a tourism destination as part of the western global modernization process. Industrialism, economic growth, and globalization in many aspects of society fostered growth in scientific endeavours, polar exploration, and related tourism in the Arctic. However, the significance and extent of arctic tourism are mainly features of post-modern times. Whether or not one agrees with the notion of post-modernity as a historical epoch, at least some of the characteristics and forces of post-industrial society are salient in terms of understanding the tourism system in Svalbard.

Post-modernism in some respects advocates less emphasis on economic growth, less faith in the capability of the industrialized societies to satisfy modern people, more contact between cultures, and a healthy disrespect for science as the key to right and wrong. Knowledge is being made available to increasing populations and is marked by de-specialization and de-differentiation. Some claim that while society is becoming more complex, incomprehensible and possibly alien to most people, increasing amounts of information are made available to virtually everyone (Arac, 1989). Consequently, norms and values are constantly up for revision.

The expanding global tourism culture is characterized by individual travellers seeking to expand their horizons, seeking new experiences in new corners of the world. There is a strong element of commonality as many people seek roughly the same types of experiences in ever new places. In some respects, the individual place seems to lose some of its significance, as more and more people gain the skills and financial ability to go to new places. Today's recreationists appear to be increasingly conscious of quality, more difficult to satisfy, busy, and far-reaching. They also contribute to a greater complexity in the global tourism system with a greater diversity of backgrounds, demands, skills, and values. The modern, adventurous tourist often invests great resources in planning and preparation for a trip, displaying a greater desire for real contact with the natural world than simple mass-tourism models tend to claim. Large segments of the western public are concerned about modern industrial development and the global resource situation. The expressed and latent need for nature is growing, and in the western world there is a growing recognition that access to unspoiled nature is a scarce good (McCloskey, 1989).

Future tourism in Svalbard will be shaped within this context. Already, in a short period from the early 1980s to today, tourism in Svalbard has, in economic terms, evolved from virtually nothing to a relatively stable activity supporting the community. Both Norwegian and foreign tour operators are well established in Longyearbyen. Several statistics from the past five years, since the main studies for the management plan were conducted, indicate that the tourism population is increasing in diversity and expanding their travel patterns throughout the archipelago. Svalbard contains attractive factors which appeal to large segments of modern tourists. The islands are highly accessible compared to other marginal, exotic areas. The area is vast, pristine, scenic, largely untrammelled, and offers opportunities for individual exploits as well as safe adventure with travel companies. Lastly, from the perspective of the tourist, Svalbard is not overly burdened with management restrictions on human recreational activities since Norway in principle practises a common access right to all public lands (Hammitt et al., 1992). This also includes the Arctic.

The tourism system in Svalbard is partly a function of the arctic environment and the outstanding natural attractions of the islands. It is also a function of outside forces such as changes in the international economy, demographic patterns, more affluent tourists, global tourism patterns with significant shifts towards more travel to fragile areas, and changes in norms and value systems. This all points towards a less predictable and stable tourism population in the future. We can expect changes in the types of tourist. Perhaps different segments than those identified in the late 1980s will dominate the scene, perhaps the distribution among segments will change. Sporadic impressions through the last five years or so suggest that more people are coming to 'do' Svalbard as part of their more or less global personal project of international adventure travel. Growing numbers also push harder to get to the remote parts of the islands for purely recreational purposes. Many of these are highly skilled and well-informed. The post-modern character of the tourism system is fast becoming more apparent.

It is evident that tourism development in Svalbard can be subject to planned management only to a very limited degree. Mostly, it is a response to a scene controlled by outside forces. This can largely be attributed to the historical attitude among public agencies of tourism as evil. Tourism has consistently been viewed as a threat to the natural environment, largely without qualification or documentation of problems. A series of important factors in tourism management has been grossly neglected. These include the complexity of tourism, its potential benefits to individuals and society, the ways and means of influencing tourism behaviour in desirable directions, the potentially very useful alliance between tourism interests and nature conservation, and the fact that tourism is an immensely powerful industry which seldom can be stopped, but frequently offers good co-operation. This state of affairs is sadly common in management regimes driven almost exclusively by natural scientists and operating in an instrumental worldview of bio-ecological science. From a social science perspective, the present situation surrounding the struggle of managers to cope with tourism in Svalbard was predictable and unsurprising.

However, there are signs of positive changes. The combination of an ecological and social science perspective in management planning signifies growing acceptance of the human dimensions of tourism management, and the need for a broader human–ecological framework for management. Furthermore, alliances are being developed between managers and tourism developers. Frequently these groups now find each other on one side of the fence, with the mining and petroleum industries on the other.

There is no question that a management plan is needed, but one should have modest visions of what it can achieve. A plan is useful in that it explicates management goals, strategies, and responsibilities. It is also a tool for highlighting values attached to resources. However, it is a framework and not a recipe. It does not instantly protect nature or create jobs in the tourism industry. Yet, it provokes choices which must be made. From a long-term resource-management perspective, the possibly greatest concerns are not caused directly by tourism. They are related to the trade-offs between fundamentally incompatible resource-uses such as sensitive wilderness tourism, extractive resource exploitation of gas, oil and minerals, and large-scale ecosystem protection for biodiversity concerns and scientific research. As elsewhere, compromises must be made, but this is best done after deciding policy priorities.

Today, the policy scene surrounding which types of societal values should be reaped from the Svalbard environment is very fuzzy indeed. The consequence is a confused and partly non-deliberate distribution of costs, in the sense of lacking opportunities or denied access to products for each of the main interests. Yet the local community desperately needs to strengthen its economic base, the islands represent some of the last pristine arctic wilderness, and international tourism has come to stay. Svalbard presents an opportunity to develop high-quality tourism in a diverse and attractive wilderness setting. If done carefully, the needs of tourism as well as science and conservation can be integrated without causing insoluble conflicts.

Tourism must be developed within definite limits. The high arctic is a vulnerable ecological environment. There is also a question of how much the local community is willing to adapt to this type of industry. Furthermore, the inherent sensitivity of a wilderness tourism product lays restrictions on the scale of development. There is always the potential of tourism degrading its own product through too many people or conflicting activities in an area where the dominant attraction is remoteness and lack of impacts. The questions surrounding tourism in Svalbard are still many and of great consequence to the future development of this northern outpost of the modern world.

REFERENCES

Arac, J., 1989 (ed.), *Postmodernism and Politics,* University of Minnesota Press, Minneapolis.

Barr, S., 1987, *Norway's Polar Territories*, Aschehoug, Oslo.

Clark, R.N. and Stankey, G.H., 1979, The Recreation Opportunity Spectrum: A framework for planning, management and research. *US Department of Agriculture Forest Service, General Technical Report PNW-98.*

CAFF (Conservation of Arctic Flora and Fauna), 1994, The state of protected areas in the circumpolar Arctic 1994, *CAFF Habitat Conservation Report 1*, Directorate for Nature Management, Trondheim.

Driver, B.L., Brown, P.J. and Peterson, G.L. (eds), 1991, *Benefits of Leisure*, Venture Publishing, State College, Pennsylvania.

Driver, B.L. and Brown, P.J., 1978, The opportunity spectrum concept and behavioral information in outdoor recreation resource supply inventories: A rationale, in Integrated

Inventories of Renewable Natural Resources, *US Department of Agriculture Forest Service General Technical Report RM-55*, 24–31.

Driver, B.L., Brown, P.J., Stankey, G.H. and Gregoire, T.H., 1987, The ROS planning system: Evolution, basic concepts, and research needed. *Leisure Sciences*, 9, 201–212.

Friedman, J., 1972, *Transactive Planning: A Theory of Societal Guidance*, Doubleday Anchor, Garden City, New York.

Greve, T., 1975, *Svalbard, Norway in the Arctic,* Grøndahl, Oslo.

Hammitt, W.E., Kaltenborn, B.P., Vistad, O.I., Emmelin, L. and Teigland, J., 1992, Common access tradition and wilderness management in Norway: A paradox for managers, *Environmental Management*, 16(2), 149–156.

Kaltenborn, B.P., 1991, The Role of Environmental Setting Attributes in Outdoor Recreation and Tourism Planning. A Case-study from the Norwegian High Arctic. Doctoral dissertation, Department of Geography, University of Oslo.

Kaltenborn, B.P. and Emmelin, L., 1993, Tourism in the High North: Management challenges and Recreation Opportunity Spectrum Planning in Svalbard, Norway, *Environmental Management*, 17(1), 41–50.

McCool, S.F., 1989, Limits of Acceptable Change: Some principles, in *Towards Serving Visitors and Managing Our Resources: Proceedings of a North American Workshop on Visitor Management in Parks and Protected Areas*, Tourism Research and Education Centre, University of Waterloo, Waterloo, 194–200.

McCloskey, M., 1989, The meaning of wilderness, in D. Lime (ed.) *Managing America's Enduring Wilderness Resource. Proceedings of the Conference*, Tourism Center, University of Minnesota, St. Paul, 22–25.

Mehlum, F., 1989, *Svalbards Fugler og Pattedyr* (The birds and mammals of Svalbard), Norsk Polarinstitutt, Oslo.

Ministry of Commerce, 1986, Om Svalbard (On Svalbard), Stortingsmelding 40 (1985–86). The Norwegian Ministry of Commerce, Oslo.

Ministry of Environment, 1982, Om miljøvern, kartlegging og forskning i polarområdene (Environmental protection, mapping and research in the polar regions), Stortingsmelding 40 (1982–83), The Norwegian Ministry of Environment, Oslo.

Ministry of Environment, 1989, Environmental Regulations for Svalbard and Jan Mayen, The Norwegian Ministry of Environment, Oslo.

Ministry of Environment, 1995, *Om miljøvern på Svalbard* (Environmental protection in Svalbard), Stortingsmelding 22 (1994–95), The Norwegian Ministry of Environment, Oslo.

Norderhaug, M., 1987, *Svalbard*, Universitetsforlaget, Oslo.

Oelschlager, M., 1991, *The Idea of Wilderness. From Prehistory to the Age of Ecology*, Yale University Press, New Haven.

Rønning, O., 1979, *Svalbards Flora* (The flora of Svalbard). Norsk Polarinstitutt, Oslo.

Stankey, G.H., Cole D.N., Lucas R.C., Peterson, M.E. and Frissell, S.S., 1985, The Limits of Acceptable Change (LAC) system for wilderness planning, *US Department of Agriculture Forest Service General Technical Report INT–176.*

7 Learning from Experience in the Monteverde Cloud Forest, Costa Rica

ANA L. BAEZ

INTRODUCTION

Monteverde lies at around 1700 m (5600 feet) above sea level in the Tilarán Mountains of northern Costa Rica, straddling the continental divide where three of the country's seven provinces (Alajuela, Puntarenas, and Guanacaste) meet. Monteverde's location means that it is exposed to climatic influences from both the Atlantic and Pacific Oceans, which is one reason that so many different ecosystems exist in a relatively small area. The six major life zones that have been identified in the region harbour great biological diversity, with more than 100 species of mammals, 400 species of birds, 120 species of reptiles and amphibians, 2500 plant species, and several thousand species of insects. The higher elevations are characterized by a temperate climate and exceptional scenery.

As recently as the early 1950s, the primary forest cover of the area was still extensive. However, the pressure of population growth and the expansion of agricultural lands were pushing back the frontiers of forest cover, increasingly restricting it to higher areas in the mountains. Concurrently, several North American Quaker families took up residence in Monteverde which, until then, had been sparsely populated by a few Costa Rican families. The pacifist Quakers had begun emigrating from the USA in search of a free and peaceful life. In Costa Rica, which had abolished its army in 1948 and enjoyed a stable social and political climate, and particularly in isolated Monteverde, the Quakers found what they sought. They acquired 1400 hectares which they divided among themselves, reserving 554 hectares as a watershed.

During the late 1960s and early 1970s, several parallel trends led to the creation of the Monteverde Cloud Forest Reserve (MCFR). On the one hand, a growing number of researchers were visiting the area to study the forest and learn about its resources. Their work revealed a wealth of biodiversity, including unique species such as the endemic Golden Toad (*Bufo periglenis*), the famous Resplendent Quetzal (*Pharamacrus mocino*), Baird's Tapir (*Tapirus*

People and Tourism in Fragile Environments. Edited by M. F. Price.

bairdii) and Jaguar (*Panthera onca*). At the same time, there was a growing conservation movement within Costa Rica. In 1972, a Costa Rican non-governmental organization (NGO)—The Tropical Science Center (TSC)—acquired the first 328 hectares of forest for a reserve in Monteverde. In 1974, TSC reached an agreement with the Quakers to manage their 554 hectares (now named the Bosque Eterno SA—the Eternal Rainforest, Inc.), and the two properties became the original Monteverde Private Cloud Forest Reserve (MPCFR). Following several very successful fund-raising campaigns, the MCFR now protects over 10 500 hectares of forest.

From the mid-1980s, major conservation efforts were also undertaken by the Asociación Conservacionista de Monteverde Conservation League. In pursuit of its principal goal—the long-term preservation and conservation of the resources of Monteverde—the League assumed a leadership role in the search for international financial and technical assistance. To date, the League has succeeded in consolidating, among others, the Children's Eternal Rainforest which encompasses a total of 17 000 hectares.

More recently, the Santa Elena Reserve was created in response to a community initiative to conserve yet another sector of forest in the Monteverde region. The main purpose of this reserve of 310 hectares is to support efforts for improving education in neighbouring communities. Additionally, several small private reserves have been established in response to new national conservation policies. Together, the private reserves form what is known as the Monteverde Buffer Zone. This is, in turn, a significant part of the 204 000-hectare Arenal Conservation Area, one of Costa Rica's eight Conservation Areas (Figure 7.1).

THE COMMUNITIES

There are three main communities in the Monteverde area. Monteverde community is in the area originally settled by the Quakers and closest to the MCFR. Cerro Plano and Santa Elena were both originally settled by Costa Ricans. These three communities and the large number of small villages and hamlets in the area have a total population of about five thousand.

Access to the Monteverde area has always been difficult because of the chronically bad condition of the winding, precipitous mountain road. This difficult access was a major factor in Monteverde's isolation and its need to be self-sufficient. Agriculture and animal husbandry, particularly dairy cattle, became the basis of the economy. In 1953, the Monteverde Cheese Factory was founded under a cooperative system and, in just a few years, became the main economic activity of the region in a 25 km radius of influence, with more than 250 members. Subsequently, the creation of the Santa Elena Cooperative united the area's coffee growers. This cooperative has extended its services to include financial assistance and the crafts programme run by local women.

To this day, it is easy to recognize the extent to which the Quaker way of life

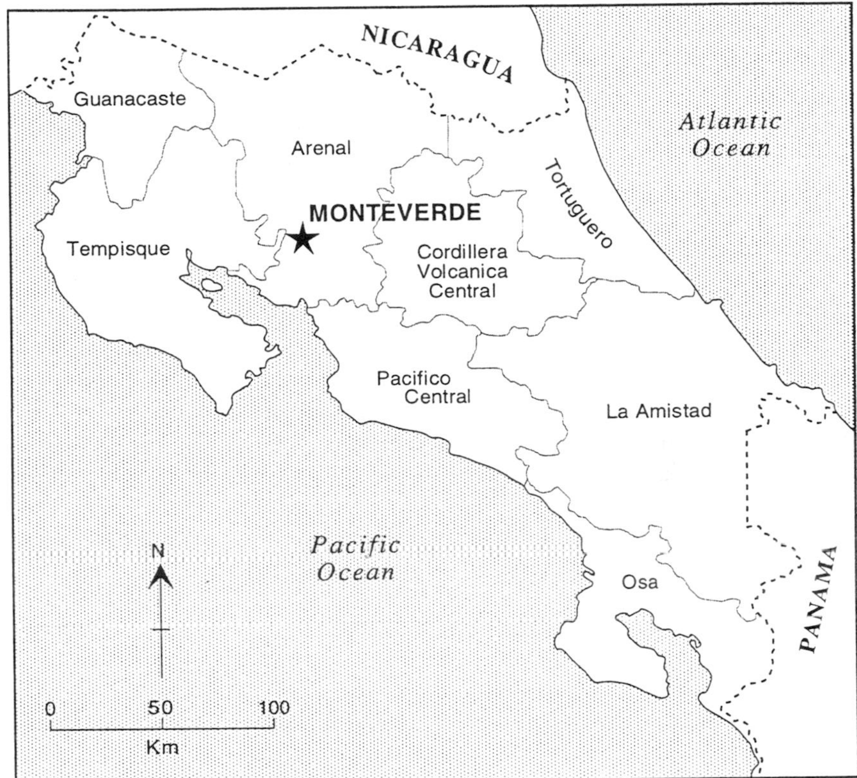

Figure 7.1 Costa Rica, showing the boundaries of the eight Conservation Areas and the location of Monteverde

has influenced the rest of the population. Both a common interest in working for the well-being of the community through organized and participatory systems, and the visionary way in which decisions are made, make Monteverde a very special community. Nowhere else in Costa Rica is characterized by so many long-standing organizations or groups working for various interests. Efforts in the areas of conservation and education predate the development of tourism and any subsequent influence it may have had. When tourism appeared on the scene, as an alternative economic activity, its development was influenced by the amalgamation of characteristics particular to the Monteverde community. As a result, a very unconventional type of tourism—now called ecotourism—developed almost spontaneously in Monteverde.

Any attempt to identify and justify the characteristics which make a given community different from others is a challenge, wrapped in that mix of limitations inherent to the interpretation of human beings and their actions. It is even more difficult when there is no baseline information. Therefore, this chapter only attempts to analyse the phenomenon of the development of ecotourism as it relates to the inherent characteristics of the people of Monteverde. Our purpose is to share with other communities some of the experiences and the challenges that seem to be developing and which, perhaps, are beginning to erode the concept of ecotourism, while in no way attempting to establish or describe a model.

THE APPEARANCE OF TOURISM

In many ways, what has happened in Monteverde reflects the history of tourism development in Costa Rica. In the late 1960s, a growing interest in learning more about the complexity and rich diversity of the tropical forests attracted a significant number of scientists from developed countries, principally the USA. Information resulting from these first studies reinforced the incipient efforts to stop the destruction of these forests. The conservation movement became increasingly strong in the 1970s, and more and more opportunities and financing began to open up for research and the protection of the forests that remained.

As with most forests in neotropical countries, Monteverde is characterized by a series of factors that made the area a refuge of biodiversity waiting to be discovered. For years, a large number of renowned researchers from a wide variety of disciplines visited the area, with the support of TSC. The results of their research were compiled and published in various scientific media. Monteverde was revealed as a site of special value for specialists in birds, frogs, high-elevation plants, and other organisms. Along with the researchers, some of whom became temporary residents of the area, appeared a growing number of visitors, most of whom were students. Groups of undergraduates and graduates from both Costa Rican and foreign universities began to visit, mainly to learn about the forest ecosystems and their components.

At about the same time, the conservation movement in developed countries was becoming ever stronger, with much media attention. Consequently, it was not surprising that Monteverde, already well-known in the scientific community, attracted the attention of the popular international press. This was encouraged by the Costa Rican Tourist Board's policy of open and direct support to journalists and representatives of other media who were interested in visiting the country. The coverage that Monteverde received in the international media (magazines, television, etc.), with an emphasis on the region's biological wealth and the spectacular abundance of the biota of the cloud forest, was another decisive factor in the development of tourism. As a consequence, new types of visitor emerged: naturalists, birdwatchers, and other special-interest groups. These groups were the most instrumental in causing the Monteverde community to take the initial steps in providing tourist services for visitors. They also largely set the tone for the type of tourism and tourist that most strongly characterize the area.

Market demand and interest in visiting Monteverde grew significantly in the late 1980s, at the same time that nature-based tourism or 'ecotourism' was rapidly gaining strength in the international market. From 1974 to 1992, the annual number of visitors to the reserve grew from 471 to 49 552: an annual increase of 578 per cent (Chamberlain, 1993). Perhaps the greatest increase in demand occurred between 1987 and 1991, with a correspondingly significant increase in tourist services such as lodging, food, and transportation. Over the past three years, there has been a tendency towards stabilization, with 49 793 visitors in 1994. The profile of the tourists has also changed to some extent. Today, a significant number of tourists have a more general interest in the forest, and are seeking a vacation that balances healthy entertainment with soft adventure and the acquisition of new knowledge (Figure 7.2). They demand a slightly higher level of attention to food service and lodging, and come from a much broader range of age groups.

Monteverde is now one of the main ecotourism destinations in Costa Rica, and the economic activity of the region has been strongly influenced by the development of the tourism industry. A recent study showed that nearly 80 per cent of the tourists visiting Costa Rica knew about Monteverde before they arrived (Echeverría et al., 1994). The same study calculated, for the first time, Monteverde's overall contribution to the economy: approximately 18 per cent of Costa Rica's total tourism revenues.

Figure 7.2 Ecotourists in the Monteverde Cloud Forest Private Reserve

THE IMPACTS OF TOURISM DEVELOPMENT

As in most rural communities, the traditional vocations in Monteverde were agriculture and ranching. People worked the land for family consumption and small-scale production, dedicating themselves to dairy farming or the cultivation of vegetables and fruits. Some crops, such as coffee, sugar cane, and bananas, were more intensively cultivated. Industry and technology were not important productive sectors of the economy so that, with the exception of the cheese factory, no experience has been gained in these sectors.

The growth and development of the tourism industry came at a crucial moment in the economy of Costa Rica, as it coincided with a drop in world market prices for the more traditional agricultural products (principally coffee and bananas). In turn, the type of tourism that began to develop was readily able to absorb a significant number of the unemployed farm workers. This small-scale tourism (70 per cent of the hotels in Costa Rica have less than 20 rooms), which developed strongly in rural communities associated with protected areas, provided not only a new source of jobs but also many opportunities for starting small businesses.

From the early 1950s, dairy farming and milk products made at the Monteverde Cheese Factory sustained the economy of Monteverde. Although tourism may appear to have displaced or had negative impacts on the dairy industry, the managers of the factory consider that only about 15 per cent of the area dedicated to dairy farming has been affected. Furthermore, total milk production has not dropped due to improvements in production systems and yield, which has increased by 10 per cent a year. However, it has been necessary to adjust employees' salaries in order to be competitive with those offered by the tourism industry.

In contrast, agriculture has declined significantly. The large majority of the products consumed by the tourism industry are now brought in from San José, or neighbouring cities, with a corresponding increase in cost. A significant percentage of the jobs generated by tourism have been filled by former farmers and the younger generation doesn't even contemplate agriculture as a job option. It is important to note that agricultural jobs are among the lowest paying and it is therefore easy to justify the displacement of workers into tourism, which offers a better income, better working conditions, and higher social status.

The tourism industry in Monteverde has resulted in the creation of some 80 different businesses, of which a significant percentage are locally owned. They include hotels, bed-and-breakfasts, restaurants, cafeterias, craft and book stores, cooperatives, a butterfly and botanical garden (Figure 7.3), private reserves, environmental education institutes, riding stables, supermarkets, bars, and places to dance and listen to music. Consequently, more than 400 full-time and 140 part-time jobs have been directly generated (Williams, 1992), not to mention those created indirectly.

Figure 7.3 Butterfly garden at Cerro Plano, Monteverde

The role of private reserves in the generation of employment and in economic contribution for the benefit of the local population is particularly worthy of mention. In 1993, for example, MCFR employed 53 people, with a total annual salary of $US 400 000. Furthermore, it is estimated that one per cent of the reserve's total budget is invested in support services and extension projects, such as education programmes, scholarships, road maintenance, and garbage collection programmes. To a large extent, these contributions derive from revenues generated by using the reserves for tourism.

The significant degree of local ownership is one of the main reasons for believing that, in spite of the costs and difficulties inherent in its development, tourism in Monteverde is there to stay. Nevertheless, tourism development, like any other economic activity, exposes the community to a series of changes and challenges that we would be remiss not to mention. No community escapes the social impact caused by facing new forms of behaviour and new habits related to the presence of tourists. It is with a tinge of melancholy that long-time residents express their feeling that Monteverde just isn't the same as it was. It seems likely that the presence of the Quakers, and the relationship that has developed between them and the other residents of Monteverde, may partly account for the fact that the relationship between locals and visitors is not submissive in character, so that the cultural impact does not displace the community as much as in many other communities.

Contrary to the norm in most rural communities, there is no emigration from Monteverde. In fact, the great increase in job opportunities in recent years has meant that the community has faced the phenomenon of immigration. The growth in both the resident and the tourist population has sharply increased the demand for basic services (telephone, water, electricity, roads, garbage disposal, etc.). While some effort has been made, the capacity to improve infrastructure is far behind the demand, so that these problems pose a major challenge. Monteverde has also not escaped another of the most common problems associated with tourism development: the increase in land value and the cost of living. Today, a square metre of land sells for $US 10–20, which is comparable to the price of land on the outskirts of San José, Costa Rica's capital city. The same holds true for the cost of living.

On the other hand, there have been significant contributions to the improvement of education in the region. With the creation of the Santa Elena Reserve, it is hoped that enough revenues will be generated through tourism to strengthen both formal and informal education programmes in the area. The incorporation of new education centres, with a particularly strong curriculum in environmental education and English instruction, are examples of the visionary manner in which this community plans its future. By the same token, the various NGOs—such as the Monteverde Conservation League and the Monteverde Institute—have also taken important steps in the field of environmental education and achieved, within the local population, an attitude of concern about the state of the environment and an awareness of necessary future actions.

Tourism has also played an important role in the conservation of natural resources, not only through the generation of revenues for self-financing but also in regard to the local community's assessment of the value of these resources. While the people of Monteverde have always shown a particular sensitivity with respect to conservation, today conservation is a way of life. Also worthy of mention are the efforts that have been made by the various productive sectors to implement models of sustainable use and management, including organic agriculture, planting windbreaks, reforestation with native species, renewing traditional techniques in the production of crafts, and using integrated and environmentally friendly systems for waste management in factories and hotels (De Rosier and Nielsen, 1994).

COMMUNITY PARTICIPATION

Monteverde does not escape the very real limitations that are particular to rural areas in developing countries. The absence of effective federal government support and, in its stead, an inefficient local government, limit the possibility of reliable maintenance and improvement of infrastructure and basic services. Rural populations also commonly run up against severe limitations when seeking sources and mechanisms of financing that would encourage active participation of community members. Although tourism is now the leading source of foreign revenue for Costa Rica, there are still no special means for small rural businesspeople to obtain loans.

In spite of these limitations, Monteverde has grown and is among the most prosperous and successful communities in Costa Rica. Much of this success can be attributed to the capacity for organization, and ability to work in groups and their particular interest in the common good—all of which can be translated to effort, constancy, and solidarity. Of particular note has been the active and ongoing participation of women in every area of endeavour: whether social, economic, or cultural development, or education. The recent development of tourism has opened up even more opportunities for women for training and active participation as hired staff or entrepreneurs (Gibbons, 1994). In addition, Monteverde probably has more NGOs that any other community in the country, with active participation from all sectors of the population. The existence of so many groups carries an inherent risk of conflict of interest and energies. For this reason the citizens of Monteverde founded an organization called 'Monteverde 2020' in the early 1990s, in an attempt to unify the interest groups from every sector and draft a cohesive development plan for the region to the year 2020. Any such effort requires special financing and leadership and, for this reason, 'Monteverde 2020' is currently undergoing a period of adjustment and a search for funding. Meanwhile, the work of all the other NGOs continues.

To summarize Monteverde's special characteristics in written form makes the community's achievements seem easy but, in fact, the process is slow, requires great effort and, like everything, is subject to all the ups and downs that characterize the human race. Care must be taken not to overestimate Monteverde's achievements, and it is certainly not our intention to present this community as a finished model. On the contrary, the local people now face their biggest challenges to date, having recognized the need to consolidate an activity which has traditionally been seasonal and often fleeting in character. They must effectively convert tourism and conservation to a solid and long-lasting productivity and, at the same time incorporate them as a way of life and a part of the Costa Rican culture, much as was done with agriculture.

THE CHALLENGES FOR CONSOLIDATING TOURISM

Tourism development in Monteverde falls within the framework of the special interest category known as ecotourism. As mentioned above, several factors combined to make Monteverde almost an automatic pioneer in this unconventional type of tourism which is based on the use of a natural resource as the principal attraction and tourism product (Cater, 1994). The Monteverde area now has more than a decade of experience in the practice of tourism as a commercial activity. As with any economic activity, ecotourism has been exposed to a process of evolution and, as a consequence, there have been changes in both supply and demand.

In the past few years, there has been an increase in the number of attractions and activities designed to complement the obligatory visit to the reserve: butterfly farms and gardens, traditional forms of cultivation and production, native species nurseries, and the reinvigoration of cultural traditions (the production of arts and crafts and culinary arts). They reflect a creativity that has sometimes led to confusion as to whether they are indeed a complementary part of ecotourism. For their part, the reserves—especially the MCFR—have been pioneers in the research and implementation of infrastructure and services for visitor management, and in their efforts to find a balance between their mandate for protecting the resource and the need to maximize the potential for visitation while maintaining a high degree of user satisfaction. Policies of restricted and controlled access, as well as increases in entrance fees to a level that valued the resource effectively, initially generated some conflict and complaints from the tourist industry, but these were rapidly overcome.

It is important for the tourist industry, whose activity depends on the existence and use of a protected area as the principal attraction, to be aware that this 'raw material' for their business is not under their complete control. As such, it is their responsibility to actively participate and involve themselves in the process of protection and in the definition of the real possibilities for the use and management of those resources. Thus, a working group consisting of tourist businessmen and members of the conservation sector has been formed. This is perhaps the fastest and most effective way for both sectors to become aware that they need each other and that they must join forces, not only to co-exist but to work towards a more solid future. This requires the identification of needs and the development of an integrated plan in order to consolidate the tourism product, recognizing that tourism has limits, which must be defined not only by the type of resource and the physical capacity for their use, but also by the type and quality of experience sought by the visitor and the quality of daily life desired by and for the resident population.

In practice, one of the greatest weaknesses, which Monteverde has not totally escaped, has been the lack of opportune training to facilitate and promote an unconventional form of production. In particular, efforts to consolidate the quality of service to the client should be promoted. The MCFR's training of local guides is especially worthy of mention. As a result, Monteverde now has a group of qualified naturalist guides, which has permitted the reserve to require that groups are accompanied by a guide. Thus, not only were new job opportunities opened up but a significant lessening of visitor impact on the resource has been noted.

The business profile promoted by ecotourism—one of small-scale businesses with a high degree of environmental responsibility— faces a major limiting factor as regards costs and the possibilities for marketing their product. The need to meet this challenge is among the concerns most recently expressed by businessmen from the Monteverde region. The possibility of competing in the international market through participation in tourism fairs and shows and advertising in the media is very costly for each small business. Consequently, local businessmen have begun to work on joint promotion of their tourism product together with each of their services and products. However, this requires much effort, maturity, and clear understanding that, in practice, the benefits of such promotion are realized gradually. An unconventional model for marketing tourism requires understanding and support from other businessmen in the industry (wholesaler tour operators, incoming operators, etc.), as well as clients. It also needs the solid support of the government which should facilitate these changes by instituting a clear policy, an incentive system, and a well-directed marketing strategy.

THEORY AND PRACTICE: WHAT CAN WE LEARN?

Ecotourism is a relatively recent activity in the economies of most countries, including Costa Rica. Nevertheless, experience permits us to compare and reflect upon what has actually been achieved, as opposed to what is proposed in theories of ecotourism (eg, Prosser, 1994), so that we can seek ways of consolidating this unconventional activity.

Among the most important contributions derived from ecotourism is the recognition of the different values of each natural resource. Indeed, ecotourism has motivated the private sector to conserve and even restore natural environments. A significant number of public and private reserves, former cattle ranches, farms, and timber operations have come to perceive this type of tourism as a profitable and responsible way of using their resources. In addition, ecotourism has resulted in important efforts in the field of environmental education, not only in the opportunity that it has afforded for millions of people to directly experience natural resources, but also in the implementation of formal and informal education programmes.

The benefits of supporting resource conservation in Monteverde can be observed in specific cases such as MCFR's self-financing in recent years, a direct result of revenues generated through tourism. The creation of the Santa Elena Reserve might be considered a direct consequence of seeing the financial opportunities that can be derived from appropriate visitor management in protected areas. Numerous businessmen, including hoteliers and ranchers, have decided to conserve the forests that still exist on their properties, and some have even declared them as private protected areas, thereby taking a step in consolidating the biological corridors and the Monteverde Protective Zone.

Yet no economic activity can exist if it is not profitable; clarification of the cost-benefit ratio is essential. As there is so little experience or precedent in the field of valuation and economics of natural resources in this context, it has been difficult to clearly define the real cost of the 'raw material' (natural and cultural attractions) on which ecotourism is based. In this regard, one must reflect on the real contribution, in global terms, that ecotourism makes to the conservation and management of natural and cultural resources.

It is difficult to imagine the conservation of natural resources in a developing country unless this could result in the generation of some type of income or improvements in the quality of life of its citizens. Also, it is important to remember that the cultural roots of communities associated with, or adjacent to, protected areas are directly influenced by these communities' relationships with these resources. Consequently, stopping the destruction of resources could assist in motivating their valuation by renewing possibilities for strengthening traditional community activities through the responsible use of these resources.

One benefit of ecotourism has been that it has permitted the rejuvenation and promotion of local arts and crafts, which has represented an important contribution to the budget of rural families. In the same vein, mention can also be made of the appearance of small businesses providing other types of service such as transportation, lodging, food, and communications. Many lessons may be learned from this experience. In particular, the insertion of the rural sector (peasants) into the field of providing services requires significant adjustments which have not yet been fully considered. The service industry is based on a condition of both aptitude and attitude. Training is important to introduce the necessary skills, but dealing with factors of basic personality and willingness to change habits and cultural patterns, without going through a process of acculturation, is fundamental to achieving the desired level of service. A practical example may clarify this point.

The tourism business literally requires work '24 hours a day, 365 days a year'. Yet most people in the rural areas of Central America have a traditional work day from 6:00 am to 3:00 pm. Weekends and holidays are sacred. The concept of quality of service is totally foreign and, therefore, one of the first challenges for the small businessman. Fortunately, the essential friendliness and helpfulness of the Costa Rican personality have compensated for these factors and contributed to ecotourism becoming the country's principal earner of foreign revenue. Therefore, it appears eminently necessary to seek a balance between the processes and programmes of training and the realities of our national personality in order not to fall into the trap of transformation—annihilation—of our own communities.

While ecotourism effectively offers an opportunity to strengthen small businesses and distribute the revenues generated by tourism more evenly, it also requires time for cultural adjustment and changes to a new way of life. Unfortunately the necessary time is not necessarily compatible with tourism, since tourism is a particularly dynamic activity, not only in economic terms but also in its process of evolution. As a consequence, community participation and the equitable distribution of revenues are among the principal unresolved conflicts in the ecotourism industry.

There are still promising possibilities for the consolidation of ecotourism as an industry representing an effective development alternative for communities and countries, as well as a means for supporting conservation of the environment. Immediate actions are needed to support efforts in the research and transfer of technical knowledge which will help orient and reinforce each of the various components (infrastructure, construction, services, marketing, relationships with other sectors of the industry, etc.) of ecotourism projects. Advances in technology and products that permit sustainable development must be equally accessible to all the different sectors. The role and responsibility of governments is obvious, with respect to the implementation both of policies and strategies that support and facilitate access to appropriate technologies, and of incentive systems and opportunities for financing.

Ecotourism has proved a popular way for travellers to combine recreation with a personally enriching learning experience. This is evidenced by the type of tourist who is attracted to ecotourism and the type of service he or she demands: brochures, maps, talks, audiovisual material, specialized guides, etc. Nevertheless, we frequently forget that ecotourism provides the opportunity for education to be a two-way street. The communities that are visited and the people who are exposed, directly or indirectly, to tourism development have yet to benefit sufficiently from this educational process. To date, resources have been directed more towards the tourist. It is time to broaden our concept of education to include communities in a truly integrated learning process that benefits each individual.

Finally, it is important to mention the persistent myth that ecotourism is less expensive than conventional tourism. This is not necessarily true. As with any commodity, mass production of tourism reduces the costs and increases competitiveness in the market. However, if the activity is to be based on criteria such as personalized services, sites of exceptional value, responsible and visionary management of the resources, low cultural impact, high-quality service, equitable distribution of revenues, and opportunity for many people, it should be understood that these very criteria constitute additional costs that the client and the market will have to learn to recognize and respect.

ACKNOWLEDGEMENTS

The author wishes to thank Terry Pratt for translating this chapter into English, and the following people for information provided in personal interviews: José Luis Vargas, Ree Sheck, James Wolf, Fernando Valverde, Wilfred Guindon, Geovanny Arguedas, Francisco Chamberlain, Agueda Marin.

REFERENCES

Aspinall, W., 1992, *Reserva Biológica Bosque Nuboso de Monteverde—Director's Report*, Tropical Science Center, San José.

Cater, E., 1994, Ecotourism in the Third World—Problems and prospects for sustainability, in E. Cater, and G. Lowman (eds) *Ecotourism: A sustainable option?* John Wiley and Sons, Chichester, 69–86.

Chamberlain., F. 1993, *The Monteverde Cloud Forest Reserve: A case study,* Tropical Science Center, San José.

De Rosier, D., and Nielsen, K., 1994, Sirven los rompevientos como corredores para animales? *Huellas de Danta* 9(2), Asociación Conservacionista de Monteverde, Monteverde.

Echeverría, J., Hanrahan, M. and Solorzano, R., 1994, *Valuation on the no-price amenities provided by the biological resources within the Monteverde Cloud Forest Reserve.* Final technical report: Biodiversity support program, grant #7530. Tropical Science Center, San José.

Gibbons, W., 1994, Las mujeres y su trabajo: Moldeano el futuro en la región de Monteverde, *Hojas de Monteverde* 1(2), Instituto Monteverde, Monteverde.

Prosser, R., 1994, Societal change and the growth in alternative tourism, in Cater, E., and Lowman, G. (eds), *Ecotourism: A sustainable option?* John Wiley and Sons, Chichester, 19–37.

Williams, W., 1992, Ecotourism and buffer zone management at Monteverde Reserve. Consultant's Report. United States International Agency for Development/Regional Central America Official Program, San José.

8 Negotiating the Development of Tourism in the Richtersveld, South Africa

EMILE BOONZAIER

INTRODUCTION

We are moving beyond the simple conservation notion that tourism should take nothing but photographs and leave nothing but footprints. New-age tourism, under labels such as benevolent, sustainable, or guilt-free, demands that due regard is given to local populations. The tourist enterprise should accommodate locals' economic interests, cultural sensibilities and pre-existing social order. And insofar as tourism inevitably involves negative consequences, these should be offset by the positive effects of development associated with tourism: the creation of jobs, injection of cash, improvement of infrastructure and generalized economic advancement of the region.

The establishment of a National Park in the Richtersveld, a remote and arid reserve in the Namaqualand region of South Africa, serves as a case study to highlight the complexity of social change associated with a single tourist enterprise. On the surface it appears to be a fulfilment of the low-impact/high-value dream. It is lauded as the first 'contract' park in South Africa: it is the outcome of democratic negotiations between the National Parks Board and the local indigenous population who now share equally in management decisions. But underneath this image of success freely disseminated to tourists, there is a much more complex tale of on-going struggles over land, economic survival and identity.

NAMAQUALAND AND THE COLOURED RESERVES

The Namaqualand region of South Africa is situated along the Atlantic coast just south of the Orange River (Figure 8.1). It is a semi-desert area of 47 000 km^2, with an average annual rainfall of less than 15 mm per year. With the exception of irrigation farming along the Orange River and some odd attempts at dry-land grain cultivation, sheep and goat herding is the only type of farming practised.

People and Tourism in Fragile Environments. Edited by M. F. Price.

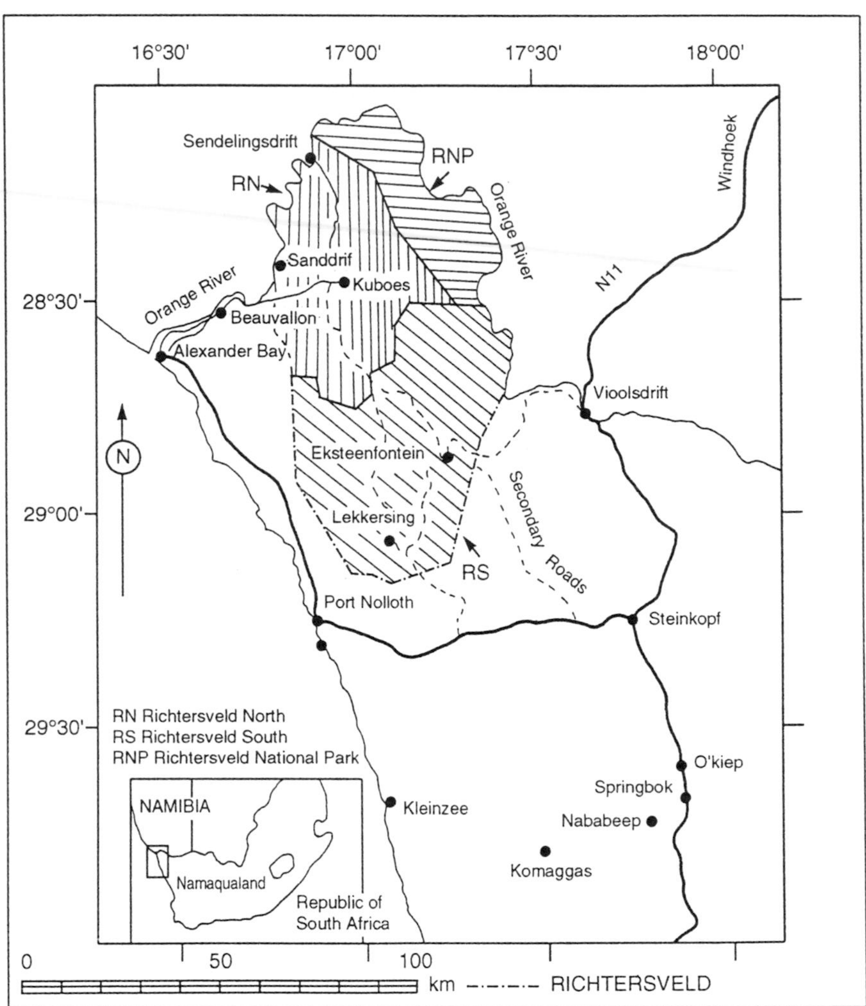

Figure 8.1 Location map of the Richtersveld

Resource extraction, especially of diamonds, copper and crawfish, has played a major role in the region's limited economy. But the benefits of these developments have not been shared widely by the local population of 60 000. Notwithstanding the visible and localized economic activity associated with mining operations at Oranjemund and Kleinsee (alluvial diamonds) and around O'kiep and Nababeep (copper), and the coastal village of Port Nolloth (fishing and marine diamonds), Namaqualand seems to have remained doggedly under-developed. The mass of Namaqualanders have certainly remained poor.

Low wages paid to unskilled workers, the importation of capital and skilled workers from outside the region, and major fluctuations in the demand for local workers (related, for example, to dramatic variations in the international price of copper and the virtual depletion of crawfish resources in the 1970s) have resulted in a healthy scepticism on the part of many locals towards new economic opportunities. It has also meant that farming activity, although subject to the vicissitudes of climate, has remained the only form of long-term security for many.

Most of the land in Namaqualand is privately owned by individual farmers or by the various mining companies. But about 25 per cent is state-owned land held in trust for descendants of the original Nama (or Namaqua), a branch of the autochonous Khoikhoi (or Hottentots). This land is divided into seven Rural Coloured Areas, commonly known as 'coloured reserves'—Steinkopf, Richtersveld North, Richtersveld South, Leliefontein, Kommagas, Concordia and Pella. Together they constitute 70 per cent of the total of 1.7 million ha making up the 23 coloured reserves in South Africa. The total population of these reserves is 27 000, less than 0.2 per cent of the total population (Steyn, 1989: 416). Richtersveld North and Richtersveld South are the driest, most mountainous and most inaccessible of all the reserves. With 3500 residents on a total area of over 9000 km^2, they also have the lowest population density.

Coloured reserves should be clearly differentiated from the notorious African bantustans of the apartheid era. Unlike the bantustans, they were never part of any grand strategy to remove all coloureds from white urban areas. In other words, there were never any restrictions on people leaving the reserves, and they did provide some protection for indigenous land rights. The various reserve communities, in an effort to control excessive strain on the limited grazing resources, developed effective mechanisms to prevent outsiders (including other coloureds) from moving in.

Figure 8.2 A Richtersveld farmer's homestead
(D. A. Gerneke)

The populations of the reserves today are very mixed and display little evidence of a traditional Khoikhoi lifestyle. People live in permanent villages with schools, shops, churches, clinics and post-offices. Their dress, housing (for the most part) and consumption patterns are visibly western (Figure 8.2). Migrant wage-labour is clearly the most important source of income, since the limited grazing resources are inadequate to sustain the existing populations. But while outsiders tend to think in terms of sub-subsistence farming, the relationship between farming and wage-labour is very important and complex. Given the insecurity of wage-employment, inadequate unemployment benefits and pensions, and the fact that much of the housing outside the reserves is company-tied, stock farming provides some form of long-term security. Farming is a supplement to poor and irregular wages: it is a vital form of insurance against unemployment, an important supplement to inadequate pensions, and a sensible investment as a hedge against inflation. Consequently, nearly all reserve residents have an interest in farming and hence a stake in the land in the reserves (Boonzaier, 1987).

THE ESTABLISHMENT OF THE RICHTERSVELD NATIONAL PARK

The idea of a park in the northern Richtersveld was first mooted two decades ago. The dominant conservation discourse of the time—expressed in terms of the need to protect the environment—was an integral part of the process for many years. People were not reckoned as part of the environment, and local populations were not incorporated into the decision-making process. While environmentalists and other outsiders were informed of the plan in elitist journals such as *Custos* (a wildlife conservation magazine) and *Panorama* (a glossy magazine published by the Bureau for Information), most local residents remained blissfully unaware of the proposal effectively to excise 165 000 ha from the reserve until at least a decade later. Under titles such as 'Richtersveld—treasure chest for the botanist' (Müller, 1982) and 'To save a mountain desert' (Claasen, 1987), the proposed park was lauded as a great achievement for conservation, of national and international importance. It was argued that the environment had to be protected from the local population 'before it is lost to posterity forever' (Claasen, 1987: 27) and the park was thus 'justified on aesthetic, moral and scientific grounds' (Müller, 1982: 23).

These arguments went unchallenged, except for a group of academics with research interests in the area, who sounded a note of concern:

> No mention is made of the opinions of the local inhabitants. Our own experience . . . . indicates that there is very strong opposition to the whole scheme because it represents yet another encroachment upon their land. Surely their opinions, and not just those of wealthy sightseers and the so-called 'scientists', should be considered.
>
> (*The Cape Times,* 19 July 1982)

Despite this 'very strong opposition' which might have been expressed verbally by some local residents, there was no active or organized resistance to the park. 'Negotiations' were characterized by the virtual exclusion of the local community, and negative local sentiments were translated into fatalistic acceptance.

Then, in 1989, everything changed. A Community Committee, derogatively referred to by some outsiders as an *opstokerskomitee* (agitator committee), was established in direct opposition to the government-backed Management Board, the local authority which had been negotiating with the National Parks Board. The Community Committee made it their task to inform the local population of the negotiations which had been taking place, and they mobilized strong opposition. Finally, on 19 March, the day before the contract for the establishment of the park was due to be signed, a delegation acting on behalf of the Community Committee travelled to Cape Town to apply for an interdict to prevent the signing.

Thereafter, there were lengthy and often heated negotiations between the two camps: the National Parks Board, government officials and the Management Board representing the one; and the Community Committee, non-governmental organizations (NGOs) and academics the other. The main issues for negotiation centred on the following:

1 the leasehold period (99 or 25 years)
2 the size of the park (165 000 hectares or smaller)
3 continued rights of access for farmers and their stock
4 compensation for loss of land
5 local employment opportunities
6 local participation in the park's management.

Consensus, which effectively amounted to local victories on all of these issues, was ultimately reached. The new contract was signed on 20 July 1991.

The process and outcome of these final negotiations have widely been heralded as *the* model for the rest of the country to follow (eg, Fourie, 1994; Koch, 1993). Everyone seems to have emerged victorious: the National Parks Board, the government, the local community, and tourism. And, in many senses, it does constitute a great achievement. But it is also important, if we are going to learn from this episode, to address certain key questions about the negotiation process and to scrutinize subsequent developments in the area.

THE BROADER CONTEXT OF CHANGING POSITIONS

Perhaps the most interesting question one might ask of the preceding two decades is why things should have changed as radically as they did. The whole episode has changed from a model of how *not* to do things, to *the* model to follow. In particular, the various parties—the local population, the Management Board and the Parks Board—have undergone major shifts. Why has this been possible?

When the local population became aware of the ongoing negotiations, it was self-evident that they stood to lose much. Significant, but muted, opposition was expressed. The real change, however, came with their recognition that they did have significant power over the outcome of the negotiations, and their subsequent willingness to embark on a confrontational course of action. This change within the local population was part of a much broader process of empowerment associated with the 1980s. Very significantly, 1990 was the year which heralded the beginning of radical transformation in South African society. It marked the end of the apartheid, the unbanning of the African National Congress (ANC) and the release of Nelson Mandela. As such, it was associated with significant sense of empowerment for oppressed South Africans.

For the population of the Namaqualand reserves specifically, the 1980s was a decade of unprecedented trade union activity, especially in terms of increased membership of the National Union of Mineworkers. Also, the creation of the Community Committee in the Richtersveld was part of a broader movement, closely allied to the ANC, to establish civic organizations in the various reserves. During the 1980s there was also a dramatic increase in the presence of NGOs, notably the Surplus People Project, which provided invaluable support and expertise for grassroots organizations.

Perhaps most significantly, the reserve populations had recently emerged victorious from a protracted battle with the state to prevent their communal lands from being privatized. Under the guise of conservation, the state had proposed that the 'tragedy of the commons' (in the form of severe overgrazing) could only be prevented by dividing the reserves into a number of 'economic units' (farms which would be hired out to a few individual stock-owners). Since such a move meant that most residents would effectively lose their grazing rights, there was very strong local opposition and, on more than one occasion, reserve populations obtained court decisions to prevent or reverse the implementation of the scheme (Boonzaier, 1987). Their successful resistance to the scheme, and their recognition of the support which the courts and the media could provide, had a carry-over effect on their attitude to the park. This was hardly surprising, given the obvious direct parallels between the two episodes: both schemes were couched in terms of environmental protection, but were viewed by locals simply as part of a general process of land encroachment.

The change in attitude displayed by the National Parks Board was even more dramatic. This was linked in no small measure to changes in international trends. The 1980s saw the emergence of new international attitudes towards tourism, the environment, and conservation (eg, IUCN/UNEP/WWF, 1980; McNeely, 1993). People, especially indigenous populations, were recognized as an integral part of the environment. There was also an increasing awareness of the destructive nature of tourism and its negative impact on local populations. Some senior Parks Board officials were very sensitive to these trends (Fourie, 1994) and they had had direct contact with successful efforts to incorporate local populations into park structures in other parts of the world (in this instance, the Uluru National Park in Australia was an important model: Hill, 1988; see also Layton, 1989).

Allied to this was a clear recognition that negative publicity regarding the Richtersveld negotiations (both local and international) would have negative impacts on the general image of the South African National Parks Board. There was also a sense that political change in South Africa was imminent, and several ANC spokespersons had expressed the view that there was a need to reassess whether the land in parks (the Kruger National Park was specifically mentioned) could not be more productively used as farming land for impoverished blacks in the area (see Engelbrecht and van der Walt, 1993). There were also significant changes within the Parks Board hierarchy, so that by late 1989 they were openly stating that no park could exist without the support of local communities. They had also learnt the lesson that merely speaking to the relevant local or central authority did not mean that community consultation had taken place (Fourie, 1994).

ASSESSING THE OUTCOMES

The final phase of the negotiation process and the terms of the final contract for the park obviously represent a major advance on the situation prior to 1989. Until then, the local population had been treated with all the disregard for the interests of ordinary people (especially people not classified as white) that was characteristic of the institutions of the apartheid state. In this sense, therefore, the Richtersveld Park represents a salutary achievement. But there is also a need to consider the longer-term impacts now that the park has been established.

In the discussion that follows, it is important to bear in mind that one cannot demonstrate direct links to the park's existence in all cases. For example, although roads and telephone links in the northern Richtersveld have been substantially upgraded since 1991, there is an argument that these improvements were long overdue and would have taken place irrespective of the park's existence. Also, there is the question of how widely the impacts have been distributed. In the case of the Richtersveld, 'the local population' has been readily circumscribed as residents of the northern reserve. But, as we will see below, such a conception has not been without its problems: why should residents of Richtersveld South, the whole population of Namaqualand, or, for that matter, all South Africans be excluded from our conception of 'local'?

THE INTENSIFICATION OF LOCAL COMPETITION AND DIVISIONS

Some cynical locals have commented that the final contract has merely allowed them to protect what was theirs in the first place. The provision of additional grazing outside the reserve and the annual payment of R80 000 (about £14 000) are fair compensation for the loss of land. But this does not mean that the population is better off than before.

One could take issue with this viewpoint. For example, the R80 000 represents money which would otherwise not have been available: it has been used to fund study bursaries for their children, and local community projects. Also, the Parks Board has strictly adhered to its undertaking to provide preferential employment opportunities for locals: to date, all nine ranger posts have have filled by people from the Richtersveld. Yet many locals are quick to point out that these are modest benefits which have been associated with significant costs. A mere nine jobs have not significantly improved the very high rates of unemployment in a population of 3500. They point out that most of the jobs went to men who already had some form of employment elsewhere, and that the posts they vacated have, of course, not necessarily gone to locals: the unemployed in the Richtersveld are still unemployed.

Equally, as is always the case when limited resources become available, the result has been intensified competition and resentment between locals. There were many unsuccessful applications for the Parks Board posts and for financial assistance from the Trust administering the R80 000. Not surprisingly, these applicants (or their kin or neighbours) readily translate this into local jealousies or criticisms of the constitution of the Park Management Board and the Trust. Some of these latter criticisms would seem to be entirely justified. For example, until recently the Trust had no representatives from the Richtersveld community. This policy was justified on the grounds that local representatives would have been excluded from submitting applications for financial assistance for themselves.

The establishment of the park has also set the stage for intensified competition between the populations of northern and southern Richtersveld. Some years ago, the people of the northern Richtersveld formally seceded from the rest of the reserve. The main issue of contention was the unrepresentativeness of a joint Management Board dominated by people from the south. Events had come to a head over the question of economic units, and many people in the north felt that their land would be much safer in the hands of their own separate Management Board. But the partition has never really been complete, and consequently southern residents have felt that they are entitled to share in the material compensations offered by the Parks Board. Although the north has agreed to the principle of sharing, many individuals are strongly opposed to this magnanimous gesture and point out that it was the south that had forced the partition in the first place: 'Now they want to muscle in on what we have achieved'.

Another issue which has caused much local dissatisfaction is the stipulation in the contract that local farmers will have continued access to grazing in the park area. As could be expected, there is a conflict between conservation and farming interests: the conservation lobby wants fewer stock in the area, while the farmers want more. This issue has been complicated by disagreement over the number of stock (and the number of farmers) that have used the park area for grazing in the past. Locals point out that the stock count, undertaken at the time of the negotiations over the contract, underestimated the use that locals made of the area (Figure 8.3). They argue that the estimate of 15 000 sheep and goats was unrealistic, since herds move around on communal grazing land, and

Figure 8.3 A stock farmer with his herd in the Richtersveld
(D. A. Gerneke)

many farmers moved in and out of the park area on a seasonal basis. Also, many farmers used the area only as emergency grazing during times of severe drought. Consequently, it has been impossible to reach agreement on how many stock traditionally grazed in the area, what the theoretical carrying capacity is, which farmers are entitled to remain there, and who is entitled to use the land offered in compensation. It has also been pointed out that the establishment of the park has effectively removed the necessarily flexible relationship between farming and wage-labour: residents who currently have large herds are being favoured, while wage-labourers in the process of building up their herds will find it increasingly difficult to do so in future.

BOOSTING TOURISM IN THE REGION

The past four years have been associated with an unprecedented increase in tourism in the region. But this increase in the number tourists represents a significant qualitative change. Until the 1990s, tourism in Namaqualand was restricted to a brief period of about four weeks (usually in September) when the barren countryside suddenly bursts out in spectacular displays of wild flowers. Tourists flocked to Namaqualand for this brief and unpredictable period (being dependent on good rains), thereby overloading the existing tourist infrastructure. And, after a few weeks, the tourists, like the flowers, would disappear until the following year.

This picture has changed substantially. Officials, operators and entrepreneurs claim that the tourist season has been extended because people are no longer only interested in pretty flowers—they come to see nature. The publicity surrounding the park has drawn the public's attention to Namaqualand as tourist destination with attractions beyond 'pretty flowers'. The park area does not have particularly significant flower displays, and publicity has thus focused on its rare succulent plants, scenic beauty and rugged isolation: attractions which characterize, albeit to a lesser extent, much of Namaqualand. Consequently, many tourists are now being directed to other similar, but less inaccessible, areas. New nature reserves have been established (and old ones revitalized), guided tours now criss-cross the whole region, and other coloured reserves are devising ways of attracting tourists.

But the Richtersveld Park itself, although arguably an important catalyst for these developments, has remained surprisingly insignificant as tourist destination. Given the fragile physical environment of the park area, the number of vehicles entering at any one time is currently restricted to 12. This means that the total income generated from gate takings (the daily charge per vehicle is R100: less than £20) is insufficient even to cover the salaries of Parks Board staff. The Richtersveld Park is clearly not being promoted as a mass tourist destination by the Parks Board, who recognize that it will effectively have to be subsidized by their other parks (such as the Kruger National Park).

The Richtersveld Park is also situated in the most inaccessible location in Namaqualand, and the roads within its borders (which will not be significantly upgraded) demand rugged (preferably four-wheel-drive) vehicles. This means that it caters for a select and hardy group of tourists with the necessary means and equipment. But these tourists spend very little money locally, except for entrance fees and petrol. Everything else—four-wheel-drive air-conditioned vehicles, food stored in portable refrigerators, and all camping equipment—is bought in urban centres such as Cape Town and Johannesburg.

But large numbers of tourists, mostly travelling in organized groups from Cape Town or other large centres outside Namaqualand, are entering the southern Richtersveld and adjacent areas. This is not only due to the restricted number of visitors that the park can accommodate, but also because these areas are much closer to the national road from Cape Town to Namibia. A visit to the park adds an effective 400 km to one's journey (200 km either way), since the usual route is via Port Nolloth and Alexander Bay. In addition, several tour operators offer trips down the Orange River or guided tours of the area just south of the park (accessible from Vioolsdrif or Steinkopf). Access is effectively unrestricted and absolutely no revenue accrues to the local population. On the other hand, the nuisance value of so many tourists—overuse of the untarred roads and tracks, tampering with wind-pumps, leaving gates open, swimming in reservoirs, and littering—is a much more serious problem than in the park itself. Not surprisingly, some residents are now proposing that the whole of the reserve should fall under the control of the National Parks Board. Ironically, such sentiments have been stimulated by local fears that the new government might call for the abolition of coloured reserves, as they have in the case of the African bantustans. It is felt that the Parks Board could offer more protection than an ANC government.

LOCAL EMPOWERMENT AND NAMA IDENTITY

The process of negotiations culminating in the signing of the contract for the park were, as we have seen above, part of the broader process of empowerment experienced by coloureds in Namaqualand. At the same time, the establishment of the park has also been associated with renewed interest in the issue of 'Nama', 'Khoikhoi' or 'Hottentot' culture. For the people of the Richtersveld, many of whom are descended from the original Hottentot or Nama inhabitants of the area, association with traditional Hottentot culture represents a double-edged sword.

On the one hand, the labels 'Nama' and 'Hottentot' have, for many years, had essentially negative connotations. The notion of Namaness has been reviled by outsiders; not only by white outsiders such as missionaries, state officials, and employers, but also by other coloureds. Those identified as Nama (or 'Hotnot', to use the local derogatory version) were seen as primitive, backward, underdeveloped and destructive of the environment. They were also assigned the lowest places in the social hierarchy. The Nama themselves were induced to participate in this process of denigrating 'indigenousness': they have suppressed the Nama language and relinquished distinctively Nama customs in an attempt to gain acceptance as members of the broader category of coloured people (Sharp and Boonzaier, 1994).

On the other hand, the establishment of the park has introduced a set of positive connotations which stand in stark contrast to these. Residents could emphasize their descent from the original inhabitants of the area in order to affirm their inalienable rights to the land. They could also use the argument that Nama farmers had utilized the area for many centuries without the supposed degradation to the environment claimed by some (Boonzaier et al., 1990). They have also come to recognize that 'traditional Nama culture' could become a marketable asset. Nama tour guides could be employed in the park; accommodation could be provided in traditional huts (*matjieshuise)* built by local Nama residents; and miniature reed mats and other locally produced artefacts could be sold to tourists.

Such a slant squared well with the view, increasingly accepted and expressed by Parks Board officials, conservationists and tourists, that local populations living 'in tune with nature' were an integral part of the environment. The reserve population was no longer a group of primitive and ignorant farmers overgrazing the land; they were a source of esteemed and detailed knowledge of the local environment.

The local residents' response to this reassessment of their 'traditional culture' was measured and cautious, since the prior negative association of being Nama had by no means disappeared. They recognized that Nama culture was a resource which could be used to address their economic concerns within a framework set by tourism. But they refused to acquiesce to the notion that this meant that they had to *become* traditional Nama. They do not, for example, want to live in *matjieshuise*, or wear animal skins. Nama cultural symbols are therefore tokens of identity which are highly valued (and very valuable) in certain contexts; they are not indicators of essential difference to be misconstrued by tourists.

This message was clearly communicated at the public signing ceremony of the contract for the park which was held in the village of Kuboes (Figure 8.4). The programme, which had been carefully orchestrated by local residents, accorded central stage to a 'traditional Nama hut' which had been specially constructed for the occasion. As was anticipated, guests from outside Namaqualand showed great interest in the structure; and like tourists, many had themselves photographed in front of it.

Towards the end of the day's proceedings, everyone was asked to move to the Nama hut for the 'coming-out ceremony of a Nama bride'. The senior representative of the Parks Board was asked to go inside where he would meet his 'bride', and the entrance was shut behind him. One of the local men then stood up on a chair and explained what was happening. A coming-out ceremony, we were informed, is essentially a coming-of-age ceremony: it symbolizes the adult status that has been achieved by the couple. The park has now eventually achieved adult status after a difficult birth and not untraumatic childhood. Most importantly, however, the ceremony is symbolic of the individual's first steps in ultimate acceptance by the adult community.

The Parks Board was eventually now being accepted as an adult by the Richtersveld community. And, in a thinly veiled reference to the problems experienced with the original contract and the initial unwillingness to recognize the local population's continued rights to grazing in the park area, he pointed out that the Parks Board had had to learn much before it could be accepted. At this

Figure 8.4 The village of Kuboes
(D. A. Gerneke)

Figure 8.5 The conclusion of the public signing ceremony establishing the Richtersveld Park (D. A. Gerneke)

point the Parks Board official was asked to emerge from the hut with his new 'bride'. All of this had obviously been unanticipated by the visitors, and the rather sheepish-looking official emerged from the dark hut with a middle-aged 'bride' at his side. He was holding a gift of a hand-crafted hanging, made of goat skins, which depicted boundaries in the Richtersveld (Figure 8.5).

Addressing the official, the speaker elucidated the significance of the 'bride' and the gift. The skin, he pointed out, was from one of the goats that they (the Parks Board) had wanted to kick out of the park area, and it had been crafted by his 'bride'. It demonstrated the kind of craftwork of which local people were capable: craftwork for which there would be a ready market to tourists visiting the park. The 'bride', he added, was the wife of one of the farmers they originally wanted to remove from the land, but the farmer was offering his wife to show that he did not hold any grudges. Furthermore, the exact boundaries of the park are still in dispute—the people of the Richtersveld have drawn this map so that there can be no doubt in future: 'We know where the boundaries are'.

Such skilful use of cultural symbols speaks of a degree of conscious manipulation, and hence control (or power), over the situation which bodes well for the future. The whole performance was explicitly directed at the visitors who, as had been anticipated, were drawn to the scene by the promise of 'exotic custom'. As the final event on the programme, it clearly re-established the people of the Richtersveld as being in control of the day's proceedings. But it is also important to emphasize what it did *not* do or say. It did not, for example, emphasize the exclusivity of the Nama of the Richtersveld. Nor did it suggest that the people of the Richtersveld were still living in mat huts and practising traditional ceremonies.

CONCLUSION

It should be clear that this performance did not simply pander to outsiders' images of indigenous culture: the people of the Richtersveld used cultural symbols in a creative way to address the dangers implicit in tourism's vision of primitive 'otherness'. But such a skilful response seems, in this case at least, to be associated with a very special set of circumstances relating to the perceived ambiguities of the situation. Nonetheless, it is still my contention that much of the literature which lauds case studies of cultural conservation or revitalization in the context of encounters with tourism speak more of passive acceptance of outsiders' demands, rather than of genuine empowerment (see Volkman, 1984; and Whittaker, 1994 as obvious exceptions).

There is also a need to question simplistic assumptions regarding 'the community' (Thornton and Ramphele, 1988): a harmonious group of like-minded people fully involved in the negotiation processes, sharing equally in the benefits of tourism, and having preferential claim to such benefits while costs are distributed more broadly. The Richtersveld case supports none of these assumptions. Furthermore, while the case obviously contains a number of very positive aspects, it can hardly be held up as an unmitigated success story. 'Success stories' might, in the short-term, serve the goal of promoting new-age tourism. But at what stage will tourists also start asking, as they have of nature-based tourism: 'Are they are faking it?' (see Weiler, 1993).

REFERENCES

Boonzaier, E., 1987, From communal grazing to 'economic' units, Changing access to land in a Namaqualand reserve. *Development Southern Africa*, 4(3), 479–491.

Boonzaier, E., 1991, People, parks and politics, in Ramphele, M., (ed.) *Restoring the Land, Environment and Change in Post-apartheid South Africa*, Panos, London, 155–162.

Boonzaier, E.A., Hoffman, M.T., Archer, F.M. and Smith, A.B., 1990, Communal land use and the 'tragedy of the commons', Some problems and development perspectives with specific reference to semi-arid regions of southern Africa. *Journal of the Grasslands Society of South Africa*, 7(2), 77–80.

Claasen, I., 1987, To save a mountain desert, *Panorama*, August 1987, 20–27.

Engelbrecht, W.G. and van der Walt, P.T., 1993, Notes on the economic rise of the Kruger National Park, *Koedoe*, 36(2), 113–120.

Fourie, J., 1994, Comments on national parks and future relations with neighbouring communities, *Koedoe*, 37(1), 123–136.

Hill, R.C., 1988, Uluru National Park, Australia, Of ecosystems conservation, land rights of indigenous people and a charter for living. Paper presented to the Endangered Wildlife Trust International Symposium on National Parks, Nature Reserves and Neighbours, Johannesburg, 31 October – 2 November 1988.

IUCN/UNEP/WWF (International Union for the Conservation of Nature/United Nations Environment Programme/World Wildlife Fund), 1980, World Conservation Strategy, IUCN, Gland.

Koch, E., 1993, Campfire, parks and people, *Tourism Recreation Research*, 18(1), 62–63.

Layton, R., 1989, *Uluru, An Aboriginal History,* Aboriginal Studies Press, Canberra.

McNeely, J.A. (ed.), 1993, *Parks for life, Report of the IVth World Congress on National Parks and Protected Areas*. IUCN, Gland.

Müller, J., 1982, Richtersveld—treasure chest for the botanist, *Custos*, 11(2), 21–25.

Sharp, J. and Boonzaier, E., 1994, Ethnic identity as performance, Lessons from Namaqualand, *Journal of Southern African Studies*, 20(1), 405–415.

Steyn, L., 1989, Privatisation and the dispossession of land in Namaqualand, in Moss, G. and Obery, I., (eds), *South African Review*, 5 (Johannesburg), 415–425.

Thornton, R. and Ramphele, M., 1988, The quest for community, in Boonzaier, E. and Sharp, J. (eds), *South African Keywords, The uses and abuses of political concepts*, David Philip, Cape Town, 29–39.

Volkman, T.A., 1984, Great performances, Toraja cultural identity in the 1970s, *American Anthropologist*, 11(1), 152–168.

Weiler, B., 1993, Nature-based tour operators, Arc they environmentally friendly or are they faking it? *Tourism Recreation Research*, 18(1), 55–60.

Whittaker, E., 1994, Public discourse on sacredness, The transfer of Ayers Rock to Aboriginal ownership. *American Anthropologist*, 21(2), 310–334.

9 Finding Common Ground in the Last Best Place: The Flathead County, Montana Master Plan

KURT CULBERTSON, DEANNA SNYDER, STEVE MULLEN, BILL KANE, MART ZELLER AND SUZANNE RICHMAN

THE RESETTLEMENT OF THE AMERICAN WEST

The American West is undergoing spectacular change. National magazines such as *Time* and *Newsweek* are heralding the merits of the region's clean air, wide open spaces, and plentiful jobs. Long considered the nation's playground, the intermountain West is rapidly becoming a haven for tourists and second-home owners who wish to escape the congestion, traffic, crime, unemployment, and high taxes of states such as California, New York, and Massachusetts. These migrants are driven primarily by non-economic interests, particularly the desire to live in beautiful places with a high quality of life, yet connected by state-of-the-art telecommunications to the rest of the world. This migration is a phenomenon of historic proportions: the 'resettlement of the American West'.

The Rocky Mountain West, including the intermountain states of Montana, Idaho, Colorado, Utah, Wyoming, Arizona, and New Mexico, is now the country's fastest-growing region, with a growth rate comparable to that of Africa. It is estimated that 15 000 people a month are leaving California and resettling in the intermountain states, in a process referred to by sociologist Patrick Jobes as 'the infilling of the skeleton' (Parham, 1994). Throughout the Rocky Mountain states, post-World-War-II land-use patterns, such as sprawl, are transforming classic 'Marlboro landscapes' and the character of rural towns and moderate-sized cities. Two distinct futures confront the American West. One future recalls John Wesley Powell's vision of sustainable development west of the hundredth meridian: growth should match the capacities of the landscape (Stegner, 1954). The second alternative is the prospect of continued sprawl with its accompanying economic and environmental costs.

The first wave of these new residents has landed in the major cities of the region such as Denver, Colorado and Salt Lake City, Utah, where jobs and housing are readily available. Yet many have been drawn to towns and areas of

People and Tourism in Fragile Environments. Edited by M. F. Price.

the West where they were first introduced to the benefits of Western life as tourists, in communities such as Santa Fe, New Mexico; Jackson Hole, Wyoming; Aspen, Colorado; and the Flathead Valley, Montana.

FROM TOURISM TO SECOND-HOME COMMUNITIES IN FLATHEAD COUNTY

Flathead County, Montana, 1.5 million ha (3.8 million acres) in area, epitomizes the 'neofrontier' of the American West. The county has changed from a drowsy outpost for loggers to a magnet for tourists, retirees and California refugees, and the population has swelled 14 per cent in the last decade. Second-home development cleaved farms that once produced mint, barley, and alfalfa into 20-acre 'ranchettes'. 'At risk is not just a quiet way of life, but some of the nation's purest water and air quality' (Leccese, 1994).

Flathead County, named after the Flathead Indians, is just south of the Canadian border (Figure 9.1). It contains half of Glacier National Park and Flathead Lake, the largest freshwater lake west of the Mississippi. The region's pristine mountains, valleys, and streams are home to approximately 64 000 residents and an increasing second-home population. The dramatic landscape, with award-winning fly-fishing streams, and broad, open valleys with prime agricultural land, has attracted numerous film producers who have shot films here. While Glacier National Park remains the largest tourist attraction, with 2.1 million visitors per year, resort towns, such as Whitefish and Bigfork, are becoming increasingly popular with tourists who are drawn by their small-town character, charming shops, restaurants, bed and breakfasts, and beauty of the West.

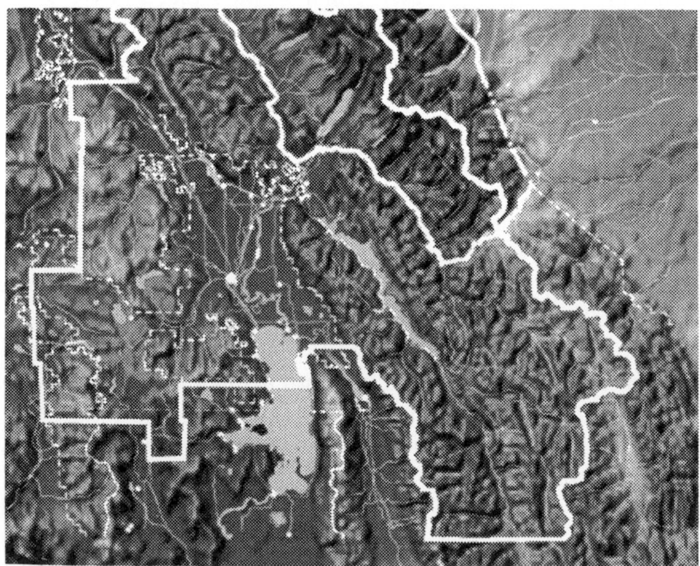

Figure 9.1 Map of Flathead County, Montana

Many of these communities, particularly the old mining towns, are enjoying real prosperity for the first time in a century. But current times are not without uncertainty. Many residents feel that the rapid growth of the last three years will continue unabated into the future, irrevocably changing the character of the Flathead Valley they love. Others are not convinced. Will the growth in Flathead County continue, or will the boom-and-bust cycle which has been the historic legacy of the West, reassert itself? Recent layoffs at Columbia Falls Aluminum and Stoltze Lumber, two of the major employers in the valley, only support such fears. As Paul Polzin, of the University of Montana Business Research Center, has stated, 'only in Montana would the last three years be considered prosperous', because the rest of the United States was suffering from a recession. Yet Tom Powers, economics professor at the University of Montana, has suggested that a new economic paradigm may be developing, in which the traditional economic base model is being replaced by an amenity-driven economic model (Leccese, 1994).

THE TOURISM INDUSTRY

Tourism is the fastest-growing industry in Montana. In 1991, approximately six million people visited Montana, with estimated visitor expenditures of $1.88 billion. According to state estimates, Glacier Country, which includes Flathead County, produced 31 per cent of all tourism expenditures in the state (Design Workshop, 1994c). It is estimated that 16 per cent of these expenditures are made in Flathead, Lake, and Lincoln Counties, although the area still lacks some of the components necessary to capitalize completely on its potential as an international destination resort (Design Workshop, 1994a). Major visitor attractions include Glacier National Park, the Bob Marshall Wilderness, Flathead Lake, the Big Mountain, and the Wild and Scenic River corridor on the Flathead River (Figure 9.2).

Table 9.1 Visitor industry revenue in Flathead County

Year	Expenditures for accommodation ($)	Total visitor expenditures ($)	Increase (%)
1987	7 259 350	42 702 059	N/A
1988	14 908 700	87 698 235	N/A
1989	16 898 450	99 402 647	13.3
1990	20 163 250	118 607 353	19.3
1991	23 764 375	139 790 441	17.9
1992	26 442 225	155 542 500	11.3
1993	27 165 475	159 796 912	2.7

Source: Institute for Tourism and Recreation Research, University of Montana

Figure 9.2 Flathead County's pristine mountains, valleys and streams are home to 64 000 residents and an increasing second-home population

Since 1987, the State of Montana has funded its travel and tourism promotion through a 4 per cent accommodation tax. This is a strong contributing factor to the growth of tourism in Montana, by providing a predictable revenue stream which allows for advertising and promotion. It also permits the calculation of the importance of the tourism industry to Flathead County, as the tax is 4 per cent of a visitor's lodging bill (whether hotel, motel, campground, or other accommodation), and research has shown that lodging costs consume only 17 per cent of the tourism dollar. Consequently, total visitor expenditures in Flathead County can be roughly calculated as shown in Table 1 (Design Workshop, 1994a).

The University of Montana's Institute for Tourism and Recreation Research has determined that visitor expenditures are distributed as follows: retail sales, 30 per cent; food service, 28 per cent; lodging, 17 per cent; gasoline, 14 per cent; incidental expenditures, 7 per cent; and transportation, 4 per cent. Similarly, based on the Institute's determination that, on a statewide basis, 24.4 per cent of visitor expenditures go into payroll costs, in 1993, tourism in Flathead County should have created $38 990 446 in wage and salary income: 19.7 per cent of the total private sector wages paid in the county for jobs covered by unemployment insurance (Design Workshop, 1994a). It appears, however, that the visitor-industry boom of the last several years is slowing. After four years of double-digit expansion, visitor expenditures in Flathead County increased only 2.3 per cent from 1992 to 1993. A continuing moderation of tourism growth can be anticipated (Design Workshop, 1994a)

However, the state-wide strategic plan notes that tourism overcrowding is perceived to be a problem in parts of Glacier Country. The Flathead County Economic Development Plan states that: 'the successful promotion of the state and specifically the Flathead has been met with some mixed reactions. Pride, cooperation and enthusiasm at the local and state levels are bumping heads with crying concerns by residents and visitors alike who want to maintain the quality of life and abundant natural resources which are the primary attraction of the area' (Flathead County, 1994).

SIGNIFICANT CHANGE

Regardless of one's position on the benefits or problems associated with current growth trends and the increasing tourism industry in the Flathead Valley, two facts are clear: significant change is taking place, and with change comes environmental and economic stress. Land that was once open space or used for agriculture is being converted to housing. Sales of subdivision lots have increased 15 per cent in one year. New construction requests almost doubled in the last two years. Access to traditional hunting and fishing grounds is being lost as private property owners exert their rights. School enrolment is up 12.4 per cent since 1988. Property taxes are skyrocketing. Former rural two-lane roads are becoming major four-lane highways. The traditional industries of forestry, mining, and agriculture are under assault.

These changes are placing extreme stress on the Flathead Valley and other communities of the intermountain West. Yet, ironically, when local residents are in greatest need of a process for dealing with these changes, they often find that traditional decision-making mechanisms of local, state, and federal governments are also undergoing dramatic change. While a rapid response is needed, these government institutions lack the ability to move quickly because of financial crises. Orders from Washington, DC, the State of Montana, and even the county seat are out of touch with residents' needs. In community after community, top-down planning has failed. There is a need for a new kind of decision-making process or processes. It must be born with the populace, the principle of empowering the people that is enshrined in the Montana Constitution:

> The people of Montana, grateful to God for the quiet beauty of our state, the grandeur of its mountains, the vastness of its rolling plains, and desiring to secure to ourselves and our posterity the blessing of liberty for this and future generations do ordain and establish this constitution.
>
> (State of Montana Constitution, cited in Kemmis, 1990: 5)

The context for planning, or rather the lack of planning, in the county and state is important to note. First, there is no county-wide zoning in Flathead County and many others in Montana. Second, there is a substantial lack of case law in land use-law in the State of Montana (Design Workshop, 1994b). These two issues became significant during the approval process of the master plan discussed below.

THE LARGEST PRIVATELY SPONSORED, PUBLIC PLANNING PROCESS

Flathead County has been one of the hottest real estate markets in the United States over the last three years. Growth has occurred so rapidly that it has outstripped the resources of county government and made ineffective the county's 15-year-old Master Plan (Flathead County, 1978). The quality of life and the beauty of the Flathead Valley were under siege by uncontrollable growth. While 70 per cent of the county is of such environmental importance that it is federally protected—and Glacier National Park has also been internationally designated as a Biosphere Reserve by UNESCO—the remaining area, which is historically pristine farmland and is the gateway to internationally known tourist destinations, is threatened by increased growth and development pressures. As a result, many local residents were deeply concerned about the changing landscape of their valley. The government of Flathead County did not have enough financial or staff resources to do the kind of visionary planning needed to guide future land-use decisions. As a result, the first known privately sponsored public planning process was born.

The need for a privately funded planning effort grew out of a lack of public funds to undertake an effort of this magnitude and out of the citizenry's general distrust of government's responsiveness to their needs. Some months earlier, the county commissioners had sought to impose interim zoning for all lands within the county. This attempt to impose planning on a top-down basis galvanized the public to action and, in autumn 1992, a diverse group of citizens—from timber company representatives to environmentalists and businesspeople—formed a grass-roots organization, the Cooperative Planning Coalition. Their goal was to develop a master plan to plan and guide growth in a sustainable manner. Support from the Flathead Valley community was overwhelming, resulting in over $350 000 in private donations to fund the project: a citizen-based, citizen-initiated, and overwhelmingly citizen-funded effort to chart a future course for the Flathead Valley.

The new plan was drawn up with exhaustive community participation, including volunteers ranging from realtors to natural scientists from the US Fish and Wildlife Service and Glacier National Park. Its difficult charge is to accommodate both preservation and development, a conundrum noted by Marilyn Wood, field representative for The Nature Conservancy: 'Some of the most critical sites for biodiversity are also prime places people want to live. Everyone wants a home on the waterfront or along a river.'

The Cooperative Planning Coalition grew out of these growth concerns threatening the quality of life and the environment in the Flathead Valley. The coalition was comprised of a multitude of local organizations and individuals, including business and industry groups, civic and service orders, environmental organizations, and interested citizens. Each of these groups was motivated by one or more desires: to simplify and streamline the local land-use approval process; to protect the natural resources and rural character of the valley; or to plan public facilities and services in a cost-efficient and proactive manner. Regardless of which of these three motivations was most important to the individual or group, they were bound together by a common belief that a clear future must be charted for Flathead County. They recognized the beautiful valley they call home as common ground.

Yet, at the same time, the public's general distrust of government also led to the growth of numerous militias and military groups. Unfortunately, they also distrusted planning, viewing it as a form of government which takes away individual's property rights. What these groups fail to recognize is that responsible, sensitive planning is critical to protecting and preserving the quality of life.

A process of community decision-making was needed which created a plan of, for, and by the people. It required a reawakening of citizenship, and the working of a participatory republic, which heeds the desires of the majority yet also respects the needs of the minorities. This is hard work. One cannot simply go to the county courthouse and complain about the latest top-down edict at a public hearing. Local citizens must roll up their sleeves, sit face to face, and resolve their differences as neighbours. In public meetings and private conversations, one often heard the belief that an individual's private rights end where his neighbour's begin. Montanans are certainly fiercely independent, but they know how to be good neighbours as well, as noted by Kemmis (1990: 20):

> The strengthening of political culture, the reclaiming of a vital and effective sense of what is to be public, must take place and must be studied in the context of very specific places and of the people who struggle to live well in such places.

How does one create a bottom-up planning process to meet local needs? First, begin by educating and informing the populace. Knowledge is power, and the dissemination of information should empower local citizens to make intelligent decisions:

> And say, finally, whether peace is best preserved by giving energy to the government, or information to the people. This last is the most certain, and the most legitimate form of government. Educate and inform to preserve peace and order, and they will preserve them . . . They are the only sure reliance for the preservation of our liberty.
>
> (Thomas Jefferson, cited in Kemmis, 1990: 2)

Design Workshop Inc., a landscape architecture and planning firm, was retained to complete the master plan for the entire county in 12 months. The planning process consisted of seven steps: 1) data gathering, 2) analysis, 3) developing plan alternatives, 4) public comment, 5) plan revisions, 6) plan adoption, and 7) code development (Figure 9.3). Although this programme is not unique, the grass-roots impetus for the project has resulted in an unprecedented, citizen-based planning process. For example, the plan was based on information generated during eight rounds of public meetings in ten neighbourhoods in the

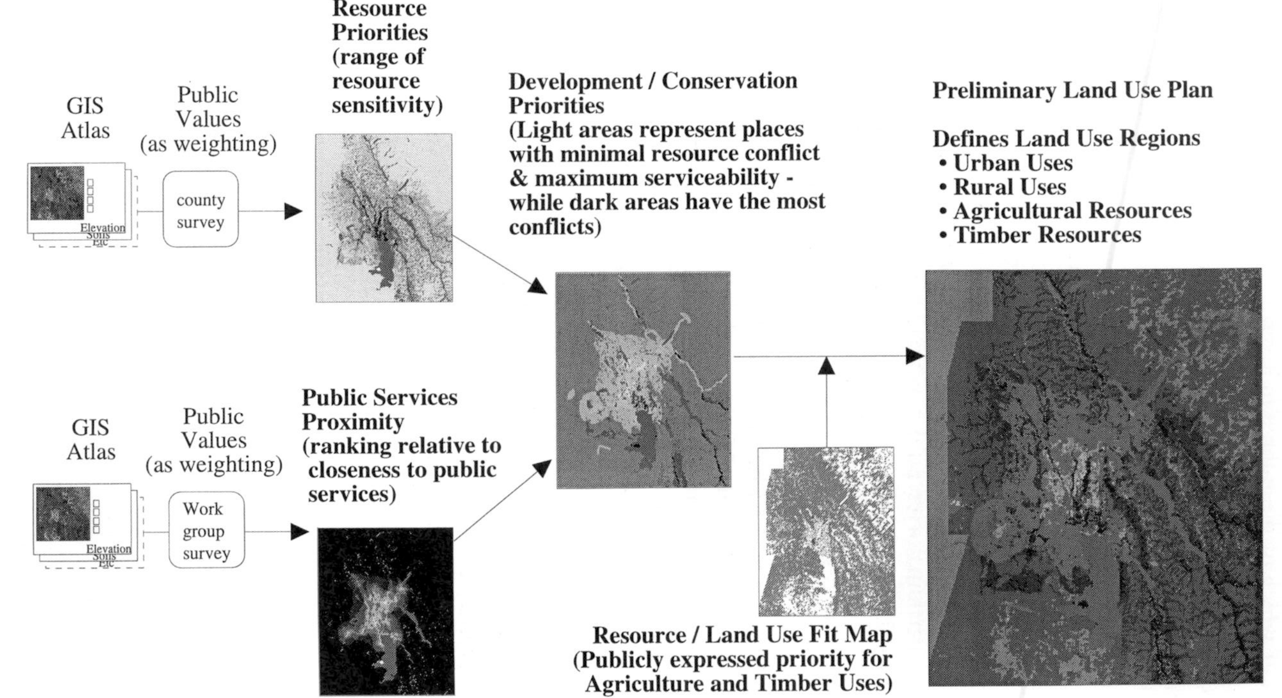

Figure 9.3 A Geographic Information System (GIS) database incorporated public values and was used to produce a county-wide land use plan

county, for a total of eighty public meetings. This approach allowed for the development of a county-wide master plan, while still providing a flexible framework within which neighbourhood plans addressed the specific needs of each area. As a result, information was generated in great detail and reflected individuals' unique views and concerns. In a county where there is such a spectrum of opinion on private property rights and environmental protection, this approach began to build community consensus.

QUALITY INFORMATION TO MAKE SUSTAINABLE DECISIONS: THE GIS DATABASE

The consultants played the roles of strategist, facilitator, coordinator and editor. Every month, team members spent a 60-hour week in the valley, interviewing local groups, meeting with each neighbourhood, and presenting current work products for public comment. Back at the office, the computer team developed an extensive computer-based Geographic Information System (GIS) database which comprised over a hundred base maps documenting both natural and man-made conditions.

The database, developed for all of the private and public land in the county, gathered enormous amounts of information on topics from vegetation, wetlands, and wildlife to transportation, utilities, and cultural and historic sites. Information on both public and private lands was gathered because of the close environmental and economic relationships between these land holdings. Wildlife obviously migrates freely regardless of ownership. Federal land policy on such issues as timber harvesting and ski-area expansion can have significant impacts on the local economy. Ironically, this comprehensive approach to planning went some way towards addressing the goals of two historically opposing political forces. By addressing public and private lands as a whole, the environmental community's desire for an ecosystem-management approach to land-use issues could be addressed (Figure 9.4). At the same time, the desire of the Wise Use Movement for local control over federal land-use issues could also be considered (Catron County, 1992).

The development of the database involved the National Park Service, the United States Forest Service, and several local agencies who will all be future users of this ongoing planning tool. For the first time, the county will have a document and database with which sustainable decisions for the future can be made, based on natural and cultural resources. In addition, the database was used to assist in analysing the comprehensive range of planning issues addressed in the plan. These included:

1 economic issues, such as the future of the timber industry, agricultural preservation, and diversification offered by the tourism industry
2 environmental issues, such as the protection of air and water quality, sensitive wildlife habitats, scenic areas and ecosystem management

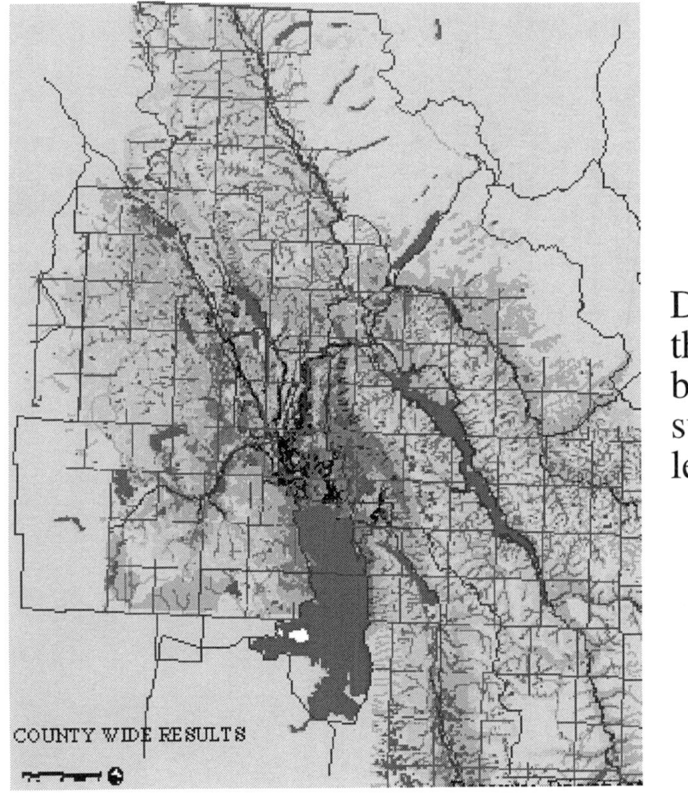

Figure 9.4 Public values obtained from a country-wide survey were used to rank resource conflicts. (darkest areas require the most protection, while light areas require the least protection)

3 development issues, such as the impacts of strip development, tourism and second homes and the need to protect private property rights
4 political issues, such as coordination with the Flathead Indian Reservation and establishing new forms and procedures of local government.

The plan's overriding theme was to create a socially, economically, and environmentally sustainable future that will be implemented as a model for gateway communities of the American West.

SETTING GOALS AND IDENTIFYING CONCERNS

The planning process began by asking the people of Flathead County in public meetings to identify their goals and concerns for the plan. The first phase of public involvement included over a hundred participants in goal-setting sessions in eight different neighbourhoods. In total, 435 goals were expressed by the public, with the following issues surfacing as the most important goals:

1 preserve the Flathead Valley's rural character
2 protect natural resources including air and water quality
3 plan for growth with creative alternatives
4 establish a diverse economy
5 protect private property rights
6 address current tax policy
7 provide for affordable housing.

Citizen involvement also played a critical role in research and analysis for the project. To ensure that database information was complete, accurate, and grounded in local knowledge, 25 work groups were assembled. The groups were comprised of local experts in fields such as ecosystem management, tourism, land-use law, demographics, affordable housing, transportation, and commercial and industrial development. Participation in the work groups served three main objectives. First, the group provided a forum where citizens throughout the county could discuss topics of county-wide concern, in many cases for the first time. Second, a framework was implemented for ongoing planning in each of these areas. Now that the master plan is complete, the work groups, or their successors, will remain to continue the planning effort. Third, alternative master plans were tested for their ability to meet the needs of each topic area before being reviewed by the general populace. The roles of the work groups will continue through plan adoption and they will be a key force in ensuring implementation of the community's goals. Other methods of public involvement included newsletters, radio and television interviews, and a land-use survey which was sent to every household in the county: 33 000 surveys were sent out and over 4000 responses were received.

These goals of positive public involvement was complicated by three major events. First, the passage of the Brady Bill. This was the first major piece of gun-control legislation in the United States by Congress, and resulted in the formation of armed militia in the county. Second, in the midst of the planning process, new property tax assessments were announced. Some homeowners say their taxes increased as much as 400 per cent. Third, the county government, without a process of extensive local involvement, enacted a county-wide building-permit system. For the first time, a new regulatory process and accompanying fee system was applied to all new construction. These three events helped to galvanize the will and encourage the organization of those opposed to expanded government activity. These actions further solidified the impression that the government was acting independently of the public's desires.

ALL POLITICS ARE LOCAL

Although the mandate of the Cooperative Planning Coalition was to develop a county-wide plan, it became quite evident that neither the average citizen nor a well-trained planning professional or environmental scientist can comprehend a landscape of 1.5 million hectares. For the process to be meaningful, it must be comprehensible to individual property owners, so that they can understand the impacts the plan will have upon their lives. They must be able to see the relationship their homes will have to their neighbours, and vice versa. The master plan had to have enough significance for each citizen to see it as a plan for action: to protect natural resources, develop a sustainable tourism industry, work for the improvement of public facilities and service, and build a diverse economy.

Repeatedly in the initial public meetings, there was a call to create a county-wide master plan tailored to meet the needs of individual neighbourhoods. The question then arose of how to define a neighbourhood to meet the needs of local individuals. Three criteria were utilized. First, attendees at the public meeting were asked to participate in a series of public meetings and to draw on maps what they perceived to be their neighbourhood. Second, existing jurisdictional and service boundaries were mapped. Tax appraisal districts, school districts, fire districts, water and sewer districts, zoning districts, postal delivery areas, telephone prefixes, municipal planning areas, census tracts, multiple-listing service areas, waste-management service areas, and utility service areas were all mapped in an effort to delineate areas of common interest. It became readily apparent why it is often said in Montana that 'never have so few been governed by so many'. Finally, physical features such as roadways, river channels, and mountain slopes were mapped. Together, these three groups of factors—cognitive boundaries, jurisdictional boundaries, and physical features—were used to roughly divide the county into neighbourhoods for discussion purposes (Figure 9.5). These 'fuzzy' boundaries, still incorporating enormous land areas, provide a way of making the plan cater to their neighbourhood. Thus there was a newfound respect for the statement by

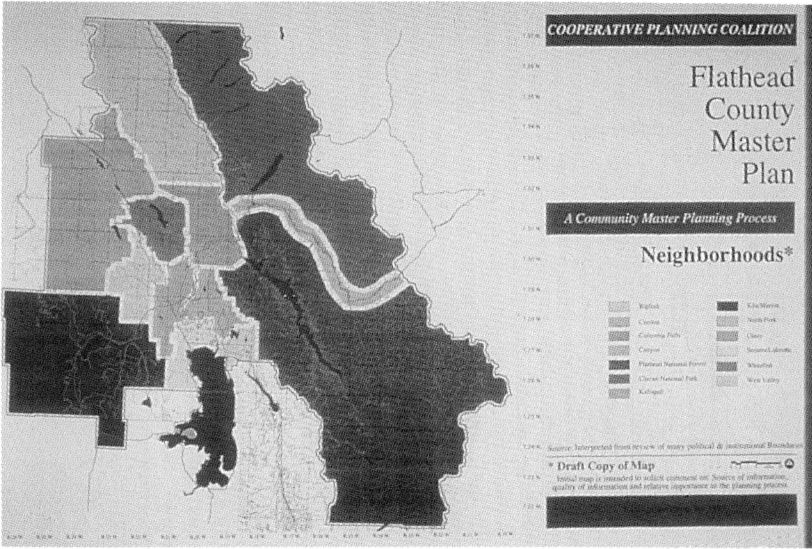

Figure 9.5 A neighbourhood map was developed from cognitive mapping, jurisdictional boundaries and physical features, providing a framework for decision-making

Tip O'Neill, former Speaker of the House of Representatives, 'all politics are local'. In the context of a county with rapidly urbanized areas, expanding tourist industries, and remote rural districts, these neighbourhood boundaries provide a framework for local decision-making.

FROM DEFINING ALTERNATIVE FUTURES TO AN IMPLEMENTATION STRATEGY

Once the general neighbourhood planning areas were identified, steps were taken to define alternative futures for each neighbourhood. What kinds of land uses do residents feel are appropriate for each area of the county? How can the tourism of the area best benefit residents? Should industrial development occur wherever the market dictates or be directed toward existing urban areas? What public facilities and services are required or desired by residents? Should these facilities be randomly dispeRsed throughout the neighbourhood or clustered in one or more centres? The arrangement of these public facilities will provide a framework around which residential, commercial, and industrial development can be built (Figure 9.6).

Once the general framework has been established, should housing development occur in all areas that the market dictates, or be at a density in keeping with the desires of local residents? What ultimate population is perceived as acceptable? What is the carrying capacity of the land? These questions were answered in a variety of ways. First, one can simply ask the populace: what

Combination of All Proximity Maps

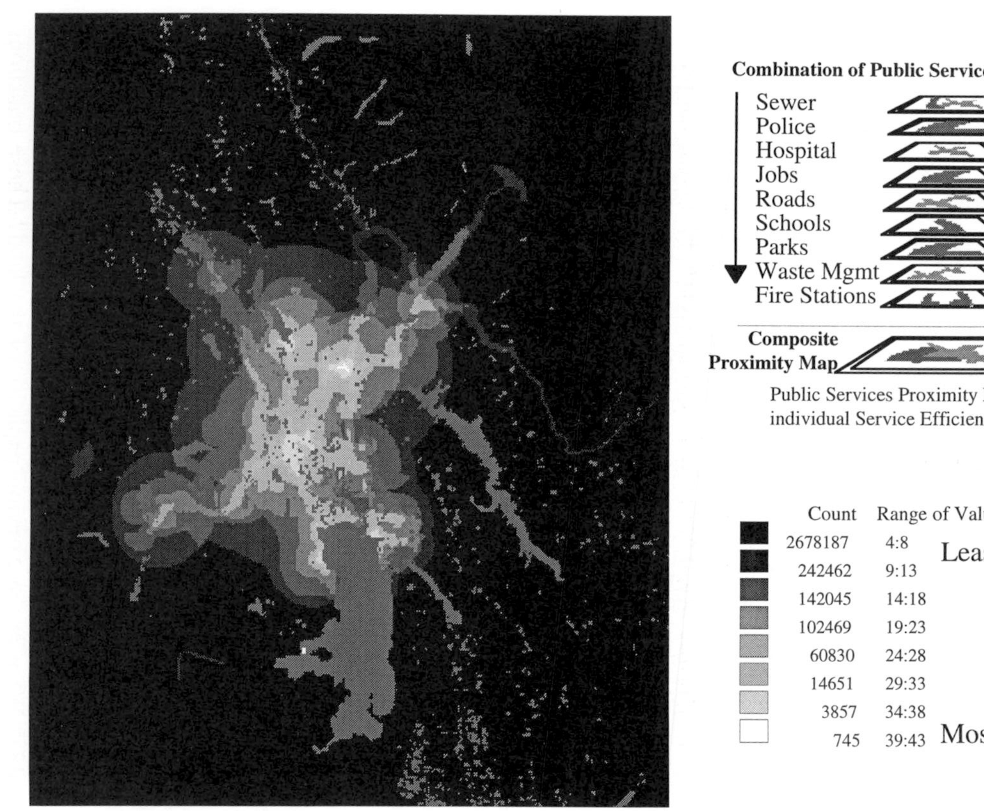

Figure 9.6 Services and utilities were mapped to allow for expansion of existing services to new development

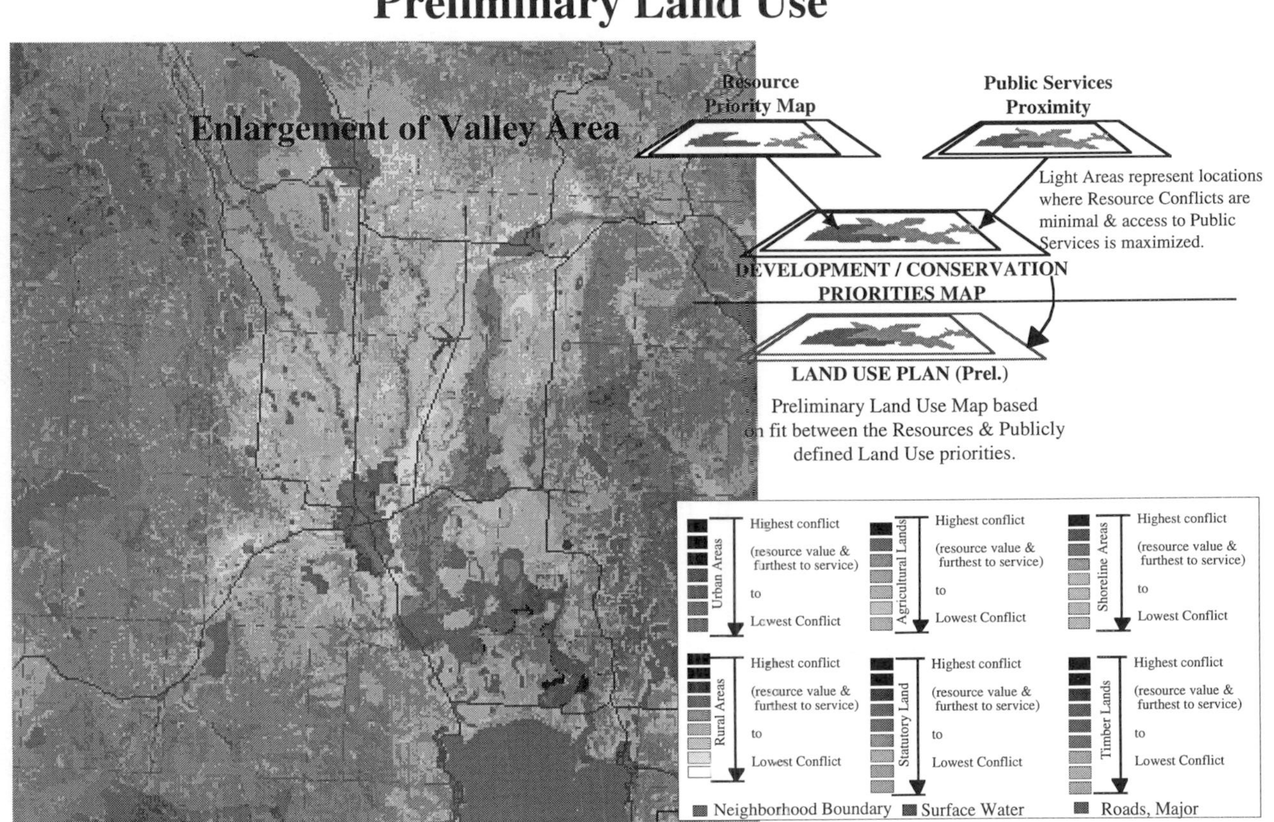

Figure 9.7 The preliminary land-use plan was developed by combining public input with resource priorities and public services

level of population can your neighbourhood support before the quality of life is irrevocably damaged?

Once the alternative futures were described on a neighbourhood basis, a best-case scenario was selected (Figure 9.7). To accomplish this, we helped citizens visualize the implications of their decisions. By generating a series of 'build-out' scenarios, residents can begin to understand the implications of their decisions. Is this the future that the people of Flathead County envision? The process of choosing between alternatives has been referred to as 'working through', as a community arrives at a common public judgement regarding a preferred alternative for its future (Yankelovich, 1991). The selection of an appropriate future was, in large measure, dependent upon how well citizens can realize these visions. By finding volunteers who allowed their land to be used as demonstration models, we could illustrate on a neighbourhood-by-neighbourhood basis how quality development is consistent with local residents' vision of the future.

With a vision described and illustrated, how then did we realize the vision? First, we compiled an inventory of all of the innovative tools available to the people of Flathead County. Second, all implementation techniques were considered. These included euclidean zoning, performance standards, purchase and transfer of development rights, rrban growth boundaries, development impact fees, growth management plans, and real estate transfer taxes—to name a few. After numerous public meetings and surveys, the chosen implementation method was a performance standards review system to be catered to each of the ten planning neighbourhoods (Figure 9.8).

IMPLEMENTATION OF THE MASTER PLAN

The recommended implementation programme included four major elements: performance review standards to create a review process in lieu of conventional Euclidean zoning; an agricultural protection programme; a forestry protection programme; and a series of amendments to existing rules and regulations to establish a better fit between existing codes and the goals of the master plan.

Both the agricultural and forestry protection programmes are non-regulatory in nature. Their aim is to recognize the importance of these economic and social activities for the preservation of the rural character of Flathead County and to create a policy framework to assure their long-term sustainability. These preservation programmes emphasize establishment of districts and notification procedures to ensure that new residents in the county are properly informed that they are locating next to either an agricultural management area or a timber management area. There are also recommendations for tax deferral and establishment of a purchasable development rights programme to be supported potentially with a real-estate transfer tax.

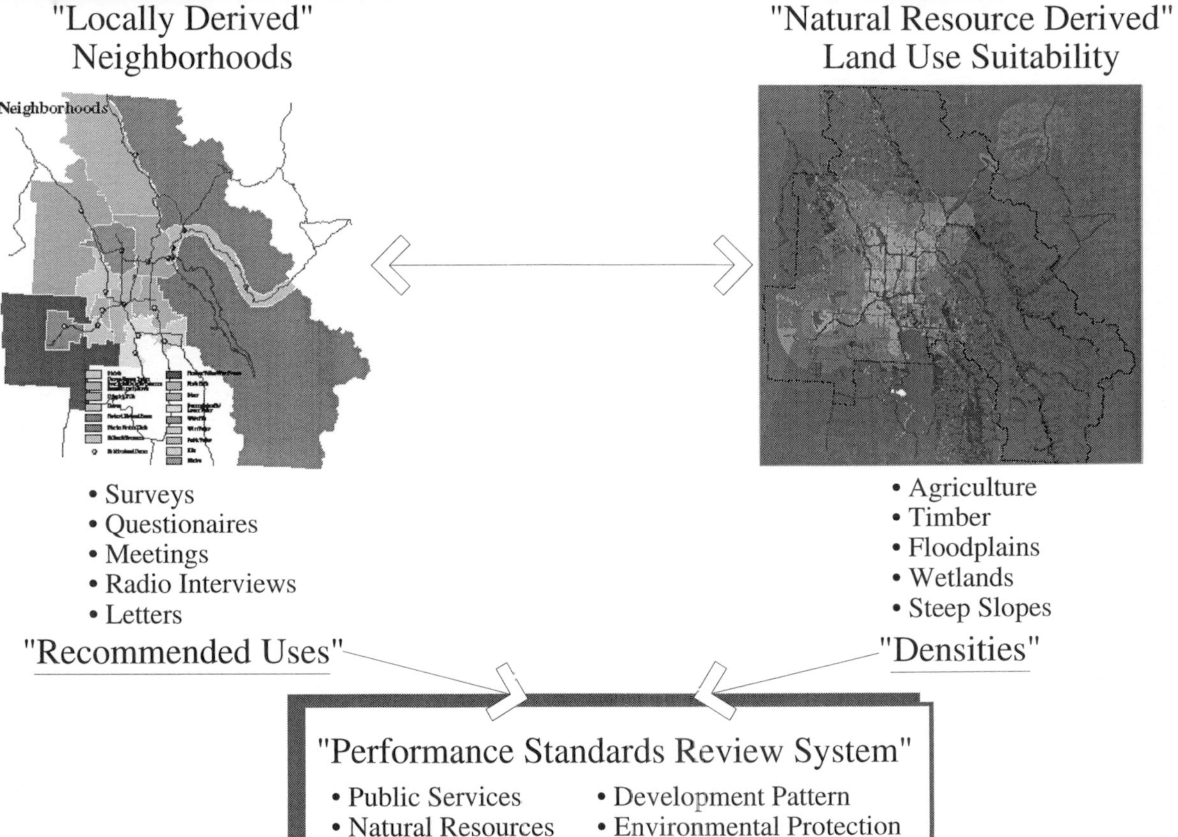

Figure 9.8 The implementation plan is a performance standards review system utilizing the land-use suitability assessment, and catering to the locally derived neighbourhoods

The performance standards review system acknowledges private property rights within the context of a review process which is neighbourhood-based. The system does not rely on conventional Euclidean zoning, such as maps, but rather says that you can do with your land as you see fit, as long as it does not have a negative impact on your neighbour or create an unfair economic impact on the balance of the citizens of the county. Within this system, ten neighbourhoods are created, with formal representation from each neighbourhood on the County Planning and Zoning Commission. The commission's composition is designed to allow decisions to be made as close to the ground as possible, and thus be responsive to local needs, while at the same time providing for a comprehensive county-wide view of land-use issues.

The ultimate result was the updated Flathead County Master Plan, containing community-generated tools to guide land-use planning decisions. The plan included the development of clusters to preserve agricultural land, a real-estate transfer tax, an increase in the use of land trusts, and a density bonus system compelling residents who petition for development to prove they have addressed resource-protection issues.

THE FUTURE OF FLATHEAD COUNTY

More than 80 public meetings were held, 165 community organizations contacted, 4000 surveys tabulated, and 800 Flathead County residents were sent monthly newsletters. The Master Plan was unanimously approved by the Flathead County Board of Commissioners, who set a 1996 date for a public vote to reaffirm the plan. While seen as a victory for the opponents of planning, this provision is ironically consistent with Design Workshop's own recommendation that the plan contain a 'sunset provision'. Under such a provision, the plan would expire unless reaffirmed by the county commissioners. This serves two purposes: to ensure constant citizen vigil so that the plan is regularly updated and relevant; and that the government bureaucracy remains consumer driven and responsive to the needs of the citizens. After the Board of Commissioners' approval opponents advocating protection of private property rights groups filed a lawsuit not only against the plan but all past and current planning efforts in the county. However, this was subsequently dropped, and the master plan will be voted on during the 1996 general elections.

The sheer size of the planning area and the enormous amount of public involvement in the master plan have established a new way for Americans to become involved and address the significant changes taking place in their communities during the resettlement of the American West. This grass-roots, bottom-up planning process is starting to find common ground in a land where once-rugged individualism is now seeking the advantages of cooperation and coordination.

MAKE NO SMALL PLANS

The preparation of a master plan for Flathead County was a monumental undertaking. The process was inspired by the planning techniques of Harvard's Carl Steinitz (1979), Lawrence Halprin's (1963) 'Take Part' workshops, the University of Pennsylvania's McHargian overlays (McHarg, 1969), and Design Workshop's own experience with Arizona's Verde River Greenway (Design Workshop, 1991).

As the great Chicago city planner Daniel Burnham once said: 'Make no small plans they lack the spirit to stir the hearts of men.' We know of no other situation in which a vast area in the throes of such change, with so many factors to consider, has launched such a citizen-initiated planning effort. The Flathead County Master Plan has captured the attention of the state and the nation, and is quickly being looked upon as a model planning effort by other Western communities that face similar change.

The successful completion of the plan required a major act of citizenship by every resident of the valley. It required the rigorous application of common sense in the context of quality information and a willingness to listen to the desires and concerns of your neighbours and to find common ground in a shared love of the land—a chance to create a society to match the scenery:

> Angry as one may be at what heedless men have done and still do to a noble habitat, one cannot be pessimistic about the West. This is the native home of hope. When it fully learns that cooperation, not rugged individualism, is the quality that most characterizes and preserves it, then it will have achieved itself and outlived its origins. Then it has a chance to create a society to match the scenery.
>
> (Stegner, 1954: 243)

REFERENCES

Catron County, 1992, Catron County Master Plan, Catron County, Reserve, New Mexico.

Design Workshop, 1991, Arizona State Parks: Verde River Greenway, Design Workshop Inc., Aspen.

Design Workshop, 1994a, Flathead County Master Plan Update Policy Document, Design Workshop Inc., Aspen.

Design Workshop, 1994b, Land Use Law White Paper, Flathead County Master Plan Update Resource Document, Design Workshop Inc., Aspen.

Design Workshop, 1994c, Tourism White Paper, Flathead County Master Plan Update Resource Document, Design Workshop Inc., Aspen.

Flathead County, 1978, Flathead County Master Plan, Flathead County, Kalispell.

Flathead County, 1994, Overall Economic Development Plan, Flathead County, Kalispell.

Halprin, L., 1963, Cities, *MIT Press, Cambridge.*

Kemmis, D., *1990, Community and the Politics of Place*, University of Oklahoma Press, Norman.

Leccese, M., 1994, Settling the Big Sky, *Landscape Architecture Magazine*, 84(6) (June 1994), 44–45.

McHarg, I.L., 1969, Design With Nature, The Natural History Press, New York.

Parham, D.W., 1994, Growth Issues in the Rocky Mountains, *Education Policy Forum Series No. 631*, Urban Land Institute, Washington D.C.

Stegner, W., 1954, Beyond the Hundredth Meridian, The Penguin Group, New York.

Steinitz, C.F., 1979, Predicting the visual quality impacts of development: A simulation of alternatives policies for implementing the Massachusetts Scenic and Recreational Rivers Act, paper presented to the National Conference on Applied Techniques for Analysis and Management of the Visual Resource, Incline Village, Nevada.

Yankelovich, D., 1991, *Coming to Public Judgment: Making Democracy Work in a Complex World*, Syracuse University Press, Syracuse.

10 Does our Community Want Tourism? Examples from South Wales

MARTIN FITTON

Tuesday April 5, 1870 broke cloudless after a sharp frost. For Reverend Francis Kilvert, the Curate at Clyro, the weather was sufficiently tempting for him to decide to walk from his home at the edge of the Brecon Beacons deep into Llanthony Valley to visit the Priory (Figure 10.1). On arrival, in the Reverend Kilvert's own words,

> What was my horror, on entering the Abbey, to see two tourists with staves and shoulder belts all complete posturing amongst the ruins in an attitude of admiration, one of them of course discoursing learnedly to his gaping companion and pointing out objects of interest with his stick. If there is one thing more hateful than another, it is being told what to admire and having objects pointed out to one with a stick. Of all noxious animals too, the most noxious is a tourist. And of all tourists, the most vulgar, ill bred, offensive and loathsome is the British tourist.
>
> (Plomer, 1980: 79)

These tourists had the additional impact of delaying Kilvert's lunch as they had ordered first at the Abbey Hotel, thus providing an early example of overcapacity. Kilvert returned to Clyro by way of Capel y Ffin, where he reflected on how William and Dorothy Wordsworth must have felt coming through the pass as they often did when visiting the Priory earlier in the century. However, he did not consider Wordsworth as a tourist; Wordsworth, who, for all his revolutionary democracy, had fulminated late in life at the Settle and Carlisle Railway invading his beloved Lake District to bring hoards of tourists from Manchester and afar: 'Is there no nook of ground secure from rash assault', he wrote (Croall, 1995: 39).

LLANTHONY VALLEY

For two centuries, the Llanthony valley has provided a microcosm of the problems and opportunities of rural recreation. In the last fifteen years, these continuing problems have been surveyed in some detail and indicate the friction that can occur when there are gulfs between visitors and the host population.

People and Tourism in Fragile Environments. Edited by M. F. Price.

Figure 10.1 Llanthony Priory, a tourist destination for two centuries

Llanthony valley, 55 km^2 in area, runs north–south on the eastern border of the Brecon Beacons National Park in South Wales. It is 12 km long from its southern entrance to its highest point (almost 800 metres) at Hay Bluff (Figure 10.2). The valley has a population of 240 people, of whom 40 per cent are members of farming families, 20 per cent from families with breadwinners who commute, and 20 per cent retired. The remainder undertake other work within the valley. Over the last two centuries, the area has seen a typical decline in the rural population: from 1841 to 1979, the population fell by 62 per cent, from 645 to 248 people (Grant, 1980). Subsequently, it has stabilized. The present economy remains frail, as it is largely dependent on agriculture. Only four families benefit directly from recreation, through hotel ownership or pony trekking.

The area's scenic grandeur, with its rich history, has attracted increasing recreational visits. It includes the twelfth-century Augustine priory at Llanthony, several important churches, a late Victorian monastery at Capel y Ffin, and the fact that the valley has an important place in cultural and literary history: the major estate in the valley was owned at the turn of the nineteenth century by Walter Savage Landor, the friend of Wordsworth (Drabble, 1985: 547); the monastery at Capel y Ffin was the home of the sculptor, Eric Gill, in the 1920s (Macarthy, 1994); and both Raymond Williams and Bruce Chatwin have drawn on the valley for their literary work (Williams, 1962; Chatwin, 1982). Despite this fine landscape and cultural richness, little attempt has been made to interpret the valley's history on-site.

The valley and its immediate surroundings offer opportunities for hill-walking

LLANTHONY VALLEY

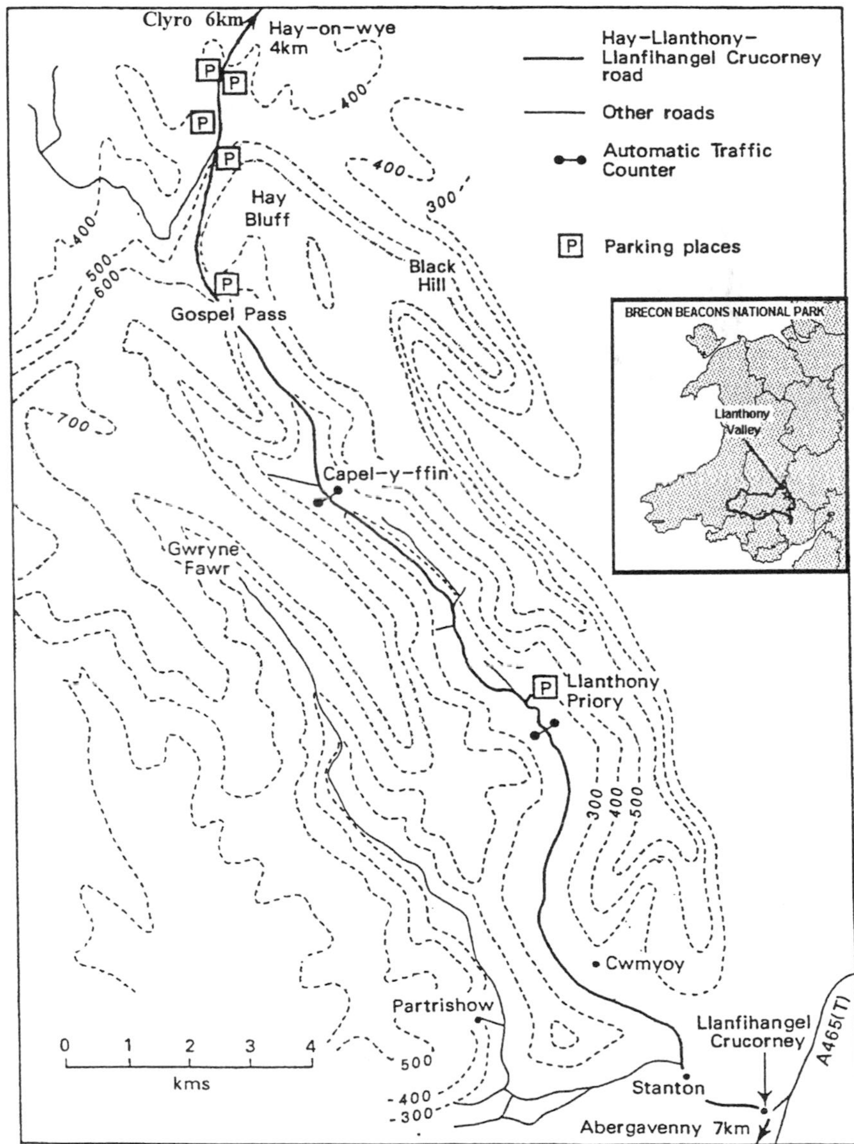

Figure 10.2 Map of the Llanthony Valley

and the Offa's Dyke National Trail runs along the ridge which forms the east side of the valley. Hang-gliding and mountain-biking are also becoming popular. From Abergavenny to Llanthony Priory, the valley road is of a reasonable width to bear the recreational traffic. However, the road beyond, through Capel y Ffin and northwards over the watershed at Hay Bluff, is barely three-and-a-half metres wide, and was surfaced only in the 1950s (Figure 10.3).

Figure 10.3 Llanthony valley road at Gospel Pass

RECREATIONAL USE OF THE VALLEY

Because of the pressure created by increased use of the valley by tourists, a detailed traffic survey was undertaken in 1978, with the objective of preparing traffic management schemes to match the capacity of the road. A survey of the attitudes of visitors and of residents to tourism was also undertaken. These surveys were repeated in 1992.

The traffic data for the 1978 survey were recorded by automatic traffic counters just south of Llanthony Priory and Capel y Ffin, and from roadside surveys undertaken on both weekdays and weekends. Use of this sub-standard road rose to just over 1400 vehicles in a 16-hour period on the May Bank Holiday, and on Sunday August 13th, the highest total of 113 travelling in both directions in one hour was recorded. Conversely, the lowest total for a 16-hour day was 120 vehicles on a weekday in May (Figure 10.4) (Gwent County Council, 1980). Over 95 per cent of the vehicles were travelling for the purposes of recreation, and three-quarters of the visitors were tourists coming from beyond the local area; more than half had not visited the area before. Most significantly, only 26 per cent of visitors interviewed had actually stopped in the valley at the Priory or on Hay Bluff. The remainder were using the road as a scenic through-route.

In addition to questions about their use of facilities, the visitors were asked

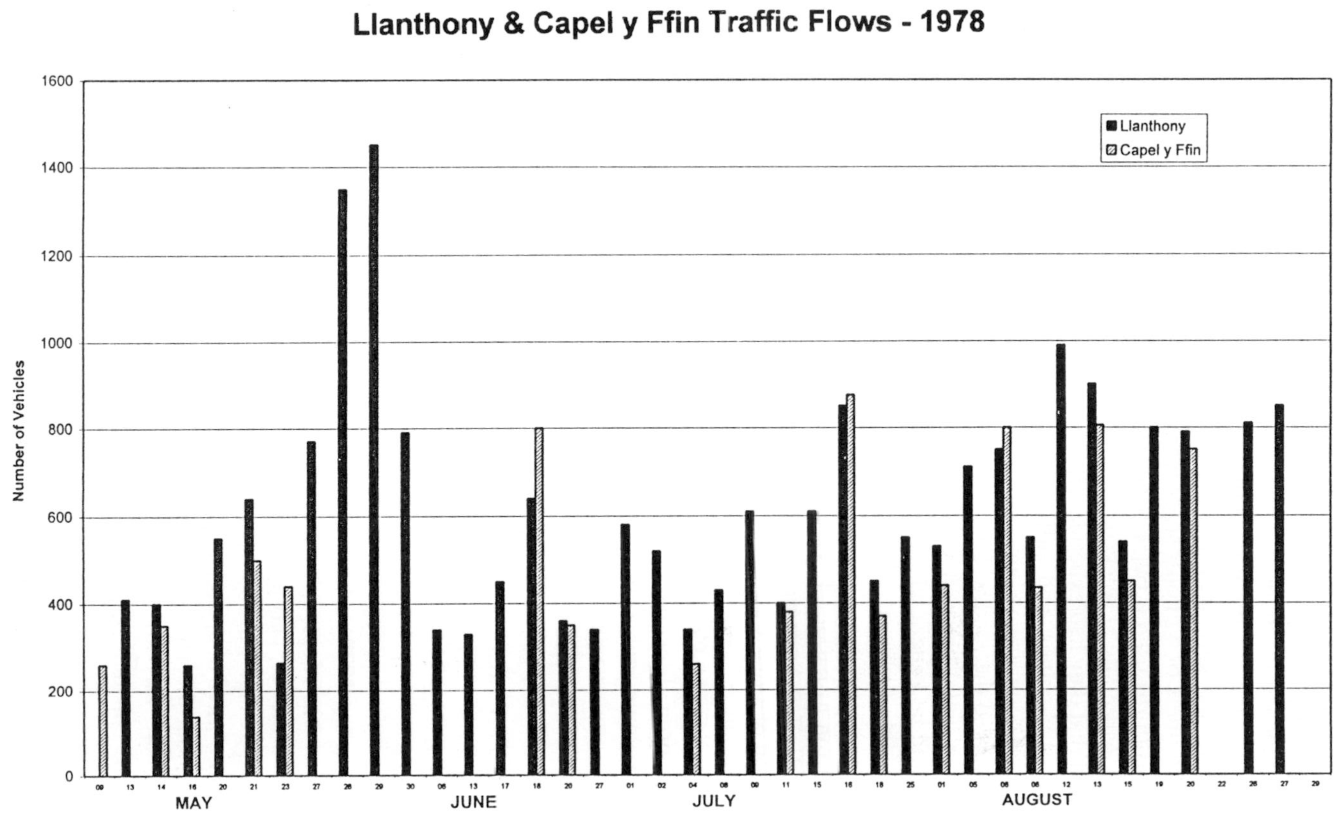

Figure 10.4 Traffic flows at Llanthony and Capel y Ffin, 1978

what they would do to improve the situation. They were sensitive in their response: though just under a third suggested that nothing needed to be done, half suggested that passing bays might be provided. Only 10 per cent wanted the road widened throughout, which is perhaps not surprising, given that this would destroy the quality of the valley which attracts visitors in the first place.

Alongside the survey of visitors, the views of the valley's residents were sought. Members of 42 households were questioned about their use of the road. Nearly two-thirds used it twice a day or more, and 80 per cent had been inconvenienced, especially at weekends and holidays in summer. Farmers specifically mentioned that they had experienced problems herding animals or moving large agricultural machines, and suffered from parking in gateways, disruption by pony trekkers, and from sightseers driving very slowly (Figure 10.5). Some 12 per cent wanted the road widened throughout, but more than four-fifths thought the problem could be resolved by additional passing bays. A third considered that it would be beneficial to close the road in busy periods. Not surprisingly, this latter option was not favoured by any of the visitors (Brecon Beacons National Park, 1980).

In addition to passing bays and the closure of the road between the Priory and Hay Bluff at busy times, a number of other options were considered: the introduction of a one-way system; restrictions on coaches, trailers and caravans; and the introduction of a toll system. In their assessment of traffic and management proposals, the County Highways staff concluded that 'Vehicle flows were negligible, even allowing for the condition of the road', and it was 'questionable on traffic volume such as this whether justification can be found for expenditure on road improvements on any large scale' (Gwent County Council, 1980). In their final recommendation, they suggested a least-cost solution.

The overall impression left by the 1978 survey was that, for most visitors to the valley, their use of it consisted of viewing the landscape through a car window—when not viewing the exhaust pipes of other vehicles. They were almost wholly unaware of the culture and heritage of the valley, and unaware of the impacts on, and concerns of, local residents. Equally, very few of the residents felt they benefited in any way from these visitors.

Following the 1978 survey and assessment of the results, only part of the least-cost solution was adopted, because of financial constraints. Three lengths of road, totalling 300 metres, between Llanthony and Hay Bluff were widened to provide passing places. Apart from this and the Warden for the area installing an informal sign which warned of congestion at peak periods, no other action was taken.

Throughout the 1980s, recreational use of the road remained heavy at peak periods. There was still congestion, and roadside verges and banks were damaged by the constant pressure of cars forced into the hedges as they squeezed past each other. As a result of this pressure, a series of unsightly informal passing places were created by cars, with eroded hedge banks and thick mud at the base. When questioned about these matters, residents indicated that they quite often deferred work journeys because of their perception of the long delays to

Figure 10.5 Pony trekkers on a narrow section of road just north of Llanthony; with two horses the road is blocked

which they would probably be subjected. The community's feeling of frustration was further increased by the deteriorating vitality of the farming economy. The locations of farms, the distribution of land, and the absence of alternative routes necessitated periodic movement of stock and farm vehicles on the public road. This was often impeded by recreational visitors, and the feeling of discrimination was increased by the fact that the cost of materials delivered to farms is higher than average, as smaller delivery vehicles have to be used because of the state of the road. At a public meeting in 1992, preparatory to further surveys, residents expressed a general view that tourism and visitors would bring little or no benefit to the area; an argument with both economic and environmental aspects.

In 1992, traffic in the valley was resurveyed. The results were not wholly comparable with the data collected in 1978, given the different data-collection periods. However, the data for August in the two years were comparable, showing a slight diminution in the amount of traffic. The average number of vehicles was 400 a day in August 1992, compared to 500 in 1978; north of Llanthony at the peak it rose only to 700, compared to 900 during 1978 (Figure 10.6). However, weekday traffic south of Llanthony was about 50 per cent higher than in 1978 (Moyes, 1992). Whilst a complete comparison is impossible, the relatively static pattern in the use of the valley which the data suggest is in line with national surveys of countryside recreation during the 1980s. However, the resi-

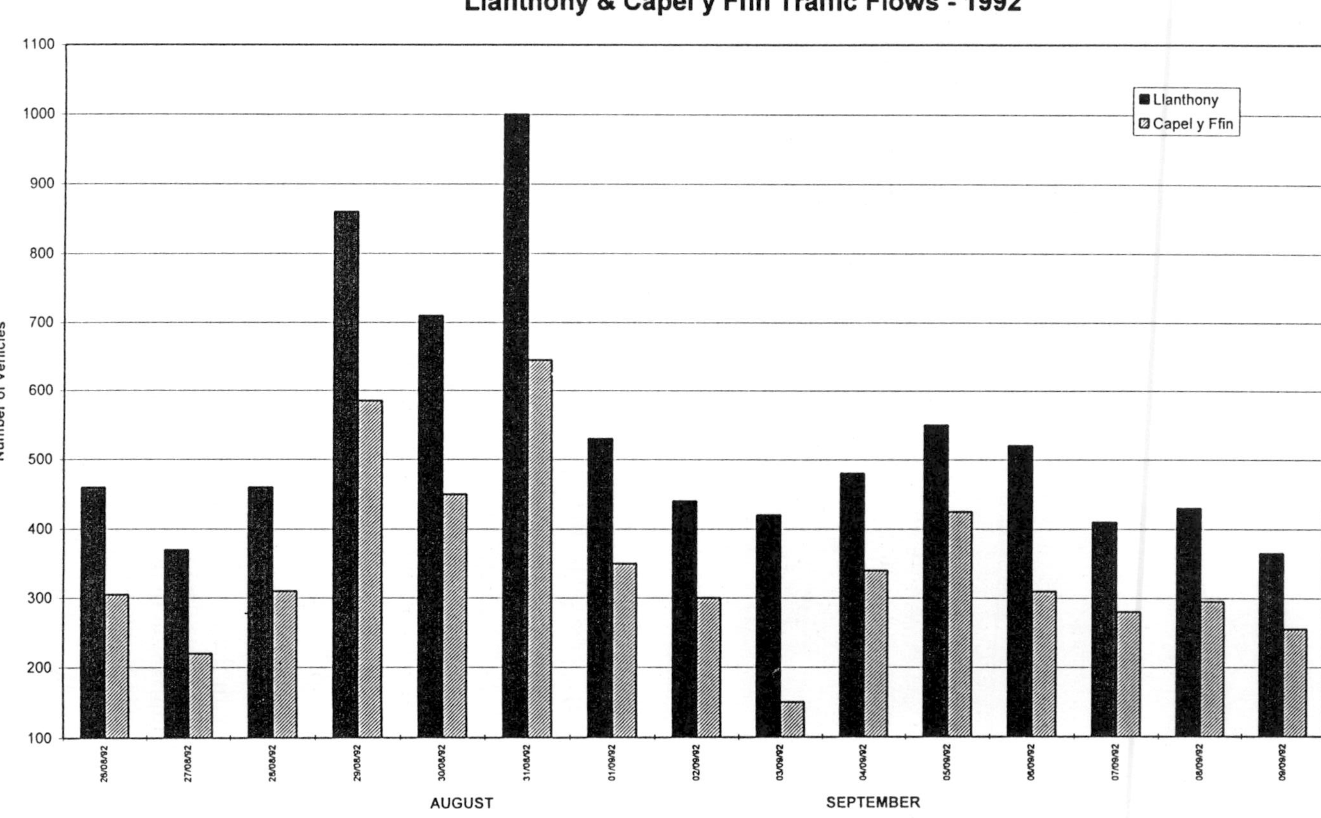

Figure 10.6 Traffic flows at Llanthony and Capel y Ffin, 1992

dents of Llanthony Valley did not see this as a consolation. There was an anecdotal view that cars were bigger; as one resident said, 'They used to come in Minis and now they drive Volvos.'

Equally marked was a continuing picture of the majority of visitors simply using the valley as the venue for a pleasure drive. Over 65 per cent of visitors on the 1992 August Bank Holiday did not stop whilst passing through the valley, and thus provided no recompense for the disruption they caused to the community. Of those who stopped at the Hay Common car park, two-thirds barely left their vehicles. The majority of these stopped to buy ice cream; if the ice-cream van had not been there, they probably would not have stopped. Of the remaining third, half managed a short walk of less than 100 yards to peer at the view before returning to their cars.

In microcosm, therefore, the Llanthony Valley exhibits all that is problematic about tourists' use of the place they visit. Over an extended period, residents in the valley have suffered disruption to their daily lives; only a minority have benefited from tourism. Not only is this economic benefit to the valley extremely small, but it is provided by a minority of those who use the valley as visitors. For the majority cocooned in their motor cars, the experience is one of pleasure motoring, which leaves them with no understanding of the community through which they are passing and the impact they are having on it. In summary, the balance between the visitor, the place, and the host community has broken down. As noted elsewhere with regard to sustainable tourism in protected areas, 'Traffic congestion is usually the first and most obvious sign of imbalance, initially disrupting local road networks, causing visual intrusion and at certain peak times, resulting in complete immobility' (Aitchison and Beresford, 1992: 9).

HOW TO INVOLVE THE COMMUNITY?

The issue is whether the impact of tourists on the communities they visit can be reduced, and the benefits increased. To do this requires engaging the attention of the local community in an activity so that they see it as ultimately to their benefit, and adding to the quality of life through their interchange with the tourists. How might residents be engaged in the development of tourism? British democracy does not continuously engage or encourage people in effective control of decisions about their own communities. This leads to both the frustration and the inertia that have been evident in the Llanthony valley.

A number of techniques have been used to involve communities more closely in decision-making about the use of their areas. The 'local jigsaw' approach (Greeves and Taylor, 1987), which encourages communities to ask questions about themselves and their aspirations as the basis for practical action, is now a well-tested tool. Across the United Kingdom, many communities have assessed their needs and developed programmes which draw on the points of consensus in their communities. This approach has been used elsewhere in South Wales, as described below.

Figure 10.7 Local residents at a 'Planning for Real' meeting in the Brecon Beacons National Park

In Llanthony Valley, the National Park Authority has used a slightly less direct technique called 'Planning for Real' (Neighbourhood Initiatives Foundation, 1995), as the basis for preparing the National Park Local Plan, in which policies for tourism have a central place (McGhie, 1994, Tawdwr-Jones, 1995). The technique is designed to involve all residents in a community, rather than an active, vociferous minority, in the planning process. The process involves bringing the community together before any part of the plan is written. These meetings have been described as a planning 'bring and buy' sale where, after the shortest of introductions by planners, the meeting becomes that of the community rather than the planners, with an exchange of ideas between residents being the main driving force. To focus issues, large-scale maps of the area are provided, into which residents place colour-coded pins to indicate, for instance, where new housing should go, where industry is needed, and where tourists are making a nuisance of themselves (Figure 10.7). At the end of this session, a detailed round-table discussion takes place. During this, because of the informal nature of the meeting, all are encouraged to participate and many do. This creates a cogent statement of community needs, better to inform the planning process.

In Llanthony Valley, the Planning for Real meetings helped to re-identify the issues. As could be expected given the history of tourism in the valley, everybody in attendance indicated they wanted no more tourism. Discussion took place about disruption and possibilities of closing the road with Traffic Regulation Orders, instituting one-way systems, and providing minibus services. The meetings also considered the possibility of increasing the benefits from tourism by improved interpretation of the many features in the valley and seeking to link this to a tourism package, developed by the community, which would attract longer-stay visitors to the valley. However, since the majority saw tourism as generating a limited benefit, the exercise has not yet provided the basis for greater action. This is compounded by the lack of suitable accommodation and the fact that the fluctuating nature of recreational use of the valley does not justify expenditure on the traffic management schemes that might alleviate congestion.

If the Planning for Real technique has not provided a basis for action in the Llanthony Valley, it has provided the opportunity for the community to clearly state its concerns. In the short term, a number of ameliorative measures have been taken, including the removal of signs which indicate the valley is a through route; and discussion has continued about signing to re-emphasize the potential for congestion in the valley. In the end, signs might be erected saying very explicitly 'Sorry Llanthony Valley is full'. Clearly, if communities do not want to be involved in tourism it is difficult and counter-productive to insist.

IS COMMUNITY TOURISM A REAL OPTION?

In some communities, such as Llanthony, the process of community involvement clearly emphasizes the community's view of the limited utility of tourism for their economy. In other communities, community involvement is providing the basis for new tourism initiatives which properly integrate the needs of the local community and visitors to the benefit of both. One such example can be found west of the Brecon Beacons in Pembrokeshire. The South Pembrokeshire Partnership for Action with Rural Communities (SPARC) is a community development project based on Narbeth and 36 neighbouring communities in Dyfed (Figure 10.8). Apart from its coastal fringe, this area had a limited tourism base despite a beautiful countryside and an interesting history. The area straddles the Landsker boundary, which marks the division between the English and Welsh created by the Norman invasion in the eleventh century. The Landsker borderland provides the foundation for the tourism promotion.

The SPARC area is much larger than Llanthony Valley, covering 400 km^2, of which 40 per cent is within the Pembrokeshire Coast National Park. The area, like Llanthony, exhibits many of the problems of rural areas. Income is 75 per cent of the European Union average, and the unemployment level is 16 per cent. Compared to Llanthony, a smaller proportion of the population—only 8 per cent—is involved in agriculture. Though the whole area is much larger, with a comparably greater population of 23 000, the individual communities are very similar in size to Llanthony, and the tourist projects are keyed to those communities (Asby, 1995).

The SPARC initiative has been sustained by a range of grant aid. Most significantly, the SPARC area has been designated a LEADER area under the

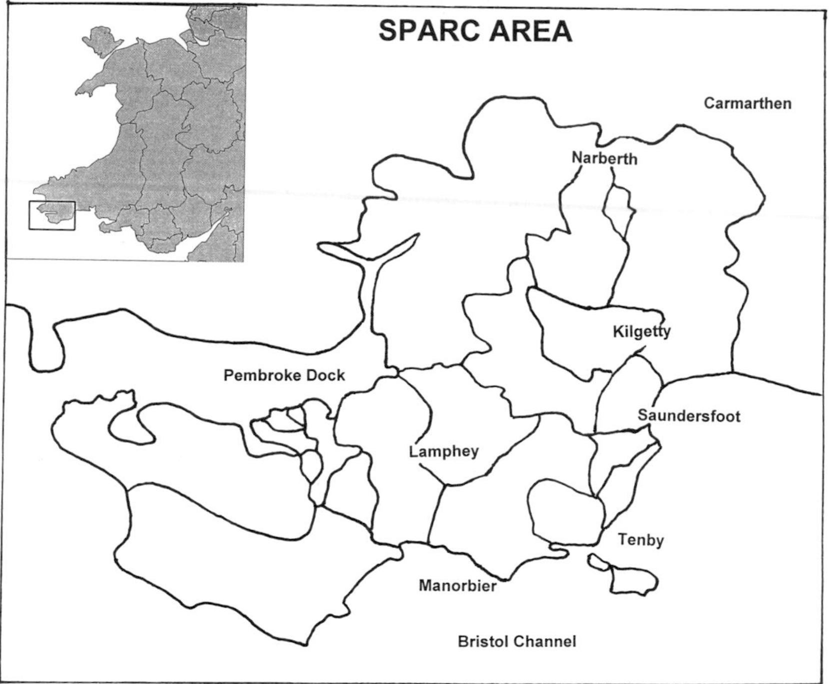

Figure 10.8 Location map of South Pembrokeshire Partnership for Action with Rural Communities (SPARC) area

European Union initiative designed to capitalize on local experience and economic opportunities. The quality of community tourism that has been developed was recognized by the British Airways UK 'Tourism for Tomorrow Award' for sustainable tourism in 1994. SPARC has promoted a quality tourism product based on the people of the area, and their culture, countryside, heritage, and cuisine. The aim is to provide a sophisticated experience for tourism, not to equate rural with rustic. The modern visitor is looking for quality; a prerequisite for successful community tourism.

In developing the tourism initiative, the involvement of the local community is paramount. Within the SPARC area, each village has its own local community association, to which all residents are entitled to belong and which has established community needs through a process of community appraisal. This is a questionnaire survey of householders carried out by local people. The analysis of this stocktaking forms the basis for future action. It helps identify issues that are important to an area, highlights the needs of the community, and pinpoints opportunities for improvement. The appraisal leads to the production of an action plan. The technique has been promoted by countryside agencies in Wales and England and has done much to increase community involvement in issues like tourism (Greeves and Taylor, 1987). In the SPARC area, this technique has been used to prepare action plans for every community. Most of these plans have a tourism component.

To aid implementation of proposals in the action plans, the local associations appoint representatives to sit on the management committee of SPARC and five working parties on agriculture, community, countryside, business, and tourism. This approach gives everyone in the community an opportunity to participate, and encourages them to think in depth about local issues and the environment. Over a thousand people regularly and actively work with SPARC for the benefit of their communities.

In their action plans, most communities identified tourism as a potential economic opportunity. Their preferred form of tourism is non-intrusive, based on the natural resources of the area, and its landscape, heritage, and culture. Working on this base and by focused use of resources and training, local buildings, some of which were redundant, were identified and refurbished, not only for tourism use but also providing environmental benefits. In addition, most of the communities researched and published a local heritage leaflet, which identified the aspects of their community which, as residents, they especially valued and wanted tourists to enjoy. The central support team provided by SPARC undertook work on the infrastructure, footpaths, and routes that linked sites, creating over 350 km of linked and waymarked footpaths (Figure 10.9). Small-scale tourism information points have been established in 24 village shops and post offices across the area, providing an effective system for presenting information to tourists while helping to supplement the income of these rural businesses.

This type of tourism provides immediate benefit to the local community by giving residents the opportunity to influence and become involved in tourism developments. It provides social and recreational environmental amenities for both locals and visitors, and develops employment opportunities for local people with limited leakage of finance from the area. In summary, all these gains come from a general philosophy in which:

1 local produce is used wherever possible
2 the majority of visitors stay in locally owned and managed accommodation
3 visitors spend their days within the area
4 the service sector is locally owned
5 local manufacturers are encouraged to tap the tourist market for gifts, souvenirs, crafts and other projects.

IS COMMUNITY TOURISM SUSTAINABLE?

The contrast between SPARC and Llanthony is clear. Llanthony is a host community which is an unwilling recipient of visitors who understand little about the area through which they are passing and the disruption their visits are causing. In contrast, the communities of the SPARC area have been directly involved in the development of new tourist opportunities, with the result that the

Figure 10.9 Dutch tourists on the Landsker path at Llawhadden in the SPARC area

area has not only benefited economically, but also achieved a widespread community commitment to tourism.

The experience of these two areas is typical of Wales and, no doubt, of other areas which host tourists. A survey of residents in three tourist areas (Llanberis, Newcastle Emlyn, and Rhondda) by the Wales Tourist Board showed that, whilst a distinct minority of respondents identified problems with tourism, the majority welcomed tourism because it could make a positive contribution to community life. Significantly, the problems most frequently identified by those opposed were traffic congestion, over-capacity, and damage to the environment (Wales Tourist Board, 1988). Few of those interviewed felt that tourism directly undermined local culture and language. This suggests that, with sufficient involvement, the local community will feel that their culture is being valued. This has led the Wales Tourist Board to recommend that community involvement becomes a foundation for a Welsh Tourist Strategy (Wales Tourist Board, 1993). The techniques developed by SPARC show the way.

Community tourism is now sufficiently developed to be promoted through training packs and enshrined in good-practice guidance issued by the Tourist Boards. Community tourism not only benefits the population and local economy, but is also more likely to be environmentally sustainable. Use of local products, the focusing of all holiday activities within a small area, and the encouragement of walking and other benign forms of transport all reduce energy use. In addition, the close involvement of the local community helps them manage the potential for over-capacity that can lead to environmental damage.

The wide consensus on the need for sustainable tourism keyed to community needs is evidenced by the fact that the majority of tourist boards have policies for sustainability; for example, the Wales Tourist Board: 'the Board's policies recognize that the resources upon which tourism depends are finite and can be fragile. It is important that the character and scale of development be such that our assets are not diminished in the longer term'(Wales Tourist Board, 1993).

Given the self-evident ability of tourism to damage the Earth (Croall, 1995), sustainable tourism is clearly an idea whose time has come. Yet, although there is widespread consensus on this topic, it remains largely as an aspiration rather than providing the general framework for tourism. Tourism is a huge global industry: 'If tourism was a country it would be the third richest on earth' (Sykes, 1995: 14). It also presents a significant problem in energy consumption, as it requires people to be transported over long distances for enjoyment. The energy used to move people to tourist destinations is enormous.

Given the scale of tourism and its use of resources, a change to a more sustainable mode will be difficult. In all tourist areas, much greater emphasis needs to be given to communities and the environment. There needs to be a turn from the provision of mass tourism to the establishment of local tourism, based on local economies and minimal flows of energy. The re-establishment of these local economies must be at the heart of any global move towards a more sustainable use of resources in tourism, as in other economic activities.

Community tourism seeks to fit tourism with the needs and aspirations of host communities in a way that is acceptable to them, sustains their economies rather than the economies of others, and is not detrimental to their culture, traditions or, indeed, their day-to-day convenience. It starts from the existing resources, in terms of the skills of that local community, and of buildings that can be re-used. All these resources must be assessed before thinking about new investment. However, we cannot assume that we have achieved anything if sustainable community tourism is simply an oasis in the huge desert of mass tourism, which is not sustainable.

Sustainability is indivisible. It means that we must look at tourism as a local product, and that people should be encouraged to move short rather than long distances and to consider whether there are really benefits of visiting more and more exotic locations. We might encourage a 'tourism begins at home' movement. Whether this can be achieved remains to be seen, but it is ultimately the only supportable way forward. Perhaps large signs promoting 'tourism begins at home' should be placed at airports so that all those flying to distant and exotic destinations will get the message. Many of us understand and have a conscience about what we do to the environment. Yet, individually and collectively, day by day, we continue to damage and destroy it.

REFERENCES

Aitchison, J. and Beresford, M., 1992, Sustainable Tourism in Protected Areas: Towards Principles and Guidelines, in International Centre for Protected Landscapes (ICPL), *Sustainable Tourism in Protected Areas*, ICPL, Aberystwyth.

Asby, J., 1995, *The SPARC Experience in Developing a Quality Tourism Product*, SPARC, Narberth.

Brecon Beacons National Park, 1980, *Survey of Local Road Users Concerning Traffic Problems in the Llanthony Valley*, Brecon Beacons National Park, Brecon.

Chatwin, B., 1982, *On the Black Hill*, Jonathan Cape, London.

Croall, J., 1995, *Preserve or Destroy: Tourism and the Environment*, Calouste Gulbenkian Foundation, London.

Drabble, M., 1985, *The Oxford Companion to English Literature*, Oxford University Press, Oxford.

Grant, R.L., 1980, *Depopulation in the Honddu Valley, 1840–1979*, Social Science Research Council, Final Report H6650.

Greeves, T. and Taylor, R., 1987, *The Local Jigsaw: An Information Pack on Village Appraisals and Parish Maps*, The Countryside Commission and Development Commission for Rural England, Cheltenham.

Gwent County Council, 1980, *Llanthony Valley: Report of Survey*, Report B4423, Gwent County Council, Cwmbran.

Macarthy, F., 1994, *Eric Gill*, Faber, London.

McGhie, C., Powys to the People, *The Times Magazine*, 21 May 1994.

Moyes, A., 1992, Recreational Travel in the Llanthony Valley, in International Centre for Protected Landscapes (ICPL), *Sustainable Tourism in Protected Areas*, ICPL, Aberystwyth, 31–53.

Neighbourhood Initiatives Foundation (NIF), 1995, *Working with Communities*, NIF, Telford.

Plomer, W., 1980, *Kilvert's Diary, Volume 1*, Jonathan Cape, London.

Sykes, L., 1995, The Holiday Crowd, *Geographical*, 67(2), 14–15.

Tawdwr-Jones, M., 1995, Brecon Beacons Planners Get Real in Rural Plan Consultation, *Planning*, 3 February 1995, 1104–1105.

Wales Tourist Board, 1988, *Study of the Social, Cultural and Linguistic Impact of Tourism in and upon Wales,* Wales Tourist Board, Cardiff.

Wales Tourist Board, 1993, *Tourism 2000: A Strategy for Wales*, Wales Tourist Board, Cardiff.

Williams, R., 1962, *Border Country*, Readers' Union, London.

11 The Challenge of Integrating Maasai Tradition with Tourism

DHYANI J. BERGER

INTRODUCTION

'Ilaretok lo inkishoronot e Nkai'—the Keepers of God's Creation—is the name given to Maasai conservation action leaders working in the rangelands below Mount Kilimanjaro. Who could be better suited as partners in conservation than the indigenous peoples who have coexisted with wildlife and natural ecosystems for millennia? The greatest opportunity for nature tourism in Maasailand is to develop a partnership with the people whose pastoral traditions make them 'natural ecologists', whose land use and cultural tradition can teach much about sustaining natural resources and livelihood (Homewood and Rodgers, 1991).

Maasai tradition, like other traditions, is a dynamic phenomenon that evolves to adapt to new circumstances and includes a set of values and practices that is associated with a particular way of life. It embodies an intimate knowledge of land, natural resources, and climate. The Maasai have long been masters at manipulating their environment to sustain livestock, their primary source of livelihood. Their use of the range has followed the movement patterns of many species of wild herbivores. Aspects of Maasai communal social organization, their production system, and their culture are valuable human resources that can be a foundation for a modern livelihood which integrates livestock keeping with wildlife management and tourism.

Wildlife-based tourism is Kenya's most valuable industry, bringing in considerable direct or service-linked local employment and foreign exchange earnings (Gakahu and Goode, 1992). Visitor numbers increased from 36 000 in 1955 to 805 000 in 1991. Over the same period, tourism income grew from 80 million to 11.8 billion Kenya Shillings. Wildlife tourism, much of it based in Maasailand, accounts for 40 per cent of the Kenya's earnings from tourism (Western, 1992). The majority of tourists to wildlife destinations visit the parks in Maasailand at Nairobi, Maasai Mara, Amboseli, and Tsavo West. Yet, until recently, the participation of the Maasai in the tourist industry, as managers or beneficiaries, has been minimal. This is changing, as tourism responds to issues

People and Tourism in Fragile Environments. Edited by M. F. Price.

of environmental impact, sustainability, and the need for more equitable sharing of benefits. Community education and activism, changes in national wildlife management policies, and new forms of tourism mean that the Maasai are now beginning to take control of and benefit from resources that are rightfully theirs.

THE MAASAI: THEIR LAND AND LIFE TODAY

The Maasai are the best-known of about ten pastoralist groups in Kenya. They are an 'Eastern Nilotic' people (Ehret, 1974) who have occupied the Great Rift Valley of Kenya since the fifteenth century. By the mid-eighteenth century, diverse, usually autonomous and geographically separate Maasai groups or sections *(iloshon)* were united through the vision of the great *Laibon* (diviner and ritual expert) Batian, occupying a huge territory which extended from northern Kenya into the central rangelands of Tanzania. However, severe drought, famine, and disease drastically reduced their population and livestock at the end of the last century, and over the last hundred years they have lost much of this territory (Figure 11.1). Controversial treaties with the British in 1904 and 1911 removed them from parts of the Rift Valley and their northern grazing lands to make way for colonial settlement. In 1904, with the building of the railway between Mombasa and Kisumu on Lake Victoria, the Maasai were compelled to vacate the highlands along the railway as it traversed the Rift Valley, so that the Maasai territory was divided into southern and northern reserves. Although the 1904 Treaty included a written guarantee to respect indefinitely Maasai rights, the second treaty, negotiated with some leaders in 1911, evicted the Maasai from their northern highland reserve (Sanford, 1919; Tignor, 1976; Ole Parkipuny, 1988).

Today, with less land, the Maasai are changing their pastoralist way of life. For many, their values and practices now have more in common with the culture and way of life of Kenya as a nation. They are intermarrying, adopting the languages and livelihoods of neighbouring groups, and participating in national development programmes. An estimated population of 400 000 live in four districts of Kenya: Kajiado and Narok on the Tanzanian border in southwest Kenya; Transmara, north of the Maasai Mara Reserve; and Laikipia, where a small community represents the Maasai who once occupied north-central Kenya (Figure 11.1). All these districts, with the exception of Transmara, are primarily arid or semi-arid rangelands (ASAL) (Braun, 1982). Within these arid areas there are patches of cooler, wetter highlands, forests, rivers and perennial springs. These create greener zones that have been profoundly important biophysical features, enabling pastoralists, their livestock and wildlife to occupy and survive on drylands.

The Maasai are better known than other pastoralist groups because their land includes Kenya's best-known protected areas, famous for a spectacular diversity and density of wild animals. It is important to distinguish between the two cate-

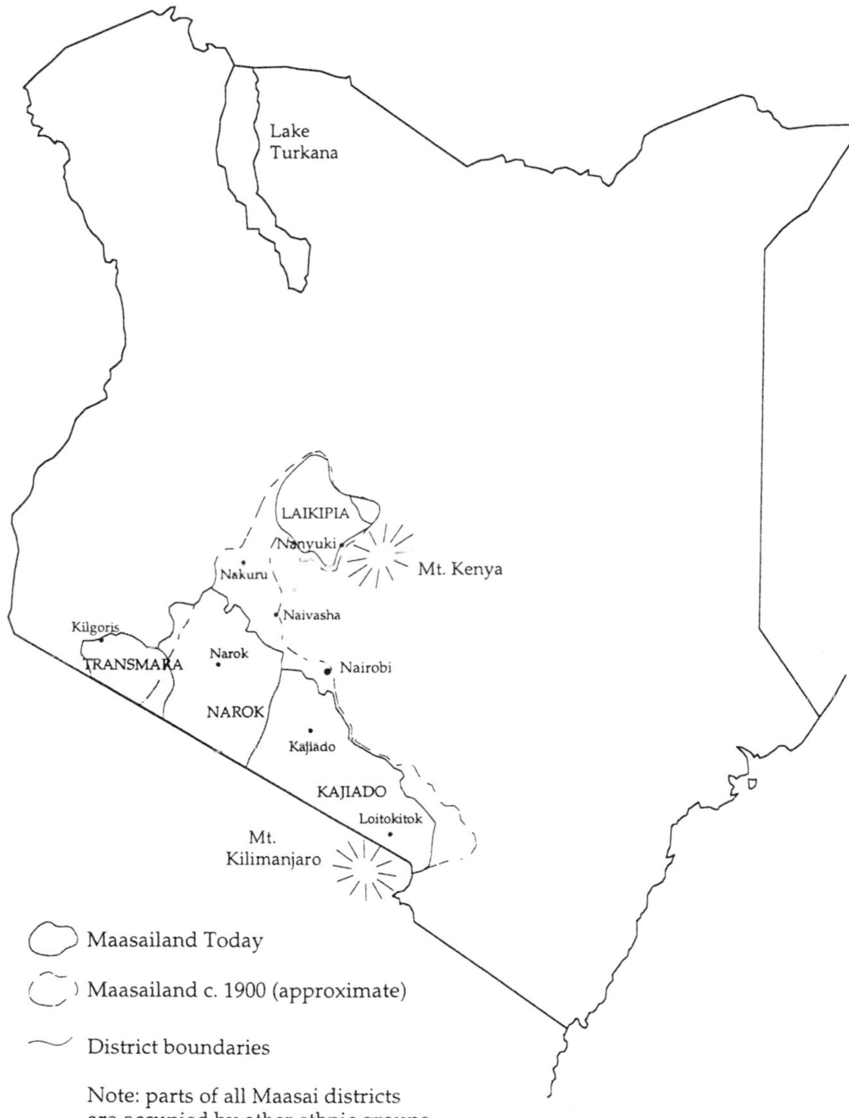

Figure 11.1 Maasailand past and present

gories of protected area: national park and national reserve. While both are protected by the same laws governing wildlife management, ownership is different. National parks are protected for the national interest and funded through and managed by a national authority, the Kenya Wildlife Service (KWS). The title for national reserves is held by local authorities on behalf of indigenous peoples. Local authorities are expected to provide funds for management and in some cases are responsible for management. Outside the protected areas, the more fertile parts of Maasailand have attracted colonial settlement and neighbouring agriculturalists. Conflicts over land ownership in areas that were previously inhabited by the Maasai have a high profile in current Kenyan politics, and many Maasai communities are now embroiled in conflicts over ownership of land and natural resources (Loita Naimina Enkiyio Trust, 1994).

To understand the challenges facing tourism in Maasailand, it is important to recognize the discrepancy between the much-advertised image of the Maasai pastoralist sustained on milk, meat, and blood and the present experience of the people of Maasai descent who live in wildlife-rich areas of Kenya and Tanzania. The classic portrayal of the Maasai is often sold as part of the safari experience. Tourists pay to visit Maasai villages of dome-shaped mud houses encircling a cattle enclosure, where women plaster their roofs with dung, while the elders wait for the cattle to come home. Tourists see the herdsman leaning 'one-legged' on his staff. They hear the sound of tinkling cowbells and watch girls and warriors dance bedecked in red ochre and coloured beads. However, behind these famous images of pastoralism are changing values, aspirations, and livelihoods shaped by modern circumstances, propelled by influences such as tourism.

CHANGES IN LAND OWNERSHIP, LAND USE AND LIVELIHOOD

Pastoralism is adapting to modern requirements and developing new forms and meaning. The herdsman with his spear and the shaven-headed mother milking the family herd are taking on altered social and economic roles. The Maasai are shifting from cattle-based subsistence towards a profit-oriented diversified economy which provides them with money to buy food and consumer goods, pay school fees, and meet other requirements (Figure 11.2). Many Maasai own buildings, bars, and shops in the trading centres mushrooming along tourist routes. They organize groups and special 'cultural' villages to earn income from tourists. The elite have cashed in on the 'gold mine' of tourism, becoming partners in safari businesses. Some are owners of lodges and four-wheel-drive vehicles used for game viewing. The Maasai, as either individuals or groups, lease their land to companies to build hotels and camps (Berger, 1990) or establish their own wildlife sanctuaries and tour ventures. Others engaging in entrepreneurial enterprises might herd ostrich with their goats or harvest kongoni and zebra for meat and skins.

These changes have become possible with new forms of land tenure. During the colonial era, communal areas were legally registered as trustland administered by local authorities on behalf of the people who lived there. After independence in 1963, government policies encouraged privatization of land through adjudication of trustlands into individual or group ranches. These new

Figure 11.2 Today's Maasai family

forms of land ownership introduced both opportunities for development and dangers of over-exploitation of rangelands, forests, water, and wildlife. Most of the Maasai trustlands are now privately owned. Many group ranches have been divided into smaller parcels of land which have been sold to agriculturalists who have introduced new forms of land use to replace pastoralism (Campbell 1979; Berger, 1993).

The majority of pastoralists no longer have the land or flexibility of movement to support themselves from their livestock alone. Inadequate pricing and marketing systems for livestock have made it necessary for pastoralists to adopt other means of livelihood. Government and aid agencies have, since colonial times, seen pastoralism as economically unproductive and environmentally dangerous (Talbot, 1973). Development policies and programmes have tended, even on dry land, to encourage conversion of pastoralist production into commercial ranching or mixed farming.

Although more than three-quarters of group ranch and trustland in the area surrounding parks and reserves is arid or semi arid, with unreliable and poorly distributed rainfall, huge tracts of this land have been cleared for commercial farming (Ole Parkipuny and Berger, 1989). The Maasai herdsman may continue to herd cattle but his homesteads have become islands in a 'sea' of ploughed land, often leased for commercial bean, wheat, or maize production (Thurow, 1994). Around perennial springs and rivers, irrigation schemes have prolifer ated, where cattle keepers supplement their income by growing onions and chillis for export, as part of Kenya's booming horticultural industry (Berger, 1993).

Agriculture in wetter zones occupied by pastoralists can be profitable

(Norton Griffiths, 1993) but high levels of production in the short term may not be sustained because the conversion of the rangeland for cropping eliminates natural grasses, woodland, and forest and can expose the soil to erosion. The reduction of grazing land has concentrated livestock and wildlife permanently on land which has little or no permanent water and was, in the past, only used in the wet season. This practice has eliminated the fallow period needed for forage regeneration and is causing range deterioration exemplified by the spread of wiregrass (*Penesitum)* in Transmara (Thurow, 1994).

DEVELOPMENT OR DISENFRANCHISEMENT?

The ochre and blanketed attire is being replaced by trousers and dresses which symbolize the adoption of new values and a national ethos that does not recognize or respect the strengths of the pastoralist way of life for exploiting and surviving in ASAL areas. Pastoralist organization has been undermined and, to a great extent, destroyed by 'foreign' social systems introduced with adjudication of land, the establishment of individual and group ranches, and the further division of land into smallholdings. Community cohesion and cooperation are being weakened by new values which encourage competition and entrepreneurship, and protect the interests of the individual rather than the group. Those who benefit most from agriculture are often outsiders who lease land or the Maasai elite who rent their private land for commercial farming. Communal groups have followed this example, leasing pieces of their land allocated informally to individual members.

The official view is that the Maasai are modernizing, developing their land, and making a contribution to the national economy. In practice, many people have lost, or are in danger of losing, access and rights to much of their land and resources and, as a result, their livestock-based livelihood and cultural heritage. These economic and social changes are neither in the interests of pastoralists like the Maasai, nor are they sustaining the rich natural resources of the rangelands. The nature of modernization in Maasailand is 'killing the goose that lays the golden egg'; or, in Maasai translation, 'killing the cow that bears the golden calf'.

This has been made abundantly clear by many failures of livestock development programmes in ASAL areas (Sandford, 1983). In contrast, awareness of the potential value of aspects of pastoralism and other indigenous land management systems in drylands is growing. Traditional knowledge and practice are now being recognized as holding important keys to life and survival (Cunningham, 1985; 1993; Williams and Baines, 1993; Sindiga 1994; Waters-Bayer and Bayer, 1994). This awareness is spearheaded in Kenya by pastoralists themselves and sympathetic non-governmental organizations (NGOs). It appears at a time when conservation is shifting from policies of protectionism towards sustainable utilization (KWS, 1991) and tourism is becoming more environmentally and socially sensitive (Kahindi and McIlvaine, 1993; Kenya Association of Tour Operators/Friends of Conservation 1994).

Indigenous land use systems, such as pastoralism, that have supported peoples for hundreds of years can be used as a basis for developing sustainable resource management systems. In Kenya, pastoralism includes forms of land use that integrate more easily with ecotourism and wildlife management than agriculture or intensive livestock-keeping. Kenya's park system, conservation programmes, and wildlife-based tourism depending on extensive land use are severely threatened by agricultural expansion which is encroaching on wildlife dispersal areas and blocking wildlife migration routes. Combining wildlife enterprises with extensive livestock rearing appears to have promise as a way to sustain human livelihood and to protect unique flora and fauna and biodiverse ecosystems (Gakahu and Goode, 1992). Other forms of land use, such as agriculture and conventional beef ranching, pose either ecological or social threats which tend to degrade the natural resources on which life depends.

TOURISM: ITS EVOLUTION AND IMPACT ON LIVELIHOOD AND NATURAL RESOURCES

To understand the potential for integrating wildland management and tourism with some form of pastoralist livestock-keeping, it is instructive to look more closely at the history of wildlife-based tourism in Maasailand and to evaluate the opportunities and threats it represents. During colonial times, the government controlled access to land in Maasai districts and governed through a few elders who were prepared 'to play ball'. These men, many of whom also held customary authority, were the first to learn how to access the modern system of governance and to acquire resources through it. Those who became administrators, chiefs, and other civil servants, together with the few Maasai who passed through the formal education system, formed an elite who began to accumulate power and resources including land. These leaders were the first Maasai to form alliances with the forefathers of today's safari operators, the 'white hunters' who came in search of adventure and trophies. Hunters, with the assistance of colonial administrators, established the first safari camps. Their children and grandchildren still run a significant proportion of Maasai tourism today.

The formalization of the first friendships and informal partnerships between early hunters, safari companies, and the Maasai was the first step in disenfranchising the Maasai majority from their land rights. Operators formed alliances with people they could communicate with and who were willing to provide land. Maasai leaders claimed pieces of trustland and, through leasing land, acquired shares in tourist establishments. Modern legal contracts enabled individual Maasai men to be designated as owners of land. The new landowners or their constituents might not have foreseen that the outcome of these land transactions would be a loss of majority rights or access to resources. Most Maasai must have been oblivious of these arrangements and their implications for the community at large. Land ownership through titledeed was a foreign practice and state law was not understood by people who had never exclusively owned or made money from land. Recognized sections (*iloshon*) of the Maasai had occupied particular geographical zones and groups of families controlled areas that often represented ecologically distinct areas or watersheds (*enkutot*), while smaller family units controlled grazing and water in neighbourhoods (*emurua* or *elatia*). However, right of access was flexible and requests for water or grazing were rarely refused (Homewood and Rodgers, 1991). Cooperative social networks ensured security for all. Furthermore, when the population was smaller, land must have appeared plentiful.

The Maasai also lost access to significant portions of their land with the gazettement of parks and reserves. This process followed pressure from some people in the colonial government and others in Europe and America who foresaw the eventual elimination of wild species through hunting and agricultural expansion. With the establishment of these protected areas, the safari to photograph—rather than shoot—began to replace hunting, and wildlife-based tourism was born as a business.

Nairobi and Amboseli Parks were excised from land that had provided dry-season grazing and permanent water sources for the Maasai. Until recently, many national reserves permitted access to pastoralists but, with increased competition for grazing between wildlife and livestock and the growth of the safari industry, local authorities administering reserves such as Maasai Mara and Samburu excluded people and their livestock. Until 1990, there had been little official attention to the impact of conservation policy and tourism on pastoralists adjacent to protected areas. Park managers (with notable exceptions, eg, Lovatt Smith, 1986) have tended to regard their neighbours as a nuisance and to overlook the rights of the original inhabitants. For a long time, Kenyan tourism promoted and marketed wildlife and the parks, ignoring the indigenous peoples. Some early hunters must have developed an intimate relationship with the land, its wildlife, and the people, but as time has gone by and roads and facilities have developed, new generations of travel operators have had much less direct local contact and so have a poor knowledge of tribal custom and social circumstances.

Increasing numbers of Maasai are benefiting from tourism, but at a cost. A few have made external business links and political affiliations which have weakened local solidarity and enabled outsiders to exploit natural resources and culture. Tourism has raised commodity prices so that local communities have suffered economically. Roads and inadequate regulation of traffic are destroying vegetation (Muthee, 1992), causing pollution, and endangering life (Kahindi and McIlvaine 1993). Yet many Maasai perceive tourism as a potential source of money. The sale of handicrafts and other forms of cultural tourism have drawn people to settle near parks where people can supplement their livelihood with the pickings from tourism. The dramatic expansion of human population along tourism routes has been both socially and environmentally destructive (Bellerive Foundation and Friends of Conservation, 1994). Efforts to earn from tourism are epitomized by the so-called 'cultural villages' visited by tourists. These provide some income to the ordinary person, but have been the site of exploitation by tour drivers and of Maasai women and children by their menfolk. Protected area managers and the tour industry have tended to overlook the rights and needs of the Maasai community as a whole. Their activities concentrate power and wealth in the hands of a minority who have easy access to opportunities for investment. This has tended to undermine communal social security, increasing inequity between families and groups. Socio-cultural and economic marginalization of the majority is creating conflict, and this has the potential to fuel political upheaval, to which tourism is particularly vulnerable.

Government policy to reduce the environmental impact of tourism inside parks and to share the benefits as well as responsibilities for managing conservation and tourism with communities (KWS, 1991), has sometimes accelerated degradation outside parks. Settlements near park gates have become unplanned trading centres surrounded by zones of increasingly denuded land. Talek township, on the border of the Maasai Mara Reserve, illustrates the dangers of urbanization along tour routes (Bellerive Foundation and Friends of Conservation, 1994). The construction of tour facilities on private or communal land has intensified resource use. Weak regulation of tourism has allowed proliferation of establishments which consume huge amounts of fuelwood and water and often ignore the need to manage waste, so that the environment becomes polluted and degraded. Kenya is now facing competition from other countries with better reputation for environmental management of tourism.

LINKING PASTORALISM TO ECOTOURISM

In spite of many social and environmental problems, tourism is well established and growing in Maasailand. The culture of the pastoralist is increasingly a marketing feature of tourism, attracting visitors to Maasailand. Tourists expect to see an exotic culture as well as a unique wildlife spectacle. Yet tourism must meet social, political, and environmental challenges to be sustainable. Increasingly, popular forms of tourism grouped under the rubric of 'ecotourism', hold promise to limit impact on the natural environment, sustain biodiversity, respect local cultures and build equitable local development. Many tours and establishments now cater for fewer higher-paying clients to minimize impact on the environment (Shelley, 1992). Since communities in wildlife areas are increasingly aware of their right to develop and manage the potential of their land and wildlife, they are demanding both responsible management and a more equitable share of profits. The number of community-based tourism enterprises is growing, encouraged by government policies and programmes. The Wildlife for Development Fund established by the Kenya Wildlife Service (KWS) provides funds to locally owned wildlife and tourist enterprises. Some Maasai group ranches are now making a livelihood from a combination of extensive livestock-keeping and ecotourism (Berger, 1990; 1994). This has allowed the Maasai to retain a livelihood which is primarily livestock-based but also includes new lucrative, but environmentally sensitive, enterprises—new forms of economic activity which are urgently needed to help pastoralists survive modern circumstances.

Both conservation and tourism benefit from the occupation of tour destinations by Maasai pastoralists because they have used large areas for extensive grazing in ways that have sustained natural ecosystems and allowed relatively harmonious co-existence of wildlife and people. The Maasai did not hunt except in severe famine. In the past, they limited forage offtake levels by restricting access to grazing and water at certain seasons. They practised rotational grazing and the opportunistic movement of herds to take advantage of spatially and seasonally erratic rainfall. They used fire to encourage new growth of grass, depress bush encroachment, and reduce disease transmission, and kept a variety of stock: cattle, sheep, goats, and donkeys capable of grazing and browsing different types of vegetation. Though pastoralism changed the landscape, it stimulated biological productivity and to some extent promoted biodiversity. The combined impact of fire, grazing, trampling, and nutrient cycling by livestock and wild herbivores created a mosaic of vegetation types inhabited by a rich flora and fauna (Homewood and Rodgers, 1991). This is demonstrated by the concentration and diversity of wild animals that graze on the group ranches neighbouring the Mara Reserve. Plains game prefer the short-grass plains (where there has been intensive cattle grazing) to some grasslands in the reserve where burning and livestock grazing are prohibited, grasses are tall and rank, and predators can easily hide.

A knowledge of the environment and wildlife was deeply rooted in Maasai culture and daily life became the classroom from early childhood. The toddler started his apprenticeship as herdsman as soon as he could hold a stick. The little girl carrying her sibling and helping her mother collect firewood was already shouldering responsibility. Herdboys observed the birds and animals around them and learned where to find wild fruits. Young men as warriors travelled extensively, accumulating information on land and resources: the location of forage, water, minerals, and disease risk under different conditions, in different seasons, and from year to year. Their knowledge is reflected by the extensive Maasai vocabulary for living things (Mol, 1978). The characteristics and uses of plants and trees are common knowledge among the general population (Sindiga, 1994) who are aware of their properties for medicine, food, forage, fuel, building, and other needs as well as their ritual significance (Phakathi Films, 1995; Loita Naimina Enkiyio, 1994). Story-telling, riddles and sayings incalculated values and norms of society that taught a harmonious relationship with the natural world (Mbugua, 1994).

The Maasai have a rich material culture which reflects their life and landscape. Their well-developed visual tradition is apparent in the beautiful beaded patterns (*muain sidain*) which draw on designs and colour systems in their surroundings. Striped patterns in the cloudy skies, or on their cows or the zebra, are depicted as parallel lines of black and white beads known as *engoitiko*, the word for zebra in the Maa language. *Keri*—bright and dark patches in their beadwork—represent *Oldoniyo Keri* (Mount Kenya) and *olkeri*, the leopard. The Purko Maasai have created a design for earrings which resembles the pattern on the wild sodom apple (Somjee, 1993). Ornaments communicate meaning indicating social groupings and status. Each Maasai section and age set can be identified by the colours and patterns 'fashionable' during a particular era (Klumpp, 1987). Maasai decoration is a rich tradition that can be recognized and encouraged to strengthen an appreciation of culture, develop local and national artistic talent, and generate income from tourism. Maasai crafts are already a popular aspect of cultural tourism and enable Maasai women, in particular, to earn income directly from tourists (Figure 11.3).

PROJECTS AND ENTERPRISES

The potential for integrating elements of Maasai tradition into land-use systems is illustrated by the active participation of the Maasai in a variety of tourism and wildlife projects and enterprises (Figure 11.4). Ecotourism in Maasailand is expanding. The group ranches adjacent to Amboseli and Tsavo West National Parks are combining tourism with livestock-rearing based on communal resource management. Several ranches have formed successful partnerships with safari operators.

Imbirikani Group Ranch has set aside its land in the Chyulu Hills for

Figure 11.3 Women's group producing beadwork and dancing for tourists in lodges at Mara

TOURISM/WILDLIFE — PROJECTS AND ENTERPRISES IN MAASAILAND

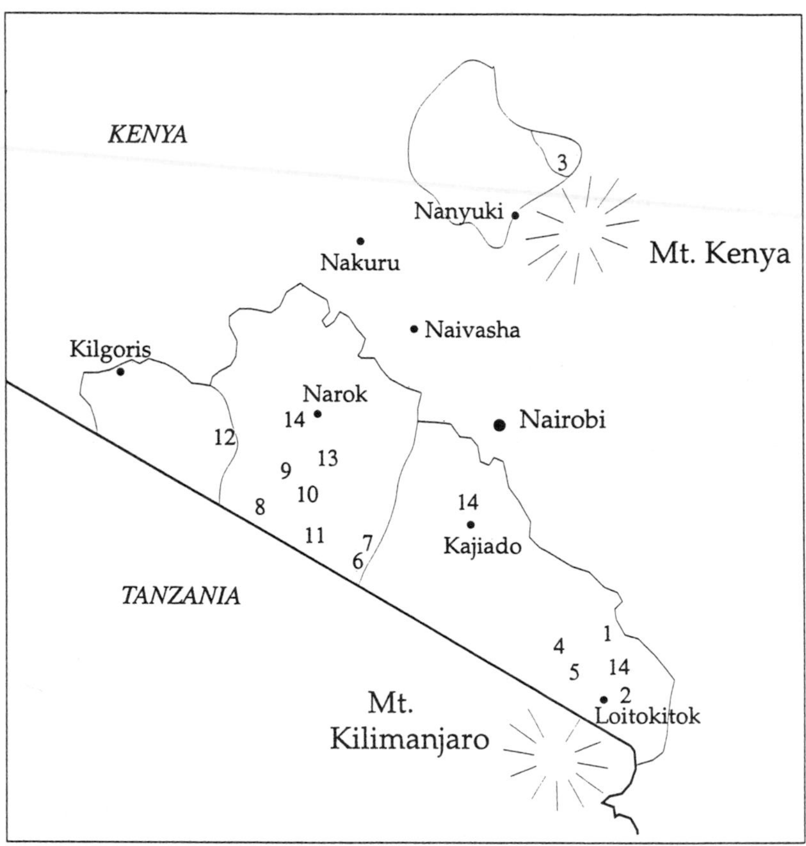

Key:

1. multiple land use — Imbirikani
2. wildlife sanctuary — Kimana
3. camel treks — Ilingwezi
4. KWS revenue sharing projects — Amboseli/Tsavo
5. group ranch wildlife scouts
6. Naimina Enkiyio Conservation Trust
7. ethnobotany project
8. waste management — Mara lodges
9. community conservatiom project — Mara
10. wood fuel survey/ energy conservation — Talek
11. rhino scouts — Naikara/Loleta
12. Olanana cultural centre
13. Explore Mara training
14. KWS Community Wildlife Service

Figure 11.4 Tourism and wildlife projects and enterprises in Maasailand

ecotourism. This has provided a source of income using the previously untapped economic potential of wildlife and spectacular scenery (Figure 11.5). A safari

Figure 11.5 Spectacular scenery in the Chyulu Hills

operator has leased land for a small tourist lodge, Oldonyo Wuas Camp, where a few high-paying visitors stay and enjoy game drives, camp, walk, and go horseback riding (Berger, 1990). The lodge employs ranch members and contributes to life on the ranch in many ways, helping to build its economy as a multi-purpose ranch. The lodge owner assisted in the preparation of a wildlife management plan for the ranch, built an abattoir and a negotiated a wildlife-cropping license with Kenya Wildlife Service. He started ostrich rearing and linked a ranch women's group with a handicraft designer who commissions beadwork. Tourist revenues, held in a Community Trust, contribute to development. Recent projects include construction of dams and reafforestation. Wildlife extension workers supported by the African Fund for Endangered Wildlife facilitated the original negotiation between the safari operator and the ranch (Figure 11.6). They were able to help overcome conflicts, clear a misunderstanding, and assist the operator to go beyond the initial contact with leaders to make his project well known throughout the ranch. In the process, trust was established, his objectives became transparent and ranch leadership had to become accountable (Berger, 1990; 1993). Mbirikani's satisfactory partnership with this man has encouraged several neighbouring ranches to renegotiate or initiate new contracts for safari lodges and tented camps. These ranches include Kuku Group Ranch, which is developing its wildlife potential through a partnership with a specialist in wildlife utilization who is helping the ranch to prepare a management plan and intends to establish a wildlife management training centre. Another group ranch at Kimana has set aside land as a wildlife sanctuary to conserve vegetation and a critical water source around a swamp and to earn income from tourism.

Figure 11.6 A discussion between local leaders and extension workers during the process of establishing Oldonyo Wuas Camp, an example of ecotourism on a group ranch

Other ecotourism initiatives include a partnership between a safari company that organizes camel treks and the northern Maasai, who live on communal land at Ilingwesi below the Mukugodo Mountains in Laikipia. Small groups of tourists walk and ride camels and camp for a few days on the ranch. The company pays the group and employs Maasai as camp staff, guides, and camel men. Trekkers live 'lightly' on the land, avoiding environmental damage and leaving no trail of waste.

Revenues earned in the parks are now shared with neighbouring communities to support community development. Over fifty projects were funded on ranches around Amboseli Park from fees generated by parks in 1993 and 1994. In exchange for access to park resources and money generated by tourism, communities are now more willing to take responsibility for protecting wildlife and land next to parks. The ranches at Amboseli are employing their own wildlife scouts for a variety of conservation-related activities. The scouts on Olgulului Group Ranch monitor the movements of elephants. On Imbirikani their duties include management of bird hunting. Another initiative is the registration of the Naimina Enkiyio Community Conservation Trust by the Loita Maasai to protect, manage, and benefit from their forest and wildlife heritage (Loita Naimina Enkiyio Trust, 1994). They are planning to develop and implement a forest management plan and, as a first step towards community stewardship, they have established an ethnobotany programme.

The tour industry is increasingly supporting conservation efforts. Friends of Conservation (FOC) was established by the owner of Abercrombie and Kent Tour Company to support conservation in the Maasai Mara National

Reserve and elsewhere in East Africa. FOC's technical assistance to the Maasai Mara has included ecological monitoring, reserve management support, a 'code of conduct' brochure for tourists, and a community conservation project. FOC spearheaded education for the responsible management of tourism through an environmental workshop for managers of hotels and lodges in the Mara (Kahindi and McIlvaine, 1993). Subsequently, several hotels have constructed improved waste management systems and have reduced fuelwood consumption through energy conservation technologies. At a second workshop, held in Nairobi for members of the Kenyan Association of Tour Operators (KATO/FOC, 1994), over thirty companies developed environmental guidelines and resolutions for action to minimize impact of tourism on the ecosystem. The planned registration of an Ecotourism Society in Kenya will further promote responsible tourism and devise incentives for changing tourism practices.

Extension work through FOC's Maasai Mara Community Conservation Programme (MMCCP) is promoting community-based natural resource management. By involving the elders in the community, the MMCCP is introducing into schools the lessons taught in the past: the need for communities to take responsibility for their environment and wildlife. To highlight and assess the need for conservation, MMCCP and the Bellerive Foundation worked with the community at Talek to survey wood fuel use in campsites and lodges, the trading centre at Talek, and nearby Maasai villages. The survey revealed that 1000 tonnes of firewood were being used annually by 243 Maasai households; 340 tonnes by 10 tourist camps; 790 tonnes in the two lodges surveyed; and 33 tons at the trading centre (Bellerive Foundation and FOC, 1994). To raise community consciousness about the problem and possible conservation strategies, energy consumption experiments were carried out to compare the amount of wood consumed in households, camps, and hotels in the trading centre under normal circumstances with that consumed using energy-saving stoves and water heaters. Both the survey and experiments illustrated that dramatic reductions in fuel use were possible. These results were discussed at a community workshop, and a plan for woodfuel conservation was agreed upon. This community is also taking part in a series of workshops and meetings to organize fire management in and around the reserve (Morgan-Davies, 1993). Another initiative undertaken by FOC is the Naikara/Leleta Rhino Scouts Project which trains and supports Maasai herdsmen to monitor and protect rhinos on their land (Figure 11.7).

A first step towards 'enlightened' cultural tourism has been made at the Olanana Cultural Centre, north of the Maasai Mara near Kichwa Tembo Camp. It is an attempt by a private company to market Maasai culture in a culturally sensitive way. The neighbouring Maasai assisted in construction of the centre and are employed there. A portion of earnings go towards local development (East African Cultural Experiences, 1994).

Figure 11.7 The Loita Rhino Scouts, who watch over rhinos on their community's land

Some of the most successful educational tourism programmes in Kenya enable university students from North America to visit Maasai communities. The rangeland ecosystem training programme organized by Explore Mara Company at Olare Orok Camp in the Mara is one example. Maasai host and teach students about rangeland ecology and pastoralism and debate issues of development and intercultural relations. Students learn to appreciate the complexities of the Maasai socio-ecosystem and that pastoralists, like other indigenous peoples, have much of value to teach industrialized peoples.

Kenya's wildlife policies and programmes increasingly support tour enterprise partnerships involving local communities. Wildlife extension by NGOs working in Maasailand laid the foundation for a nationwide community wildlife service (KWFT/UNEP, 1988; Berger, 1990; African Wildlife Foundation, 1993; USAID, 1991). The Community Wildlife Programme of the KWS now supports local conservation initiatives through its network of community wildlife wardens who facilitate communication between communities, the tour sector, and wildlife managers. This programme has assisted most of the activities mentioned above, thus helping Maasai groups organize, evaluate needs, plan projects, enter into contracts, and acquire management and technical skills. Community wardens play a key role in distributing and monitoring the use of wildlife revenues to park neighbours in the Amboseli/Tsavo area and elsewhere in Kenya.

The KWS also established the Wildlife for Development Fund (KWS, 1994) to support local development and wildlife and tourist enterprises. It has assisted organization and legal registration of Maasai groups, and will also provide funds for feasibility studies, baseline surveys and participatory rural appraisals (PRAs), setting up group management and monitoring systems, and providing basic financial, management, and accounting training to groups. An in-service training course in community conservation is equipping KWS community wardens to facilitate sustainable, community-based wildlife management and ecotourism. The devolution of responsibility for management and policing of conservation and tourism from government to communities is vital, given the limitations of government resources and difficulty of regulation from outside. The KWS training programme being planned for wildlife scouts employed by their communities will be a further step towards community self-reliance in the Maasai rangelands.

CONSTRAINTS ON INTEGRATION OF TOURISM AND PASTORALISM

TOURISM AS BUSINESS VERSUS PASTORALISM AS LIVELIHOOD

Tourism is seen by some Maasai as an opportunity to enter the modern economy and prosper in it. Others see it as a perverting force that is destroying ethnic identity and solidarity and marginalizing the majority of pastoralists. Tourism has introduced new socio-economic conventions that have had a profound effect on community and individual aspirations and social relations. A shift to a monetary economy has meant adoption of different values, particularly those associated with the business ethic. The primary aim of tourism as a business is to make money for a company or individual. Businesses tend to compete rather than cooperate to make money. From this perspective, parks, wildlife, and the Maasai culture are viewed as products to be sold and are managed primarily to make a profit. Social and environmental responsibility is likely to be a secondary consideration. The nature of the safari experience means that interaction between different stakeholders—the tour operators, tourists and people who own land and natural resources—tends to be superficial and based on economic exchange.

Pastoralism, on the other hand, is concerned with providing subsistence and a multitude of other needs for the livelihood of a whole community. Land and natural resources are used to raise livestock to ensure individual and collective wealth and security. A pastoralist community strives to provide for all, placing higher value on group identity and welfare than individual need and success. Through cooperation and social networks of support and unity, resources are managed and shared, and their exploitation tends to be controlled to ensure sustainability.

ACCESS TO TOURISTIC RESOURCES: EXCLUSIVITY VERSUS COEXISTENCE

The resource protection strategies of wildlife-based tourism and pastoralism are often in conflict. Pastoralists avoided damaging grazing and water resources by seasonal movement of herds over extensive lands which allowed people, livestock, and wildlife to coexist. Tourism has depended on parks and reserves set aside for conservation and exclusive use by wildlife and tourists. The gazettement of parks and reserves for use of wildlife and tourism has been locally opposed since its inception. Pastoralists continue to graze livestock illegally in many parks and reserves, and pressure on protected areas has increased as more land in dispersal areas has been converted to agriculture and fenced, and grazing competition between wildlife and Maasai livestock has intensified. This situation creates tension between communities and those who use the land for conservation or tourism. Cooperation through joint land-use planning between agencies, the tour industry, and local communities is vital, although it is as yet underdeveloped. Issues around access to parks and reserves by the Maasai remain unresolved and are a source of resentment which will undermine efforts to develop tourism partnerships.

DISUNITY AND INEQUITY WITHIN MAASAI COMMUNITIES

The Maasai face a leadership crisis, as a class of elite landowners has taken over the lion's share of resources in Maasailand, dominating the political scene, and controlling access to resources, including tourism and its benefits. They monopolize leadership and thwart democratic processes. The lack of formal education of the Maasai majority has been an obstacle that has barred their way to modern forms of legal redress. The monopoly of power by a few has divided communities who have not found it easy to unite, organize, and claim what is rightfully theirs. Ironically, some aspects of tradition—respect for elders, the recognition of the life-long office of a leader, and age-group or section solidarity—have made the Maasai majority vulnerable to abuse of power and customary respect, and hence to political manipulation.

One aspect of inequity that sets limits on the viability of pastoralism under present circumstances concerns the ownership of livestock. Although the area of grazing land has shrunk, livestock continue to be owned by individual families. Those with the largest herds use the majority of communal resources and contribute most to land degradation. Groups wishing to maintain biodiversity and good grazing for wildlife and livestock will have to face the thorny issues of livestock ownership and population.

Another urgent priority, although it will be difficult to implement, will be for tour companies to negotiate contracts or establish companies with communal groups rather than individuals. This is to avoid the historical pattern of tour companies developing partnerships with the small elite who have consequently been able to accumulate tremendous wealth from exploitation of resources that belong to the community as a whole. The Maasai need to form stable, united organizations capable of representing communal interests to attract investors. Training in participatory rural appraisal (PRA) and other approaches that enhance community participation and organization is needed (GTZ/Transmara Development Programme, 1994; 1995).

THE MARKETING AND MANAGEMENT OF ECOTOURISM

Maasai communities rarely have the organizational machinery or contacts to market or the skills to manage tourism ventures. Partnerships with agents who have overseas contacts, marketing networks, and managerial skill will be necessary to provide clients and to run tour facilities. However, tourism needs to be planned and regulated through joint efforts of communities, the private sector, and natural resource managers. A holistic approach to planning will be necessary, taking into account the effect of enterprises on the quality of life for the local people, the long-term impact of activities on the landscape, and the need to ensure profitable businesses (Savory, 1991; PELUM, 1995). Communities will have to be educated about the options, benefits and costs of different tourism options, and feasibility studies to evaluate market potential, accessibility, and other factors are necessary. The ecotourism market, aimed at a few high-paying visitors rather than masses of package tourists, is likely to be limited; inexpensive package tours and large tourist establishments will continue to attract many tourists. Policies, regulations and control measures will be necessary to control the impact on the landscape of mass tourism, especially because the incentive to build facilities which cater for it are high because of short-term economic returns. Communities and local entrepreneurs whose concern is immediate gain rather than sustainability will be tempted to multiply the number of tourist ventures on their land.

A related constraint to locally managed tourism is the limited capacity of rural communities to administer funds and to provide bookkeeping and project supervision. Identification, planning, and management of community projects and business enterprises using wildlife/tourism revenues or loans require management and technical skills that are not widely available in local communities. The fragility of new social structures and organizations being established to manage local initiatives can threaten the success of efforts to introduce tourist enterprise to pastoralists. If members are not yet aware of their rights or do not demand accountability from leaders and if communities are too dependent on external help, projects are likely to fail.

Inadequate policy and regulation of tourism by the central government, local authorities, and landowners means that environmental and social abuse by the tour industry is uncontrolled. Even though efforts are being made to make the industry more accountable (KATO/Friends of Conservation, 1994), laws and stronger control are needed to contain the expansion and nature of facilities and to control behaviour at tour destinations.

SURVIVAL TODAY VERSUS SUSTENANCE FOR TOMORROW

For many Maasai, the urgency of survival today and a strong economic incentive to use land for growing crops means that questions concerning sustainability of particular forms of land use are unlikely to be considered. The urgent need for cash, combined with policies that promote individual ownership of land and cash cropping, encourages pastoralists to clear their land for agriculture which appears to be the most profitable option, particularly in wetter parts of Maasailand (Norton Griffiths, 1993). There is little incentive to consider other options that would protect soil fertility and water catchments and maintain biodiversity. Changes in land tenure and agricultural expansion are occurring so fast that it is too late to introduce the option of ecotourism in some areas with potential for wildlife management and tourism.

CONCLUSIONS

In the past, the government and the tour industry have 'mined' the parks and the culture of the Maasai people without reinvesting locally. A new approach to park management and tourism is taking shape, building on traditional land-use systems and encouraging Maasai communities to take up the sustainable management of wildlife for tourism. Some tour operators are recognizing the wisdom of investing in more equitable partnerships with the Maasai. The success and sustenance of the tour industry in Maasailand is increasingly linked with the conscious development of strategies to enrich the livelihood of the majority of the people. It is no longer expedient to make alliances with those who first claim to represent the majority. Tour operators must establish more democratic relationships and partnerships, by working cooperatively to manage resources with the local people, investing in the education and training of the people from whose land they are profiting.

For tourism to continue, the land must retain its natural beauty, unique flora and fauna, and biodiversity. Pastoralist communities with traditions that enhance and protect biodiversity have the potential to be ideal caretakers to ensure survival of unique and valuable species, such as the large migratory herds of wildebeest and zebras for which Maasailand is famous. Sustainability will depend on these people taking responsibility for the management of the land, and for this to happen they will have to benefit directly. Without economic incentive, alternate forms of land use that are incompatible with tourism, such as agriculture, will continue to be chosen by the Maasai. Those concerned with conservation and tourism will need to pay landowners for taking care of their land, so reducing the economic incentive to develop it in ways that would be detrimental to wildlife and diverse ecosystems.

Rural development and resource management programmes are increasingly using participatory extension methods to educate and organize communities so that they can initiate and control their own destiny. This work is enabling communities to evaluate their situation, assess development options, plan accordingly, and acquire technical skills. To enable tourism to become a means of livelihood for communities, tourism managers would be wise to draw from and train personnel in holistic land-use planning (Savory, 1991; PELUM, 1995), participatory rural appraisal (Waters-Bayer and Bayer, 1994; Chambers and Guijit, 1995) participatory technology development (Sharland, 1990; Ruddell and Beingolea, 1995), and related approaches to community based development (GTZ/Transmara Development Programme 1994; 1995).

Awareness of individual and community rights is growing among the Maasai, and people are beginning to confront corruption within their midst. In all of the important tourist areas, conflicts now rage over fragmentation of land, ownership of lodges, and sharing of wildlife revenues. If tourism in Maasailand is to be developed and sustained, these conflicts will have to be settled. Fora are needed to facilitate dialogue and debate about the role of tourism in development of pastoralist lands. The impact of tourism must be monitored with the participation of all involved; its effect on both the natural environment and the well-being and development of local people. The expansion of ecotourism in Maasailand seems to hold promise as a land use with potential to provide a sustainable livelihood that will ensure the Maasai people as a community have a rightful place in the modern state.

REFERENCES

African Wildlife Foundation (AWF), 1993, *Tsavo West Community Conservation Project Evaluation of Phase 2 1992–3*, AWF, Nairobi.

Bellerive Foundation/Friends of Conservation (FOC), 1994, *Study of Woodfuel Utilization in Talek Region of the Maasai Mara Game Reserve*, Bellerive Foundation, Nairobi.

Berger, D.J., 1990, The Keepers of God's Creation, *Swara*, March/April 1990.

Berger, D.J., 1993, *Wildlife Extension, Participatory Conservation by the Maasai of Kenya.* African Centre for Technology Studies Press, Nairobi.

Berger, D.J., 1994, Wildlife as a peoples' resource. A first step and the journey ahead, *Research Memorandum 7*, African Centre for Technology Studies, Nairobi.

Braun, H.M.H., 1982, Agro-climatic Zone Map of Kenya. Exploratory Soil Map and Agroclimatic Map of Kenya 1980, *Exploratory Soil Survey Report El*, Kenya Soil Survey, Nairobi.

Campbell, D.J., 1979, *Development or decline: Resources, Land Use and Population Growth in Kajiado District*, Working Paper 352, Institute for Development Studies, University of Nairobi.

Chambers, R. and Guijit, I., 1995, PRA—five years later. Where are we now? *Forest, Trees and People Newsletter*, 26/27. IRDC, Swedish University of Agricultural Sciences, Lund, 4–14.

Cunningham, A.B, 1985, *The Resource Value of Indigenous Plants to Rural People in a Low Agricultural Potential Area*, Ph.D. dissertation, Department of Botany, University of Capetown.

Cunningham, A.B, 1993, *African Medicinal Plants: Setting Priorities at the Interface between Conservation and Primary Health Care*, UNESCO, Paris.

East African Cultural Experiences, 1994, *The Olanana Maasai Cultural Experience*. Nairobi, Kenya.

Ehret, C., 1974, *Ethiopians and East Africans—The Problem of Contacts*, East African Publishing House, Nairobi.

Gakahu, G.G. and Goode, B.E. (eds), 1992, *Ecotourism and Sustainable Development in Kenya*, Wildlife Conservation International, Nairobi.

GTZ/TransMara Development Programme (TDP), 1994, *Report on workshop for technical officers on participatory approaches to community based development*, TDP, Lolgorien.

GTZ/TransMara Development Programme (TDP), 1995, *Report on Training in PRA at Lolgorien and Olopikidongoe, Transmara District*, TDP, Lolgorien.

Homewood, K.M. and Rodgers, W.A., 1991, *Maasailand Ecology. Pastoralist Development and Wildlife Conservation in Ngorongoro, Tanzania*, Cambridge University Press, Cambridge.

Kahindi, O. and McIlvane, K., 1993, *Waste Management and Energy Conservation. A Guide for Lodge and Camp and Management in Wildlife Areas*, Friends of Conservation, Nairobi.

Kenya Association of Tour Operators/Friends of Conservation (KATO/FOC), 1994, *Woodfuel and Environmental Conservation Seminar*, KATO, Nairobi.

Kenya Wildlife Fund Trustees/United Nations Environment Programme (KWFT/UNEP), 1988, *People, Parks and Wildlife. Guidelines for Public Participation in Wildlife Conservation. Case Studies from Kenya,* UNEP, Nairobi.

Kenya Wildlife Service (KWS), 1991, *Policy Framework and Development Programme, 1991–96. Annex 6 Community Conservation and Wildlife Management Outside Parks and Reserves*, KWS, Nairobi.

Kenya Wildlife Service (KWS), 1994, *Guidelines for Revenue Sharing, Community and Enterprise Development*, Community Wildlife Service/KWS, Nairobi.

Klumpp, D.R., 1987, *Maasai Art and Society: Age and Sex, Time and Space, Cash and Cattle*, Ph.D. Dissertation, School of Arts and Sciences, Columbia University, New York.

Loita Naimina Enkiyio Trust, 1994, *Forest of the Lost Child. A Conservation Success Threatened by Greed,* Loita Naimina Enkiyio Conservation Trust Company, Narok, Kenya.

Lovatt Smith, D., 1986, *Amboseli: Nothing Short of a Miracle*, East African Publishing House, Nairobi.

Mbugua, K., 1994, *Inkishu. Myths and Legends of the Maasai*, African Art and Literature Series, Jacaranda Designs, Nairobi.

Mol, F., 1978, *Maa: a Dictionary of the Maasai Language and Folklore*, English-Maasai Marketing and Publishing, Nairobi.

Morgan-Davies, M. (ed.), 1993, *Maasai Mara Fire Management Workshop. The Use of Fire as a Management Tool in the Maasai Mara National Reserve, Kenya.* Friends of Conservation, Nairobi.

Muthee, L., 1992, Ecological impacts of tourist use on habitats and pressure—point species, in tourist attitudes and use impacts, in Gakahu, C.G., (ed.), *Maasai Mara National Reserve*, Wildlife Conservation International, Nairobi, 18–35.

Norton Griffiths, M., 1993, The implications of national conservation interests of economic incentives to develop the rangelands of Kenya, *Development Discussion Paper 30*, Harvard Institute for International Development, Cambridge.

Ole Parkipuny, L.H.S., 1988, *The Ngorongoro Crater Issue. The Plight of the Maasai Pastoral Community of Kenya and Tanzania under the Rule of Wildlife Preservation*, Paper presented at International Congress on Nature Management and Sustainable Development, University of Groningen.

Ole Parkipuny, L.H.S. and Berger D.J., 1989, *Sustainable Utilisation and Management of Resources in the Maasai Rangelands: The Links between Social Justice and Wildlife Conservation*, paper prepared for the Osborne Center for Conservation and Development, World Wildlife Fund, Washington DC.

PELUM, 1995, *A curriculum and network for participatory ecological land use management*, PELUM Association, Harare.

Phakathi Films, 1995, *Living in Africa: Healing the Land Film Series*, Johannesburg.

Ruddell, E.D. and Beingolea, J., 1995, Towards farmer scientists, *ILEIA Newsletter*, March 1995, 16–17.

Sandford, S., 1983, *Management of Pastoral Development in the Third World*, John Wiley and Sons, Chichester.

Sanford G.R., 1919, *An Administrative and Political History of the Maasai Reserve*. Waterlow and Sons, London.

Savory, A., 1991, *Holistic Resource Management*, Gilmore Publishing, Harare.

Sharland, R., 1990, A trap, a fish poison and culturally significant pest control, *ILEIA Newsletter*, March 1990, 12–13.

Shelley, S., 1992, Marketing Strategies for Ecotourism in Africa, in Gakahu, G.G. and Goode, B.E. (eds), *Ecotourism and Sustainable Development in Kenya*, Wildlife Conservation International, Nairobi, 133–145.

Sindiga, I., 1994, Indigenous (medical) knowledge of the Maasai, *Indigenous Knowledge and Development Monitor*, 2, 16–18.

Somjee, S., 1993, *Material Culture of Kenya*, East African Educational Publishers, Nairobi.

Talbot L.H., 1973, Ecological Consequences of Rangeland Development in Maasailand, East Africa, in Farvar, M.T. and Milton, J.P. (eds), *The Careless Technology: Ecology and International Development*, Stacey, London.

Thurow, T.L., 1994, *Understanding and Facilitating Rangeland and Pasture Management in the Transmara*, Department of Rangeland Ecology and Management, Texas A and M University, College Station, Texas.

Tignor, R.L., 1976, *The Colonial Transformation of Kenya: the Kamba, Kikuyu and Maasai from 1900 to 1939*, Princeton University Press, Princeton.

USAID, 1991, *Project Document for Conservation of Biodiverse Resource Areas (COBRA) Project*, USAID, Nairobi.

Waters-Bayer, A. and Bayer W., 1994, *Planning with Pastoralists: PRA and More. A Review of Methods Focused on Africa*, GTZ Division 422: Livestock Farming, Veterinary Sciences and Fisheries, Eschborn.

Western, D., 1992, Ecotourism: The Kenya Challenge, in G.G. Gakahu and B.E. Goode (eds), *Ecotourism and Sustainable Development in Kenya*, Wildlife Conservation International, Nairobi, 15–22.

Williams, N.M. and Baines, G., 1993, *Traditional Ecological Knowledge: Wisdom for Sustainable Development*, Centre for Resource and Environmental Studies, Canberra.

12 People, Wildlife and Tourism in and around Hwange National Park, Zimbabwe

FRANK C. POTTS, HAROLD GOODWIN AND MATT J. WALPOLE

INTRODUCTION

Hwange National Park (HNP) is one of the greatest wildlife sanctuaries in the world. Comprising some 1 465 100 ha of semi-arid savanna land, it is the largest national park in Zimbabwe and the third largest park in Africa, after the Serengeti in Tanzania and Kruger in South Africa. The ecosystem supports the largest and most diverse wildlife population in Zimbabwe, with more than a hundred mammal and some seventy reptile and amphibian species. Among these are a number designated as specially protected under Zimbabwean law, such as the white and black rhinoceros, cheetah, gemsbok, roan antelope, aardwolf, pangolin, bat-eared fox, and African python. More than four hundred species of bird have been recorded.

Wildlife is Zimbabwe's main tourist attraction besides Victoria Falls, and Hwange is Zimbabwe's most accessible, most visited, and most densely game-stocked National Park. It is 750 km west of Harare on the tourist route to Victoria Falls. The Victoria Falls National Park and HNP attracted 151 000 visitors and 98 000 visitors respectively in 1993 (Bvundura, 1994), which amounts to 35 per cent of the total visitors to National Parks in Zimbabwe in 1993.

The development of HNP for photographic tourism has led to severe problems for park management, not least visitor overcrowding and environmental degradation. In this chapter, we describe the origins of these problems together with views on how to deal with the ecological and human pressures on the park. In addition, HNP is discussed in the context of surrounding rural development. Closer links between the park and local communities offer practical solutions to the problems facing both.

People and Tourism in Fragile Environments. Edited by M. F. Price.

HISTORY AND DEVELOPMENT OF HWANGE NATIONAL PARK

LOCATION AND BIOPHYSICAL ENVIRONMENT

HNP is situated in north-west Zimbabwe, in Matabeleland North Province on the border of the country. It is bounded to the west by Botswana, to the north by the Deka and Matetsi Safari Areas, to the north-east by State Forest Land (Sikumi and Ngamo Forest Areas), and to the south-east by the Tsholotsho Communal Lands (TCL) (Figure 12.1).

HNP forms the north-eastern extremity of the Kalahari Desert, which influences the climate of the park. Daytime temperatures exceed 30°C in the summer, and fall dramatically in the evening. Temperatures below freezing have been recorded in the winter months (around July). The annual average rainfall is 620 mm.

The park lies at an altitude of around 1000 m, and consists of flat, gently undulating country, although the northern part consists of more broken terrain (Rogers, 1993). Approximately two-thirds (947 000 ha) of this semi-arid park is covered by deep aeolian Kalahari sands. No natural watercourses exit on the sands, only fossil rivers draining south to the Makgadikgadi Pans in Botswana, but the area is characterized by numerous seasonal, natural pans or waterholes. The natural pans have been, to a great extent, formed by game animals themselves. The other third of the park in the north, where relief is more pronounced, crosses a watershed dividing the Zambezi basin from the Makgadikgadi basin further south. It is drained by the Deka and Lukosi rivers which flow into the Zambezi river.

The vegetation is clearly delineated between those types which occur on the Kalahari sands and those which occur in other areas of the park. This represents the transition from dry desert flora to moist savanna woodland. The Kalahari sands support extensive *Baikiaea–Combretum* woodland thicket with *Terminalia* bushland on the dune slopes. Dune troughs contain more heterogeneous bushed grasslands with *Acacia* and *Burkea* species. Woody vegetation in the non-Kalahari sand areas is dominated by *Colophospermum mopane*, which occurs from open grassland to woodland, with *Combretum* and *Commiphora* species. The rockier areas are of a mixed miombo woodland (Rogers, 1993).

The fauna of HNP is a mixture of southern savanna and south-west arid elements, including typical Kalahari species. There is a particularly large elephant population. Wildlife is contained by a boundary game fence surrounding much of the park to the north and east, erected to prevent the spread of foot-and-mouth disease by buffalo.

TRADITIONAL AND HISTORICAL PEOPLE AND LAND USE

Historically, the area was occupied by hunter-gatherers (the San or Bushmen people) and the areas bordering Tsholotsho Communal Land in the south were used as dry-season grazing by pastoralists. In the colonial era, a number of farms

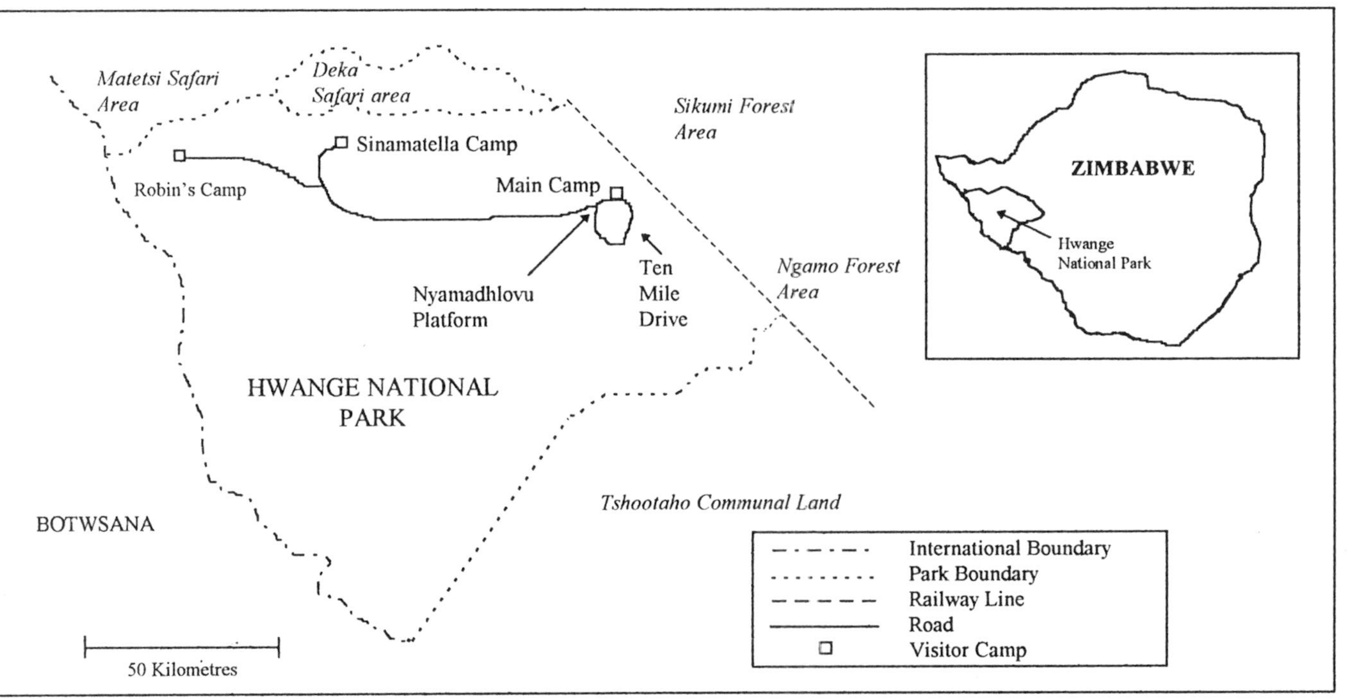

Figure 12.1 Hwange National Park and surrounding land use (adapted from Jones, 1989)

were established in the north and east of the present park for wheat cultivation and cattle ranching, with a timber concession over the east of the park. Parts of HNP were a royal Ndebele hunting reserve, and the area where Hwange Safari Lodge now stands was a favourite hunting ground of the Victorian hunter-adventurer Frederick Courtney Selous.

THE ESTABLISHMENT OF THE PARK

Soils unsuitable for agriculture, and a lack of water, led to the area being established as a game reserve. Part of what is now HNP was first proclaimed as a Game Reserve under the Game and Fish Preservation Act in 1930. A number of farms were incorporated when Hwange was proclaimed a National Park in 1949. In the early 1950s, unsuccessful attempts were made to acquire additional State Land to form a corridor for game movement from the park to the Gwaai river north-west of the park. Prior to settlement of the Gwaai Valley, it formed the northernmost permanent water source for game during their normal dry season range. Without this source of permanent water, very few game could survive in the park without migrating out to other water sources during the dry season.

To increase numbers of game and keep migrant populations in the area, artificial methods were devised by the first warden, Ted Davison, to provide water for game during the dry season (Davison, 1977). Because of the absence of natural watercourses upon which to build dams, the natural pans offered the best possibilities of improving the water supplies for game. Thick layers of mud and silt which accumulated in the pans denied animals drinking water when water levels where low, so efforts were made to make the pans last longer by scooping the mud out with ox-drawn dam scoops. This greatly improved the water supplies.

Davison and his staff then turned their attention to the underground water supplies and evolved a plan for sinking boreholes near pans. The idea was to replace some of the water lost by evaporation by erecting windmills on the boreholes and pumping into the pans. By this means it was hoped to build up a sufficient supply during the rains and early dry season—when game pressure on the pans was not very high—to carry the pan over into the next rainy season. Unfortunately, the plan was unsuccessful, because the silt in the bottom of the pans was such that, with continual trampling, the water still became too dirty for game to drink before the rains began. However, with the boreholes supplying fresh, clean water, it became possible to clean the pans out with the ox-drawn dam scoops. This was successfully achieved at a number of major pans.

The idea of pumping into the cleaned pans was an improvement, but still not good enough as the animals were able to break up the actual formation of the pan, causing the water to become dirtier than ever. Davison then hit upon the idea of building strong concrete troughs and pumping the water into these, then allowing the water to spill over into the pans. These circular, concrete troughs were constructed solidly to withstand elephant and other large animals (Figure 12.2). The dimensions of the troughs are about twenty feet in diameter, a foot

Figure 12.2 Elephants drinking at a concrete water trough

wide, and about two feet deep, with no concrete bottom. Initially, windmills were used to pump water from the boreholes, but they did not provide sufficient water to keep game satisfied, so diesel engines were used instead. This method of providing water for game still predominates.

Interestingly, there was very little game in the park in the early 1930s, but the improvement and development of the game water supplies led to a dramatic rise in wildlife populations over the years. Elephants alone rose from fewer than 1000 in the 1930s to a population of 30 000 today.

MANAGEMENT PROBLEMS

Protected areas have always faced a series of ecological and economic challenges (Cumming, 1990). In HNP, the major problems, both ecological and economic, are related to the provision of the artificial waterholes. Throughout the park there are 50 operational boreholes, with 35 situated in the Main Camp subregion. This is the largest section of the park, mainly of Kalahari sandveld, covering approximately 10 000 km^2.

The provision of artificial water supplies is a controversial issue. In a park with a dry season lasting almost seven months, it is vital to prevent migration out of the area and large-scale mortality amongst the wildlife. This is particu larly true of HNP, since the old dry-season route taken by water-dependent species to the Gwaai river has long been cut off by the commercial farms on the Gwaai (which are usually enclosed by strong game fences) and the Veterinary Fence for the control of foot and mouth disease. However, the provision of artificial water supplies can lead to a number of ecological impacts on wildlife, vegetation, and soil (Senzota and Mtahko, 1990; Kalikawa, 1990). The resultant over-population of large, wild herbivores, and the associated degradation of the ecosystem, is an inherent problem, particularly of the savanna grassland areas which constitute only 6 per cent of the entire park area. Most of this area is subjected to extreme hoof pressure, over-grazing, and the destruction of trees, mainly around water points. Habitat destruction is more noticeable in the northern sector of the park, which is prone to damage because of the nature of the shallow soils and associated vegetation types.

During the past four years, the provision of water for game in the park has grown steadily worse; every year since 1990 it has faced a major water crisis. Erratic rainfall and long periods of drought, in past years, have been major contributory factors to the problem of supplying water to game. The rainfall in recent years has been below average. The depth of the water-table has been increasing (regular borehole yield tests reveal this trend) and some holes have dried up completely (Figure 12.3). The problems are exacerbated by large herds of game, particularly elephant and buffalo, drinking at the pans during the dry season, coupled with high rates of evaporation and seepage. Elephants are

Figure 12.3 A dry waterhole

destructive and have a tendency to destroy water installations.

However, the major factor in the present water crisis is the lack of government funding for maintenance. Since the early 1930s, when the first boreholes were pumped in the park, no major borehole maintenance has been undertaken. Existing boreholes are operating unpredictably because of ageing equipment which cannot be replaced because of a limited capital budget. Boreholes considered not strategic by the park wardens have had to be shut down in order to cannibalize spares for the maintenance of others, particularly on the tourist routes. This has resulted in the unnatural concentrations of animals around key water points and the associated degradation of the ecosystem.

The park is chronically under-funded by the Department of National Parks and Wild Life Management (DNPWLM) as discussed below. Spending cannot take place unless, and until, the official notification of annual allocations is received. The annual monetary allocations granted by central government do not match the financial bids submitted each year. This leads to a depreciation in equipment and expertise. The diesel engines currently used to supply water for game were donated to HNP by the Indian government in 1986, together with a wide range of spare parts to maintain the engines. The engines have now exceeded their life expectancy and the stock of spares is depleted, hence the problem of constant mechanical breakdowns and cannibalism. Most borehole equipment is obsolete and requires urgent replacement. The lack of technically trained staff to repair engines and borehole equipment is also a major problem. There are insufficient tools and workshop facilities to carry out repairs. Furthermore, the park does not have reliable transport with which to conduct this major operation efficiently. Instead it relies on voluntary assistance from safari operators, local firms, non-governmental organizations (NGOs) and, in 1994, a volunteer team from the British Army.

Water shortages in the park lead to an increase in the number of animal mortalities, particularly of water-dependent species such as waterbuck, which are unable to walk long distances in search of water. Also, many animals may be excluded from pans by elephant which dominate scarce water reserves. This is of particular concern with regard to specially protected and rare species such as roan and sable antelope respectively. There is an ecological disaster waiting to happen because of economic neglect. If it does, the park will lose its economic value as a tourist destination (Child, 1985). To maintain viable game populations within the Park, it is essential that water is pumped for them. Without the usual large concentration of game in Hwange during the dry season, when the bush is more open, visitors will not be attracted. If normally busy pans are deserted and devoid of game, the image of Hwange as a premier National Park and tourist destination would be destroyed.

An immediate short-term solution to the problem of water-supplies for game would be a huge injection of funds to remedy the immediate crisis before it gets worse. A long-term rehabilitation programme also needs to be implemented, and new and innovative ideas to conserve underground water reserves, fuel, and funds need to be developed. Ongoing research programmes are in place, including the manipulation of water supplies (Butcher, T., 1994) and a study on the impact of artificial waterpoints on nutrient cycling (Dudley, 1990). Other pertinent research is necessary, such as a study of the seasonal movement patterns of elephant. More research is also required to investigate the current method of artificial water provision and its effects on the ecosystem.

TOURISM IN HWANGE NATIONAL PARK

BACKGROUND

The publicly accessible area of HNP skims the eastern edge of the protected area. The DNPWLM has centres at Main Camp, Sinamatella, and Robins, all with chalet accommodation and camping grounds. Networks of game-viewing roads guide the visitors through areas inhabited by good concentrations of animals, and to waterholes where large numbers of species congregate. At some waterholes, platforms have been erected, safely enabling close viewing of game (Figure 12.4). HNP, which contains over 30 000 elephant, is one of the greatest elephant sanctuaries in Africa, and herds of up to 200 animals may be seen at the waterholes, particularly at the end of the dry season. The area south to the Botswana border is inaccessible wilderness.

On the north-eastern side of the park are a range of hotels, lodges, and luxury bush camps. The development of tourist lodges on the periphery has increased the pressure for photo-safari access and, whilst the vast majority of visitors to the park use their own vehicles or hire vehicles, there are now 38 registered tour operators using 127 vehicles within the protected area (Bvundura, 1994). In 1991, there were 6 photographic safari camps operating into HNP. By 1993, there were 18.

Figure 12.4 Constructing a game-viewing platform

VISITOR USE PATTERNS AND OVERCROWDING

Although a small number of tourists visited Hwange before it was proclaimed a National Park, it was only afterwards that tourism development really got underway. In 1949, the park received 2771 visitors. Most of the tourist roads and the three rest camps at Main Camp, Sinamatella, and Robins had been built by this time, but the rest camps were only open to the public from 1st June to 30th November each year. By 1965, the number of visitors had risen to 25 351 per year, while the rest camps and part of the Main Camp area remained open throughout the year.

Tourism to HNP is growing rapidly (Figure 12.5). Since Independence in 1980, annual visitation has risen from 15 434 to a peak, in 1992, of over 110 000. Main Camp is by far the busiest centre for tourism. Between 1980 and 1993, 78.5 per cent of visitors passed through Main Camp, with 16.7 per cent and 4.9

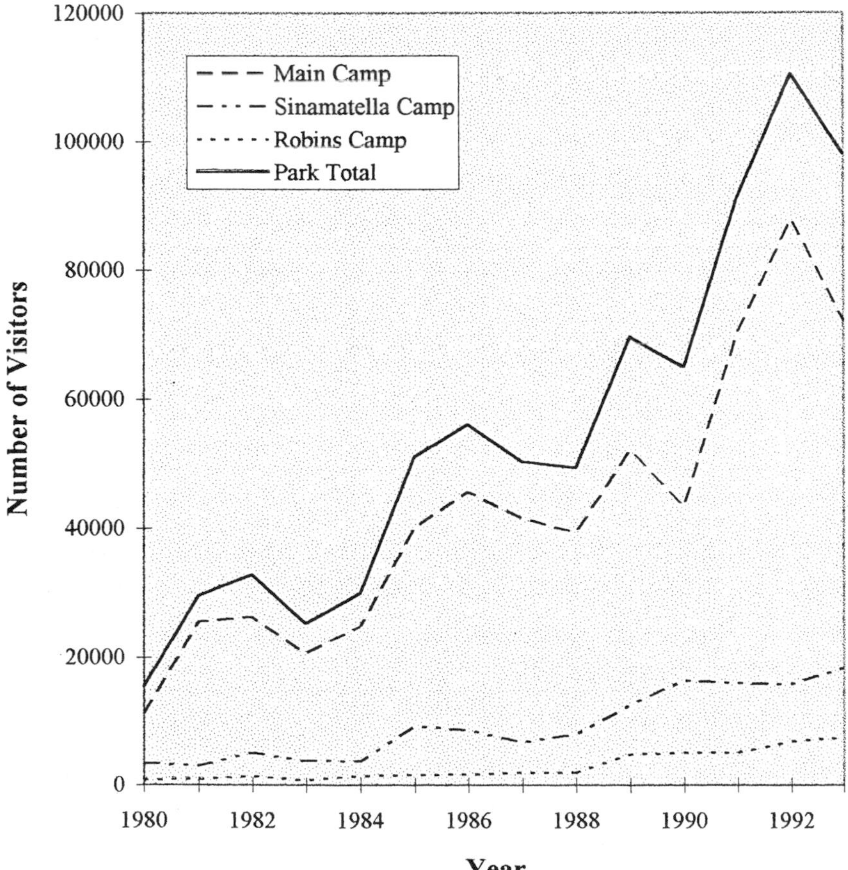

Figure 12.5 Total visitors to each camp, Hwange National Park, 1980–1993

(Source: Moore, 1990, 1991, 1992,; Bvundura, 1994)

per cent passing through Sinamatella and Robins Camps respectively. Since Main Camp is more accessible than the other two camps, it attracts many more day visitors (Figure 12.6); day visitors passing through Main Camp constituted more than 50 per cent of the total visitors to the Park in 1993.

The park authorities and some stakeholders consider overcrowding by tourists as a problem, particularly on the Ten Mile Drive close to Main Camp and in the prime areas of the park. The Ten Mile Drive, an attractive, open area of savanna rich in wildlife, is within 15 km of Main Camp and incorporates the most popular game-viewing platform, situated at Nyamandhlovu Pan. Because of its close proximity to Main Camp and its richness in wildlife, self-guided tourists, and those conveyed by the numerous tour operators, use it more often than any other area of the park, creating congestion. The road network in other areas is not very well maintained, and the next nearest platform to Main Camp is 30 km away.

A survey carried out by DNPWLM shows that half of all traffic uses Ten

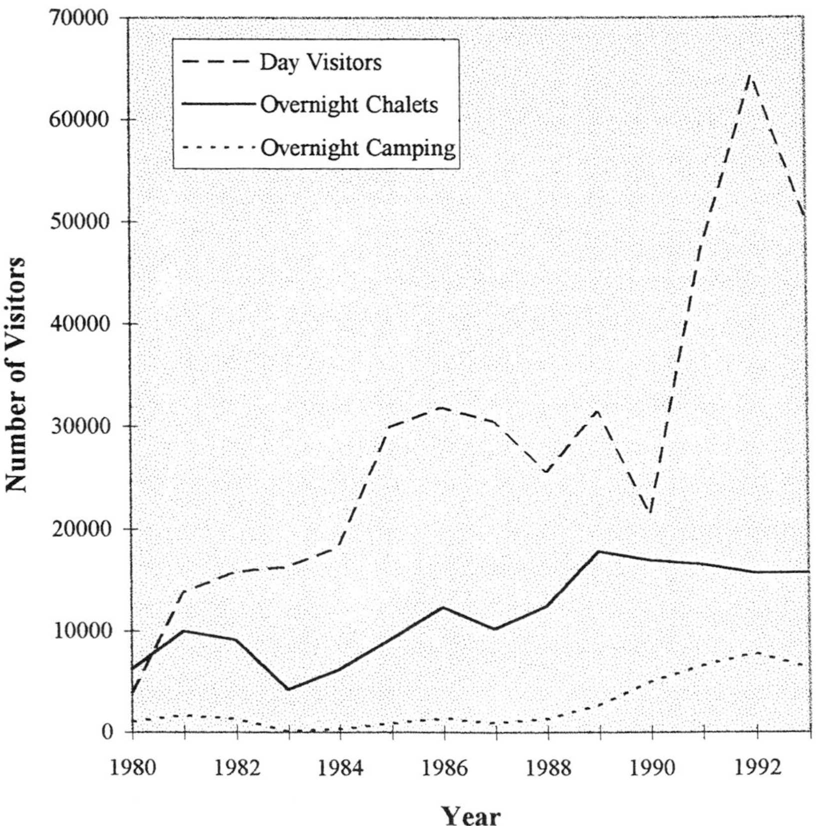

Figure 12.6 Day and overnight visitors to Hwange Main Camp, 1980–1993
(Source: Moore, 1990, 1991, 1992; Bvundura, 1994)

Mile Drive, with a utilization peak between 16:00 and the park closure at 18:00, when 50 per cent of all traffic is in the park. There is also a smaller peak in the early morning between 07:00 and 08:00 (Wetenhall, 1991; Rogers, 1992). Such peaks in utilization result in a less personal, and a less 'wilderness' viewing experience. This in turn affects the visitor carrying-capacity of the park.

The issues of overcrowding and visitor carrying-capacity are difficult to resolve. One recourse is to examine visitor perceptions based on their experiences in the park. In July and August 1994, Raleigh International Venturers carried out a survey of visitors in HNP. When asked how many other cars they had seen during their visit to the Park, the average response was 15, and only 18 per cent of those surveyed felt that the park was overcrowded. However, one-third (37 per cent) felt that Nyamandhlovu Platform was overcrowded. The opinion was also expressed that the roads are of poor quality for private cars and that wildlife at roadsides has decreased due to traffic, dust, and pollution. However, some visitors prefer gravel and dust roads because they present a more natural aspect. Many visitors from South Africa travel to HNP seeking a more 'natural' environment than is available at Kruger National Park.

Operators have expressed a variety of opinions about what should be done about overcrowding (Wetenhall, 1991). First, some argued that, although the game-viewing experience was becoming less personal, there were natural limits imposed by capacity constraints (access and accommodation) and that visitor numbers would reach a natural saturation level without intervention. Second, although increased pricing is not seen as a viable regulatory measure, the view was expressed that the park should be commercialized. If entrance fees were raised, DNPWLM could improve the wildlife resource, creating new pans, and providing better interpretation. By far the majority view was that new areas within the park should be developed for visitor utilization, since most operators believe that overcrowding has reached a critical level. Development priorities included the renovation of roads that are currently closed, construction of new loop roads, restricted access with accountability to new areas, and the opening of new areas for walking safaris, which are more environmentally sound and absorb more visitors, giving a perception of less crowding.

The antithesis of the new-development policy is the *laissez faire* option put forward by some operators. In this scenario, the overcrowding in areas such as Ten Mile Drive would encourage some visitors with the capability and motivation to go beyond into less-developed areas. In this way, development would be confined to limited 'honey-pot' areas that would attract most visitors, whilst the problem of overcrowding would be naturally regulated by those who perceived going to other areas as a problem. Despite this suggestion, the further development and commercialization of the park is widely held to be the desirable solution (Wetenhall, 1991; HATSO, 1992).

Better maintenance and carefully planned expansion of the present road network, with platforms erected at strategic waterholes, would be a solution to the problem of congestion. The interpretation service also needs to be improved drastically to educate visitors about the ecosystem in its entirety, including historical, archaeological, and other sites of interest. Research is being conducted during 1995 into the potential for improved visitor interpretation services.

PARK FINANCES

Traditionally, the charges for access to National Parks in Zimbabwe have been based upon the philosophy that the national heritage should be available free, or at a nominal charge, and that dual pricing (charging more to foreigners) was undesirable. However, Jansen (1993) has demonstrated clearly that park admission fees in Zimbabwe were below international market values, and argues that the DNPWLM should be required to 'maximize revenue within the constraints set by environmental considerations and equity goals'. As a result, a price increase and a system of two-tier pricing favouring Zimbabwean residents was implemented in 1993.

HNP generates large sums of money directly from entrance fees, accommodation fees, and other services, and also indirectly, through income generated by the lodges, camps, and tour operators who constantly use the park. HNP was responsible for generating 23.4 per cent of the entire revenue from the Parks and Wild Life Estate in 1991/92 (Jansen, 1993), and Main Camp is the top or second-highest revenue earner every year (Moore, 1991; 1992). However, all the revenue from tourism in the Park is returned to state coffers, rather than remaining with the DNPWLM to reinvest in the Estate. The operating budget for HNP in the 1993/94 financial year was Z$529 000, approximately 50 per cent of what is needed to run the park efficiently, yet this is only 25.2 per cent of the Z$2 100 000 direct revenue generated by tourism in the park. This underfunding is directly responsible for the water supply, maintenance, and overcrowding problems. In the past seven years, the funding allocated to HNP for the game water-supply has fallen from 72.6 per cent to 29.3 per cent of the formal bids (Potts and Russell, 1995). This is indicative of the underfunding of parks as a whole. Since 1980, financial allocations for managing the Parks and Wild Life Estate have declined in real terms (Child and Heath, 1990). In the same period, numbers of visitors have increased enormously.

Problems caused by the shortage of funds include the erosion of capital expenditure and the steady deterioration in the maintenance of existing facilities (rest camps, roads, picnic sites, and other park services), many of which are up to three decades old and were not designed to cope with such a high visitor pressure (Moore, 1990). Furthermore, there are acute staff shortages, and the few incumbents lack motivation and adequate training, resulting in the general decline of standards. The quality of service offered now is poor compared to several years ago, when the DNPWLM had better financial resources and did not have to cater for such large numbers of visitors. Despite the recent rise in fees, there has not been an improvement in the standard of maintenance of tourist facilities and park services.

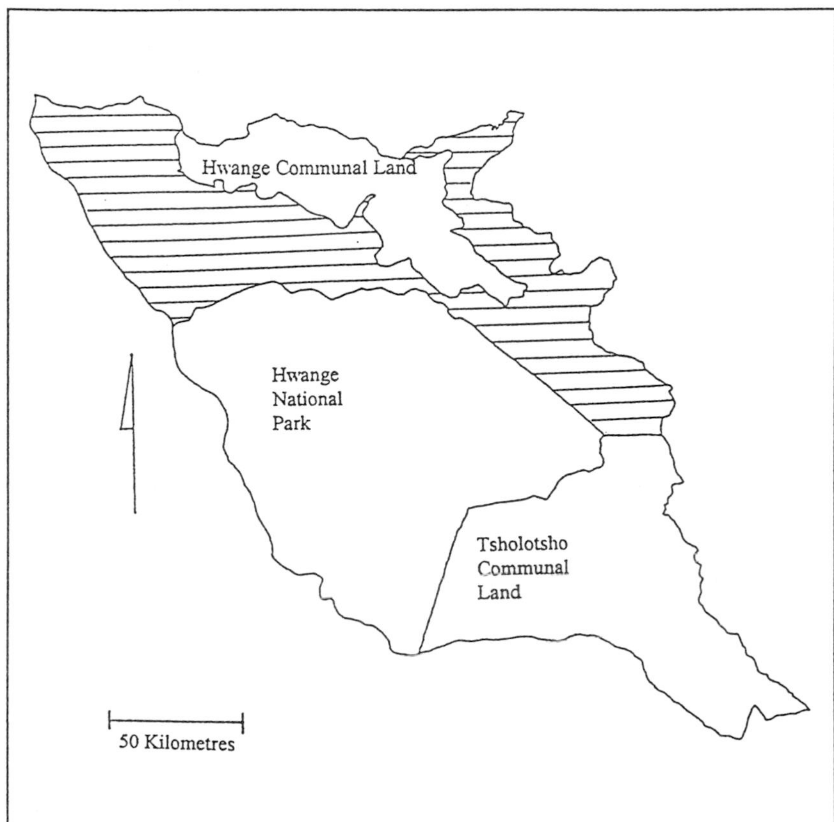

Figure 12.7 Communal Lands in Hwange and Tsholotsho Districts, Matabeleland North Province
(Adapted from Potts, 1994; Zimtrust, 1991)

During the Raleigh International survey in 1994, visitors to HNP were also asked how much more they were prepared to pay in increased park fees for improved roads, water and viewing platforms. In 1994, the single-day entry fee was Z$10. Only 18 per cent of those questioned were unwilling to pay more than Z$20 for admission; 16 per cent were prepared to pay Z$20–30; 24 per cent Z$ 30–40; 18 per cent Z$40–50; and 23 per cent more than Z$50. This suggested that there is considerable potential to raise park admission fees further, although to do so for all visitors would exclude most Zimbabweans. When asked how they would like the additional revenue spent to improve Hwange National Park, improved water supplies to the pans was the first priority of 55 per cent of respondents, followed by roads (19 per cent), more viewing platforms (14 per cent), and an interpretation centre (11 per cent).

Although visitors are aware of the problems facing the park and are willing to pay more for the privilege of visiting parks, nothing will improve without a revision to the allocation of funds generated by tourism. There is a lack of financial accountability and incentive; extra revenue earned from expanded tourism activities is returned to Government Central Treasury with little hope of it returning to cover the increased costs emanating from growth in the tourism sector. In other words, there is no incentive to promote tourism. Although tourism generates large revenues, from the DNPWLM's perspective it does not increase revenues to the Estate, but simply results in a greater demand upon already over-extended finances and manpower (Child, 1992). If the park was allowed to retain its earnings, this would promote self-sufficiency and further development.

TOURISM AND RURAL COMMUNITIES

BACKGROUND

HNP, only sparsely populated before its establishment, is no longer inhabited by local people, and adjacent areas to the west in Botswana are still very sparsely settled. However, within the Province of Matabeleland North, both Hwange District and Tsholotsho District contain rural communities living in communal farming areas close to the park (Figure 12.7). To the south, HNP abuts Tsholotsho Communal Land (TCL), which is predominantly settled by Ndebele, and some Kalanga and San (bushmen) who have settled and become part of the community. The Ndebele were resettled in Tsholotsho in the 1950s from other parts of Matabeleland, to make way for white commercial farmers and ranchers. Tsholotsho district is a semi-arid marginal agricultural area. Two-thirds of the population is dependent upon subsistence agriculture. Only 16 per cent of the population is dependent on employment, with many men going to South Africa in pursuit of work.

To the North of the park, although not bordering it, is Hwange Communal Land in Hwange District. This too is an inhospitable and underdeveloped area, inhabited mainly by Tonga fishermen and Ndebele. Hwange District has considerable mineral deposits, with coal, tin, clay, mica, and granite all being mined around the Communal Land. The coal deposit at Hwange Colliery supplies the entire country. Mining is the second most significant economic activity next to tourism in the District, which lies between HNP, Kazuma Pan, and the Victoria Falls complex. However, Hwange Communal Land is isolated from these tourist areas and receives little benefit (Zimtrust, 1991).

There is relatively little involvement of local people in tourism in and around HNP. The DNPWLM staff are drawn from a wide area and live within one of the three centres in the park. The hotels, safari lodges, and camps have been established by companies and entrepreneurs mainly from outside the local community and, whilst they employ some local people, this is marginal to the subsistence agriculture and mining which predominates.

As with most other countries, Zimbabwe's conservation policy during the first half of the century, based on the establishment of national parks, ignored the rights of local people to inhabit and utilize designated land and wildlife. The expropriation of an important aspect of their culture and livelihood, through protectionist conservation by the colonial government, served to antagonize the rural communities' attitudes towards wildlife, to the detriment of wildlife resources. Problem animals destroy crops and livestock, so it is not surprising that communities often perceive wildlife as a symbol of oppression. However, the 1975 Parks and Wild Life Act provided a unique opportunity for landowners and, subsequently, local people on communal lands to benefit from wildlife conservation and utilization. The act conferred custodianship of wildlife on the landowner or occupier. This created the legal framework within which the CAMPFIRE initiative could be developed.

CAMPFIRE AND CONSUMPTIVE TOURISM AROUND HWANGE NATIONAL PARK

CAMPFIRE, the acronym given to Zimbabwe's Communal Areas Management Plan for Indigenous Resources, is a programme designed and implemented to encourage local communities to conserve, rather than exploit, their remaining wildlife resources through sustainable utilization. It aims at improving the quality of life in communal lands by developing people's ability to manage these resources sustainably. The programme places emphasis on the participatory involvement of the local people, and on attaining success by consensus rather than by decree. One of the key elements of the programme is that proceeds earned from sport hunting, mainly for trophy elephants, go to the rural communities. Commercial operators lease concessions directly from the district councils, and pay a proportion of their income to the district, to be divided as cash dividends or used for infrastructural development. Both Hwange and Tsholotsho Districts have CAMPFIRE schemes.

TCL gained Appropriate Authority status under CAMPFIRE in 1991 and eight of the twenty wards in the district take part in CAMPFIRE (a ward is an area of land designated in the modern local government structure of Zimbabwe's communal lands) (Figure 12.8). Five of these eight wards abut the park. Concession fees paid by safari operators are shared equally between the wards in the concession areas. Half of the trophy fees are distributed to the wards in which the animals are shot. Elected local-ward wildlife committees identify and implement local projects. Revenues have mainly been used for the construction of schools, roads, and a community hall, and the sinking of boreholes.

Other benefits accrue to the community through employment opportunities and local manufacturing. When Matupula Safaris established a safari camp in TCL, the concessionaire rejected using a diesel pump to provide water for the camp. Instead, young men from nearby villages were contracted to use their fathers' carts to fetch water in drums, thus contributing to the local economy (Butcher, M., 1994). Rather than take clients into Victoria Falls to shop, Matupula Safaris has been encouraging people from local communities to bring

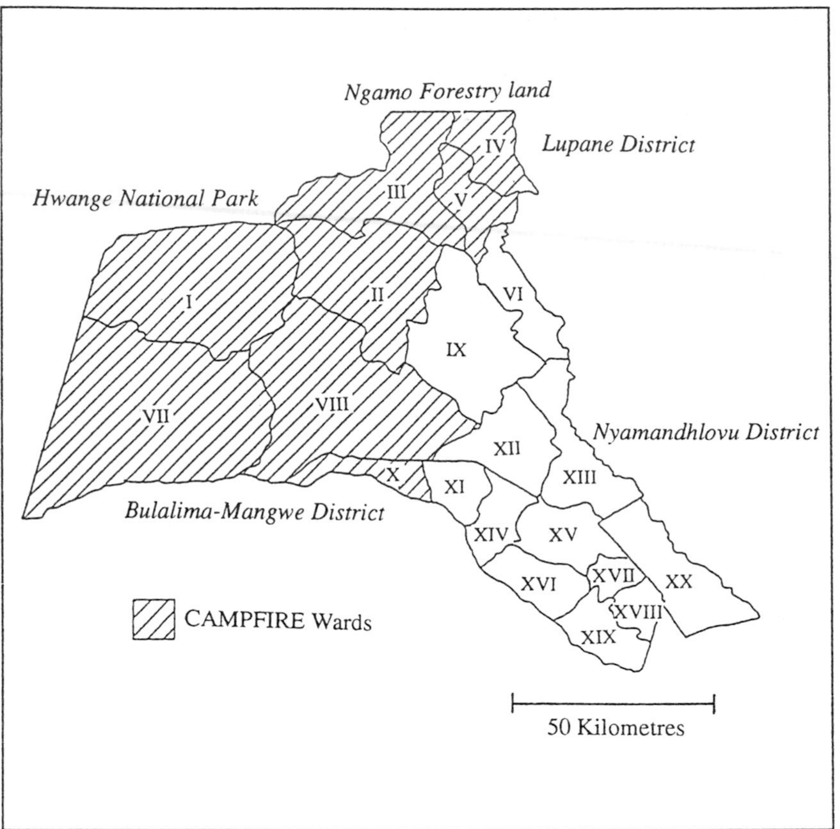

Figure 12.8 Tsholotsho District CAMPFIRE Wards
Adapted from Potts, 1994.

crafts into the safari camps. An average of Z$500 per client is being spent in the local economy. Similarly by employing and training local people to work in the safari camps and sourcing supplies locally, the local economy is boosted. Old, sick, or lame cows, donkeys and goats are purchased as bait, thus providing cash from an otherwise fully depreciated asset.

A study of the CAMPFIRE programme in TCL was conducted to measure the social, economic and ecological effects of the programme in the district (Potts, 1994). It was also used to develop and test methods for the evaluation of other CAMPFIRE projects and to research their impacts on conservation. Results showed that CAMPFIRE is perceived by residents of TCL as a conservation programme with considerable development benefits. A total of 84 per cent of household heads responding to a survey on the impact of CAMPFIRE in TCL felt that it had increased the value of wildlife, and 80 per cent felt that the poaching of wildlife for subsistence had been reduced as a consequence of CAMPFIRE, although DNPWLM has reported continued evidence of poaching from TCL

(n=56, sampling frame adopted from Kearl et al. 1976; see Potts, 1994).

The Honourable Welshman Mabhena, Governor of Matabeleland, opening a workshop on safari operations in Communal Lands in October 1993, stated that safari operations represent a working relationship between the private and public sector and promote sustainable development. He argued that the local self-reliance strategy could be furthered by local people becoming engaged in business ventures and that mutually beneficial investment could be developed through links with safari operators. He expected local people to develop their skills through their involvement in the safari operations:

> so that in the near future, the locals could be able to run these safari ventures with current operators or on their own . . . . The safari industry in communal areas is a significant rural development enterprise, and we look forward to more indigenisation of this industry.
>
> (Jones, 1994: 1–2)

DEVELOPING LINKS BETWEEN COMMUNAL LANDS AND HWANGE NATIONAL PARK

Although national parks are preserved as sanctuaries from hunting and local occupation, it is interesting to note that the districts with CAMPFIRE schemes all occur in marginal lands surrounding parks. Most rely on the parks as reservoirs for wildlife that spill over onto these communal lands. This is one reason why the Hwange Communal Land has not been able to benefit from wildlife tourism through CAMPFIRE to the same extent as Tsholotsho Communal Land. The former does not abut any areas with abundant wildlife, and is surrounded on two sides by game-control fences, further isolating the area from the surrounding parks and Wild Life Estate (Zimtrust, 1991; Child and Bond, 1994).

To increase the potential for tourism in Hwange Communal Land, a proposal has been made to reposition the game-control fences separating HNP from the Gwaai Valley and Hwange Communal Land (Zimtrust, 1991). This would provide a corridor which would enable wildlife to pass between the park and the Gwaai Valley, ultimately linking up with other wildlife areas in the neighbouring Binga District. There are already breaches in the fences around HNP which, as a result of a government policy change, have been left unrepaired to facilitate the movement of wildlife. Were a full corridor to be provided, it would be necessary to create enclaves within the communal land where subsistence agriculture could continue undisturbed by marauding wildlife. There are institutional, legal, and financial obstacles to this scenario, but recommendations have been made and a full feasibility analysis is awaited (Zimtrust, 1991).

Closer links are also envisaged between HNP and the TCL through a new initiative, the Tsholotsho Communal Land Wildlife Fencing and Buffer Zone Project (Hoare and Bond, 1994). The veterinary fence forms the boundary between TCL and HNP, and a buffer zone has been planned along this boundary. The project proposes to construct an electric fence along the extremity of the settlement in four wards, to demarcate a narrow buffer zone along the HNP boundary and, simultaneously, to curtail incursions of problem animals into inhabited areas. The proposed zone has already been set aside mainly for wildlife utilization and is presently divided into two hunting safari concession areas; Tsholotsho north and Tsholotsho south. The two concessionaires have also been granted permission to conduct photographic safaris within HNP.

The proposed Buffer Zone Project is poised to have an enormous impact on future sustainable wildlife utilization. Safari hunting, mainly for trophy elephant, has earned the district over Z$2 million since 1990 (Child and Bond, 1994). When the fence is erected, this zone will allow for the spill-over of game, particularly elephant, from HNP into part of TCL; the result will be increased revenues for local communities from the utilization of wildlife. Despite an increase in the availability of trophy elephant bulls from which the district earns most of its revenue through ‘consumptive use’ or safari hunting, the potential for non-consumptive use of wildlife, ie, photographic safaris, will be greatly enhanced. An extremely attractive part of the Tsholotsho north wildlife area has very good potential for photo safaris but this has not been tapped yet. The buffer zone project will also form a larger area dedicated to conservation, increasing the range for all wildlife species.

Several waterholes within the park along the HNP/TCL boundary are pumped in support of the CAMPFIRE initiative: the presence of water encourages and supports good wildlife populations which cross between the park and TCL. The recent survey by the Wildlife Fencing Research Project recorded 16 species of the larger mammals crossing back and forth across the veterinary fence (Hoare and Bond, 1994).

CONSUMPTIVE OR NON-CONSUMPTIVE TOURISM?

Safari hunting is an important component of wildlife-based tourism in Zimbabwe (Heath, 1992). To date, CAMPFIRE initiatives have been heavily reliant on safari hunting operations. For most CAMPFIRE communities, sport hunting is the main revenue earner, with a heavy emphasis on elephant hunting. Between 1989 and 1992, 90 per cent of total income to the 12 CAMPFIRE districts in Zimbabwe came from sport hunting, compared with 1 per cent from other forms of tourism (Bond, 1994). A number of other ways in which wildlife can be utilized by people in communal land areas have been suggested (Child and Bond, 1994). The formation of local hunting clubs, to utilize less prized species such as impala, would involve local people in the consumptive tourism industry, enabling them to gain new skills as well as providing meat for local consumption. The alternative option is to establish non-consumptive tourism.

Many areas have great potential for non-consumptive photographic tourism, but this potential has not been tapped. Part of the reason is the financial and tenure problems associated with photographic safari operations (Zimtrust, 1991; Butcher, M., 1994). Mark Butcher, of Matupula Safaris, with experience of both hunting and photographic safaris in communal lands including TCL, reports that, whilst hunting safaris can be operated on short-term leases, he has been unsuccessful in establishing good non-consumptive programmes. The present legislation pertaining to the use of Communal Land restricts District Councils to issuing renewable leases of only one year for commercial concessions. Photographic safari operations require five or more years' tenure because they require much heavier initial capital investment, and it takes longer to build the business and recoup the investment (Butcher, M., 1994).

Nevertheless, diversification out of safari hunting, and forging closer links with HNP through photographic safari operations, is vital if TCL and similar communal lands are to realize their potential and not rely purely on increasing elephant trophy quotas.

CONCLUSION

Hwange National Park is in a terribly precarious state. As a fragile ecosystem, it is unusual in being heavily dependent on the provision of artificial water holes for game. These were originally supplied, as a result of the isolation of the park from permanent natural water sources, to sustain wildlife in the Park. However, these artificial supplies are now necessary to maintain grossly inflated numbers of wild animals to satisfy the booming safari tourist industry. Paradoxically, it is the tourist revenue that will be the only way of saving the Park from ecological disaster as pumps deteriorate and pans dry up.

The Park is desperately underfunded at present. The resource cannot be properly managed on current financial allocations, and further development is impossible. A revision of the pricing policy for visitors was made in 1993, in an attempt to increase revenue and stimulate local development, in order to balance the opportunity costs of such a large protected area (Child and Heath, 1990; Jansen, 1993). However, nothing will improve without a fundamental change in the way that funds generated by tourism are allocated. Were the Park to be able to retain its earnings, it could maintain its infrastructure and develop new areas for tourism. If it is unable to maintain its ecological integrity it will lose its amenity value, and without further development the problems of visitor overcrowding will continue to worsen.

Local people surrounding the Park have increasingly seen it as an asset to which they have been wrongly denied access. The development of safari hunting operations, through initiatives such as CAMPFIRE, is a way of involving the local people in wildlife management whilst allowing them to benefit financially and infrastructurally. Community-based wildlife tourism offers a way of improving rural livelihoods in areas where agricultural prospects are at best marginal. In addition, it increases local support for the Park, decreases poaching, and may provide a way for spreading non-consumptive tourism into surrounding areas, thus alleviating some of the pressures of overcrowding, of both wildlife and tourists, within the Park. However, these initiatives depend on closer links between HNP and the surrounding Communal Lands of Matabeleland North, links that are now being strengthened in both Tsholotsho and Hwange Communal Lands.

REFERENCES

Bond, I., 1994, The Importance of Sport-Hunted African Elephants to CAMPFIRE in Zimbabwe, *TRAFFIC Bulletin*, 14(3), 117–119.

Butcher, M., 1994, Safari Operations in Matabeleland North Communal Lands: Problems, Pitfalls and Successes, in *Safari Operations in Communal Areas in Matabeleland*, M.A. Jones (ed.), Department of National Parks and Wild Life Management, Harare.

Butcher, T., 1994, The Effects of Manipulating Artificial Water Supplies on Large Mammal Drinking Behavior and Range Conditioning in the Vicinity of Artificial Water Points. Unpublished report to the Department of National Parks and Wild Life Management, Harare.

Bvundura, S., 1994, *Annual Report of the Warden (Tourism) 1993*, Department of National Parks and Wild Life Management, Harare.

Child, B., 1992, Implementation of Tourism Component of Hwange Park Plan. Draft copy submitted to the Department of National Parks and Wild Life Management, Harare.

Child, B. and Bond, I., 1994, Marketing Hunting and Photographic Concessions in Communal Lands, in *Safari Operations in Communal Areas in Matabeleland*, Jones, M.A. (ed.), Department of National Parks and Wild Life Management, Harare.

Child, G., 1985, Tourism and the Parks and Wild Life Estate of Zimbabwe, *Tourism Recreation Research*, 10(2), 7–11.

Child, G. and Heath, R., 1990, Underselling National Parks in Zimbabwe: The Implications for Rural Sustainability, *Society and Natural Resources*, 3, 215–227.

Cumming, D.H.M., 1990, *Wildlife Conservation in African Parks: Progress, Problems and Prescriptions,* Paper No.15, WWF MAPS Project, Harare.

Davison, T., 1977, *Wankie: The Story of a great Game Reserve*, Regal Publishers, Harare.

Dudley, J.P., 1990, The Impact of Artificial Waterpoints on Nutrient Cycling in Semi-arid Savanna Regions of Zimbabwe. Full research proposal submitted to the Department of National Parks and Wild Life Management, Harare.

HATSO, 1992, *A Strategic Plan for the Future*, Aries Associates, Republic of South Africa.

Heath, R., 1992, The Growth in Wildlife Based Tourism in Zimbabwe, paper presented at the *IUCN 4th World Congress on National Parks and Protected Areas, Caracas*, Venezuela, 10–21 February 1992.

Hoare, R.E. and Bond, I., 1994, An Environmental Review of Tsholotsho Communal Land Wildlife Fencing and Buffer Zone Project, A working paper submitted to Zimbabwe Trust, Zimbabwe.

Jansen, D.J., 1993, *Investigation and Recommendations on Access, Pricing and Control over Resources and Services of Department of National Parks and Wild Life Management*, Department of National Parks and Wild Life Management, Harare.

Jones, M., 1989, Hwange National Park Management Plan, draft copy submitted to the Minister of Environment and Tourism, Zimbabwe.

Jones, M.A., 1994, *Safari Operations in Communal Areas in Matabeleland.* Department of National Parks and Wild Life Management, Harare.

Kalikawa, M.C., 1990, Baseline vegetation description at artificial watering points of Central Kalahari Game Reserve, *African Journal of Ecology*, 28, 253–256.

Kearl, B. et al., 1976, *Field Data Collection in the Social Sciences: Experiments in Africa and the Middle East*, Agricultural Development Council Inc., New York.

Moore, A., 1990, *Department of National Parks and Wild Life Management Ten Year Review (1980–1989)*, Department of National Parks and Wild Life Management, Harare.

Moore, A., 1991, *Department of National Parks and Wild Life Management Tourism Statistical Report for 1990*, Department of National Parks and Wild Life Management, Harare.

Moore, A., 1992, *Department of National Parks and Wild Life Management Tourism Statistical Report for 1991*, Department of National Parks and Wild Life Management, Harare.

Potts, F.C., 1994, A Comparative Evaluation of the CAMPFIRE Programme in Binga and Tsholotsho Communal Areas, Zimbabwe. Unpublished MSc Thesis, DICE, University of Kent, UK.

Potts, F.C. and Russell, M., 1995, Current Management Problems. Provision of Artificial Water for Game in Hwange National Park, paper presented to the *Game Water Supplies Workshop*, Hwange Safari Lodge, Zimbabwe, January 1995.

Rogers, C.M.L., 1992, *Monitoring the Usage of Roads by Tourists in Hwange National Park*, Department of National Parks and Wild Life Management, Harare.

Rogers, C.M.L., 1993, *A Woody Vegetation Survey of Hwange National Park*, Department of National Parks and Wild Life Management, Harare.

Senzota, R.B.M. and Mtahko, G., 1990, Effect on wildlife of a water-hole in Mikumi Park, Tanzania, *African Journal of Ecology*, 28, 147–151.

Wetenhall, P., 1991, *Tourism in Matabeleland North*, Department of National Parks and Wild Life Management, Harare.

Zimtrust, 1991, *Tourism Potential of the Hwange Communal Land*, Price Waterhouse, Harare.

13 Good Intentions in a Competitive Market: Training for People and Tourism in Fragile Environments

CHRISTOPHER WHINNEY

INTRODUCTION

This chapter is an account of one organization's pursuit of solutions to the problem of tourism's continual destruction of its principal resource, the environment, and an examination of the reasons that preclude the implementation of readily available solutions to some of the greatest endemic problems.

The road to hell is paved with good intentions. From its foundation in 1979, Alternative Travel Group has adopted principles of sustainable tourism, long before such concepts became fashionable. Our intentions could not have been better, and the standards of our research, staff, and operations were among the highest in the tourism industry. We created the most idyllic sustainable tourism products. Yet the direct result of our good intentions was the rape of one culture and the degradation of others. We had opened the door—and the world followed. It is difficult to live with such a realization. The only way is to try to ensure that such things never happen again. But, of course, they do. Every moment of every day.

EARLY EXPERIENCES IN THE MOUNTAINS OF TURKEY

Alternative Travel Group first offered very specialized, environmentally low-impact trips—archetypal sustainable tourism—to areas which had been very seldom, if ever, visited by travellers. The local people were not totally isolated—many engaged in transhumance or had occasionally visited local towns—but none had any experience of tourism in their own regions.

Two of our early programmes were in remote mountain areas in Turkey: the Little Caucasus or Pontic Alps in northeast Turkey and the Western Taurus Mountains in central southern Turkey. Although the two areas differ climatically

People and Tourism in Fragile Environments. Edited by M. F. Price.

and culturally, their economies are similar, largely depending on transhumance (Figure 13.1). In both areas, Alternative Travel Group was instrumental in pioneering tourism and subsequently withdrew its operations for similar reasons.

The Little Caucasus lies in the 'Black Sea Low', with tea gardens giving way to rhododendron forests (*Rhododendron ponticus*), with scented rhododendron forests higher up, mountain meadows and 'forests' of dwarf rhododendron (*Rhododendron caucassium*) above 8000 feet. The summer villages, which are of very ancient origin and built principally of stone, are situated between 4500 and 7500 feet. In the Adaglar region of the Taurus, open plains give way to pine forest and high meadows up to 11 000 feet. In winter, the people live in villages built principally of pine wood with stone foundations, whilst in the summer they live in yurt-style tents. Ethnically and culturally, the people of the two areas are very diverse. The inhabitants of the Little Caucasus, the 'People of Hemsin', are bagpipe-players with Celtic origins who, until 1923, regarded themselves as Armenians and Christians, and still retain a very strong sense of ethnic and cultural identity. In the rainshadow of the southern side of these mountains, the people are principally Georgians. By contrast, the mountain people of the Adaglar are of remote Hittite origin. With 11 000-foot passes to the west and tortuous valleys to the east, they are geographically isolated and, perhaps because of this, seemed to retain a serene immunity to any semblance of historical influence—whether Selcuk, Karamano-gullari, Mongol, or Ottoman—although their early Christianity had been superceded by Islam.

Developing sensitive low-impact tourism in previously unvisited areas of such outstanding interest and beauty was both a privilege and a wonderfully exciting challenge. We carefully researched the areas, studied their flora, fauna,

Figure 13.1 Transhumance in the Little Caucasus (Pontic Alps)

history and traditions, and appraised the peoples' economies and ways of life. We visited villages and asked the people if they would be happy for groups of tourists to visit them, possibly camp nearby, use the village 'tea house' and the communal toilet facilities (so as not to pollute the meadows) (Figure 13.2). We also asked people if they could or would like to sell local produce or artefacts.

The trips were sold through direct marketing, and the travel press was actively discouraged from mentioning the trips or the areas (despite the boundless opportunities for publicity). The marketing was targeted at a civilized, intelligent and perceptive clientele, and the 'tourists' were carefully prepared, informed of the local history, traditions and way of life, told about local customs, and taught some of the language. Our widely travelled, discerning clientele assessed the trips as 'breathtakingly successful tourism'. They seemed to be enjoyed as much by the local people as by the 'tourists', with parties and dancing being given at almost every village en route (on one occasion a Scottish piper accompanied a trip to return hospitality) (Figure 13.3).

Where one tourist or tour operator goes another will follow—inevitably: 'the word gets out'. Tourism development, however, is reciprocal, affecting not just 'supply and demand' but also the attitudes and often fragile fabric of ancient cultures that, whilst flourishing in isolation or with sympathetic and sensitive appreciation, may react in self-defence when threatened with 'culture clash' or unacceptable intrusion.

In the two areas we visited, tourism began to grow insidiously. At first, tourists—German, French, English, American—came a few at a time, and only to the more accessible areas. We heard stories of tourists angrily demanding to buy food from people who had none to offer; tourists using the freshwater

Figure 13.2 Tourist camp near Tirivit in the Little Caucasus (Pontic Alps)

Figure 13.3 Local people and tourists dancing out-of-doors at Polovit, in the Little Caucasus (Pontic Alps)

sources as a swimming pool; tourists stealing firewood laboriously carried up 3000 feet from the treeline; 'improperly dressed' tourists; human faeces in the water supply; and extensive botanical robbery (of species unique to the area). We also heard widespread complaints about tourists' arrogance and ignorance of local traditions. We saw the attitudes of the local people change from overwhelming friendliness and hospitality to almost total disassociation.

Then other tour companies, presumably concerned that we had established a 'competitive advantage', started to offer our itineraries. We knew they had never visited the areas, let alone researched the routes. In several cases, they produced word-for-word copies of our brochure text, accompanied by library pictures. Finally came the cataclysmic denouement. We had stones thrown at us by people who had formerly offered us nothing but the most friendly and hospitable welcome. The story emerged: a tour company had seen our brochure and, because they had never visited the area, offered the trip as an 'adventure' holiday for 18–22-year-olds. The local people who had previously seen only our groups assumed that they were us. They welcomed them, and as usual offered hospitality and a party with music and dancing in the evening. To the 18–22-year-olds, a party meant something different—they had brought some whisky and 'dope' and seduced the local girls whom they plied with these unfamiliar substances. The result was not just the seduction of some innocent girls, it was the rape of a culture.

Our good intentions had lowered the people's resistance and presaged disaster. Horrified, sickened, and utterly disillusioned, we immediately withdrew the entire programme, and began to analyse the causes and look for solutions. We realized that the danger came from a dynamic industry driven by insatiable customer demand, so we began by looking for clues within the structures of the tourism industry, its practices and marketing.

THE ECONOMICS OF TOURISM: TRAINING AND THE ENVIRONMENT

The tourism industry is a service industry in which the demand for service usually depends on the existence of resources such as the natural environment or cultural monuments. The resources themselves create neither employment nor wealth unless and until a service (transport, accommodation, guided tour, etc.) is provided. As an industry that is predominantly price-led, the marketing advantage of matching the quality of the resource to the quality of the service is almost invariably sacrificed to mass-market consumerism that may degrade, and even destroy, the resource. Furthermore, because tourism marketing is largely image-oriented (rather than content-oriented), this tends to accelerate the exploitation of outstanding resources as people flock to see publicized 'sights'.

Tourism is an intensely competitive and fast-moving industry subject to multifarious uncertainties, whether political, commercial, or meteorological, and every business almost invariably incurs high overhead costs and hazardously seasonal cash flows. The necessity of continuous profitability on trading accounts, particularly for tour operators within the European Union who are legally bound by stringent financial controls, and of quick pay-back on investments, dictates an expedient, short-term view. The industry therefore tends to be reactive rather than proactive. The tendency is to follow marketing leads, rather than to invest in the creation of genuinely original or innovative products—which will then be plagiarized. The travel media, however, always hungry for a story, ply their customers with information about 'new' areas, creating a demand, which is then satisfied by the industry—and the areas are almost invariably degraded. To break this vicious circle, the challenge is to create a climate in which the tourism industry would react to produce sustainable tourism products. The only effective arguments would be economic.

In a service industry, the organization that provides the best service has a clear competitive advantage. Service can only be provided through training. The prime aim of such training is to create customer satisfaction, increase personal recommendations to reduce marketing costs, and enhance 'the bottom line'. Customer satisfaction must, of course, include a perceived satisfaction with 'value for money'. People will pay more if they can be persuaded that they are receiving more for their outlay.

The perception of added value can only be created through effective presentation; and presentation skills can only be acquired through training. For tourism professionals, the best elements of added value cost nothing; they are simply there, merely requiring presentation—and the most readily available 'free additions' that increase profit margins are, of course, environmental. The environment therefore acquires significant value. With this understanding of added value, profits can be significantly increased by personnel with the necessary skills in environmental presentation—which must of course include a high degree of people-management skills. Managing people within the environment acquires a significant economic value, and validates the necessary expenditure on training.

TRAINING TO RESOLVE ENDEMIC ENVIRONMENTAL PROBLEMS

Viewed from a strategic commercial standpoint, the prime objective of training is to protect margins by establishing products that are measurably superior to those of all competitors. But what has this to do with conservation? The answer is: everything. A mistake of the past has been the failure to recognize this.

'Raising the dust and complaining that we cannot see' has beset approaches to training in relation to the environment. Much attention has focused on studying the symptoms—which are sometimes perceived as almost esoteric in their complexity—and relatively little on saving the patient. The patient (the environment) is bleeding to death and, whilst resources have been channelled into qualifying a few highly skilled experts, who are unquestionably needed to study the symptoms (and conduct 'post mortems'), there are not enough people qualified in basic skills (first aid) to stop widespread haemorrhaging on the spot and prevent death from blood-loss.

The cause of the disease is people—people who have been conditioned to believe that as consumers they have rights; that as consumers they are always right; and that they have a right to what they want—now. They want to enjoy what is 'rightfully' theirs: the environment. Erudite papers, reasoned argument, even national parks and other protected areas, can do little to check the onslaught of 'voracious consumers'. Service industries, however, are expert in such matters, processing and satisfying masses of consumers every second of the day, whilst carefully conserving their resources. They succeed because they have invested heavily in training their personnel, and they have only done so because this investment yields impressive returns.

The management of people, not as 'human resources', but as 'customers' within the environment, goes to the root of many endemic problems. Training in people-management and customer service has been developed to the highest and most effective levels and is common to every service industry—except (if we are to believe some surveys) the tourism industry, education and administrators: those upon whom the environmental future of our planet largely depends. The knowledge and skills are there. They just need to be applied. Furthermore, the tourism industry has the strongest possible motivation for adopting such an approach: to create competitive advantage, endorse the concept of added value, and increase profit margins. Training, therefore, is one of the keys.

In 1987, Alternative Travel Group introduced structured training for Environmental Guides and Managers. None of the trainees is a professional environmental scientist or able to pronounce on the current ramifications of the environmental debate. They probably recycle glass, use approved aerosols, eschew whale meat, and have a general interest in the countryside, and some particular interest, such as history, ornithology, or botany. The potential sought at their interviews is their ability to manage people. The training qualifies them in a wide spectrum of areas including presentation skills, group dynamics, non-confrontational management and first aid, as well as knowledge of sound environmental practice. The programme is pragmatically based on the recognition that, through skilled people-management, we have the opportunity not only to profoundly limit the potential damage of tourism, but also to present the environment in such a way as to give it both intrinsic and commercial value. What people value they respect, protect, and conserve.

In 1988, this programme won a National Training Award, with a further commendation in 1991. It has been recognized by the Sustainable Tourism Workshop Group of the Federation of Nature and National Parks of Europe as a case study in effective training for Environmental Guides and Managers (FNNPE, 1993). It was also featured on the BBC's *Winning* programme and formed the basis for Alternative Travel Group becoming one of the first organizations to win the prestigious 'Investors in People' award. Since 1987, customers' assessment of their overall enjoyment of their trips has never dropped below 99 per cent 'good' or 'excellent', with 77 per cent of our customers assessing our trips as 'excellent'. Personal recommendations account for 95 per cent of all reservations. Advertising costs are negligible.

TRAINING STANDARDS

A second key is the development and establishment of standards. Standards are an integral aspect of every society, to protect both resources and consumers alike. Ironically there are countless regulations within the tourism industry world-wide to protect the consumer, but few to protect what is consumed: the environment, which is perceived as a complex external 'issue'. At present, the world is a playground. The governing force is the market. The situation with regard to tourism and the environment is almost totally out of control. It is analogous to everyone driving motor vehicles without instruction or a code of practice: consumerist anarchy.

Political and economic solutions to control tourism will always be open to compromise. There are, almost invariably, too many interests involved; and laws, no matter how draconian, will not resolve the fundamental problems of attitude, motivation, and education. Yet attainment of, or compliance with, established standards is frequently synonymous with a licence to trade or be involved in particular areas of activity, and in this context compliance with voluntary standards creates competitive advantage: 'All our products comply with a standard recognized by...', a logo, or an insignia.

One advantage of resolving the problem by establishing internationally accepted standards for the management of people within the environment is that this in no way interferes with the autonomy of each area, allowing each the freedom to resolve its particular problems independently. 'Differences in culture, customs, socio-economic conditions, and other factors have led many less developed countries to evolve their own approaches to protecting natural resources, and the international community has responded by advancing the notion that each country must develop its own tradition—one that will work best there' (Ham *et al.*, 1993: 232). Local conditions may vary, but people-management skills are much the same the world-over. A further advantage of an internationally recognized standard is as a 'passport' that will enable governments, local authorities and private individuals to protect areas, whatever their status, by allowing access only to qualified persons (Whinney and Reggiori, 1992).

INHERENT DANGERS OF INACTION

In the absence of any single international standard, the predictable proliferation of independent 'standards' around the world will continue to gather momentum. The boards of these 'standard-makers' may comprise fund-raisers or campaigners on specific issues or areas, whilst others may be exclusively comprised of representatives of large national or multi-national companies, whose environmental credentials are as questionable as their pockets are deep; and the cynical suspicion will remain that their participation is part of a public relations strategy. Authorization to display a logo indicating compliance with an 'environmental standard' almost invariably involves payment of a fee, often beyond the budget of many organizations, and far in excess of the administration cost. Every new 'standard'—each with its own criteria, 'awards', and 'membership fee'—diminishes the credibility of others. The environmental debate, with goalposts determining 'environmental correctness' in constant motion, is confusing enough for the general public without a plethora of possibly meretricious logos and 'awards'.

The concern now is that, instead of a voluntary solution utilizing and stimulating strong latent elements of motivation, draconian local laws will be passed to sort out the mess, and probably make matters worse. Suppressing the symptoms with repressive and restrictive measures is no substitute for educating people and curing the disease. In 1991, I wrote: 'the time for implementing an internationally recognized standard is now—before yet another culture is raped or unique environmental area destroyed. There is certainly no case for inaction to resolve endemic problems of the effects of tourism upon the environment when easily accessible solutions exist' (Whinney and Reggiori, 1992). The need for implementing these solutions is increasingly urgent; the tourism industry around the world must cooperate to achieve them, both for its own future and for the future of the communities and environments that are its essential resources.

REFERENCES

FNNPE (Federation of Nature and National Parks of Europe), 1993, *Loving Them to Death? Sustainable Tourism in Europe's Nature and National Parks*, FNNPE, Grafenau.

Ham, S.H., Sutherland, D.S. and Meganck, R.A., 1993, Applying environmental interpretation in protected areas in developing countries: problems in exporting a US model, *Environmental Conservation*, 29(3), 232–242.

Whinney, C. and Reggiori, E., 1992, *Tourism: An Alternative Way Forward.* Paper presented to the IVth Congress on National Parks and Protected Areas, Caracas, February 1992.

Index

Index compiled by Liz Granger